Critical Acclaim for
Land of a Thousand Hills

"Many lone women seem to have a deep affinity for Africa. Thankfully, they continue to record their memoirs and enrich our understanding of this vast continent . . . Carr thoughtfully examines the bliss and turmoil of life near the Rwandan-Congo border for over fifty tumultuous years . . . [She] has articulated a new world for those who have not experienced the paradox that is Africa . . . Readers will continue to be captivated."
—*The Christian Science Monitor*
(A Noteworthy Book of 1999)

"Though she delves into the ethnic and political history behind Rwanda's 1990s Hutu–Tutsi massacres, much of her story centers on a relatively tranquil, if arduous, plantation life . . . Carr has left her own mark of beauty on that tragic land."
—*USA Today*

"Riveting."
—*New York Post*

"While Rosamond Halsey Carr has made neither headlines nor history, her work has improved the lives of thousands of people. With the burgeoning of the memoir as a literary form, *Land of a Thousand Hills* exemplifies the value of the genre."
—*The Dallas Morning News*

ROSAMOND HALSEY CARR is the last of the foreign plantation owners in Rwanda, where she runs a children's orphanage. She has been featured on television programs from the *Today* show to CNN and the BBC.

ANN HOWARD HALSEY traveled to Rwanda to work with her aunt on this memoir. She lives in Downingtown, Pennsylvania.

LAND OF A THOUSAND HILLS

My Life in Rwanda

ROSAMOND HALSEY CARR

with Ann Howard Halsey

A PLUME BOOK

PLUME
Published by the Penguin Group
Penguin Putnam Inc., 375 Hudson Street,
New York, New York 10014, U.S.A.
Penguin Books Ltd, 27 Wrights Lane, London W8 5TZ, England
Penguin Books Australia Ltd, Ringwood, Victoria, Australia
Penguin Books Canada Ltd, 10 Alcorn Avenue,
Toronto, Ontario, Canada M4V 3B2
Penguin Books (N.Z.) Ltd, 182–190 Wairau Road,
Auckland 10, New Zealand

Penguin Books Ltd, Registered Offices:
Harmondsworth, Middlesex, England

Published by Plume, a member of Penguin Putnam Inc.
Previously published in a Viking Penguin edition.

First Plume Printing, September 2000
10 9 8 7 6 5 4 3 2 1

Photograph credits:
Page 11 of photo section: three images of Dian Fossey:
Bob Campbell
Page 12 (top photo): © Estate of Dian Fossey
Page 16 (bottom photo): Janice Gleason
All other photographs are from the collection of
Rosamond Halsey Carr.

Ⓟ REGISTERED TRADEMARK—MARCA REGISTRADA

ISBN 0-670-88780-3 (hc)
0-452-28202-0 (pbk)
CIP data is available.

Printed in the United States of America
Original hardcover design by Betty Lew
Map illustration by Mark Stein

To the children at the Imbabazi Orphanage;

and to Sembagare,
my valued and trusted friend

CONTENTS

LAND OF A
THOUSAND HILLS

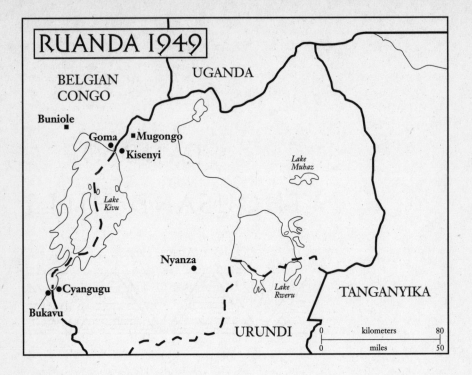

RUANDA 1949

BELGIAN
CONGO

UGANDA

Buniole ■

Goma ● ■ Mugongo
● Kisenyi

*Lake
Kivu*

*Lake
Muhaz*

Nyanza ●

● Cyangugu

Bukavu

*Lake
Rweru*

TANGANYIKA

URUNDI

0   kilometers   80
0   miles   50

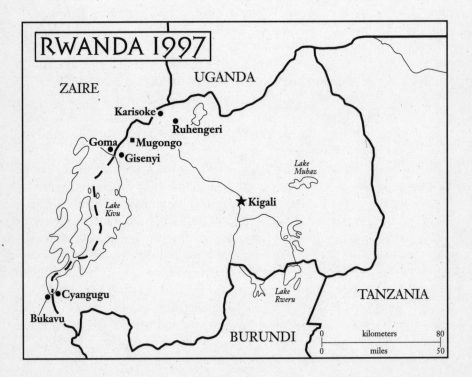

RWANDA 1997

ZAIRE

UGANDA

Karisoke ●
● Ruhengeri

Goma ● ■ Mugongo
● Gisenyi

*Lake
Kivu*

*Lake
Muhaz*

★ Kigali

● Cyangugu

Bukavu

*Lake
Rweru*

TANZANIA

BURUNDI

0   kilometers   80
0   miles   50

When Kenneth suggested that we move to Africa, everyone thought we were mad. At that time, however, I would have followed him anywhere. It was the summer of 1949, and it was the beginning of what was to become a lifetime adventure. It is true that I was very much in love with Kenneth, but this is really the story of a love affair between a woman and a country. It took some time for this love affair to take hold. But take hold it did, and it has been going on now for almost fifty years.

My name is Rosamond Halsey Carr and my home is in Rwanda, a small country in east central Africa. Rwanda is called the "Land of a Thousand Hills" (or in French, *"Mille Collines"*), and much like the pattern of my life, its landscape is a tapestry of a thousand peaks and valleys that fill the horizon and beyond. The name is derived from the Virunga Mountains, a volcanic chain which forms the continental divide between the great Nile and Congo river basins. Rwanda lies just south of the Equator at an elevation of approximately five thousand feet. My home is a flower plantation called Mugongo, situated high in the foothills of the Virunga volcanoes at an elevation of seventy-eight hundred feet.

Rwanda is bounded on the west by Zaire, on the south by Burundi, on the east by Tanzania, and on the north by Uganda. The Rusizi River empties south from Lake Kivu to form its western boundary with Zaire. The southern region is scattered with numerous lakes and dense forests. To the east, a high plateau declines gently toward the low marshy plains and grassy savannas of the Akagera National Park and Akagera River, which empties into Lake Victoria and forms its eastern boundary with Tanzania. The northern region is dominated by the lofty peaks of the Virunga volcanoes and encompasses some of the most fertile land in all of Africa.

Rwanda is one of the most densely populated countries in Africa, with a population of almost eight million people in an area of approximately ten thousand square miles. The capital city is Kigali, and the official languages are Kinyarwanda and French, although Swahili is widely spoken as well. Its fertile mountain slopes and grassy plains are home to three distinct ethnic groups. The Wahutu (Hutu), whose name translates to mean "cultivators," are of Bantu stock and make up approximately eighty-five percent of the population. The Watutsi (Tutsi) are the tribe of the feudal kings of Rwanda and make up less than fifteen percent of the population. They are a tall, nomadic people who are traditionally cattle herders and great warriors. The remaining one or two percent are the Batwa pygmies, who are hunters and potters and purveyors of magic spells. Collectively, they are known as the Banyarwanda—the people of Rwanda.

It is generally believed that the Tutsi migrated to this region in the fifteenth century and established dominance over the agriculturalist Hutu by a series of land and cattle contracts. By the seventeenth century they had founded a kingdom encompassing the area surrounding what is now Kigali and the outlying Hutu communities. The Germans claimed Rwanda as part of German East Africa in 1890, but their presence and control were limited. Following World War I, Rwanda—along with neighboring Burundi—was assigned to Belgium as part of the League of Nations mandate (later the United Nations trust territory) of Ruanda-Urundi. The Belgians ruled indirectly through the Tutsi monarchy, but encouraged the rise of the Hutu lower classes. In 1959, war erupted between the Tutsi and the Hutu. As a result, the *mwami* (king) Kigeri V was deposed and forced into exile, and vast numbers of Tutsi fled to neighboring countries, setting the stage for much enmity and bloodshed in the decades to follow. Rwanda was declared a republic in January 1961 and became an independent country on July 1, 1962.

Rwanda in 1949 was a land of enchantment—a wilderness where people and animals lived in harmony untouched by the outside world. Shepherds led their cattle to drink at the lakes and pools until evening, when elephants began to migrate toward the watering holes to drink and bathe. Time was told by the sun, and the moon was the calendar. A house could be built in a few days, made from trees and bamboo gathered from the forests and roofed with grass. Men prayed that the weather would be favorable for their crops, young boys dreamed of owning large herds of cattle, and little girls cradled and sang to their dolls made of spiky flowers called red-hot pokers, imagining a baby of their own. The markets were social gathering places and trading centers where a finely woven grass mat was exchanged for forty pounds of potatoes or a basket for storing grain.

Many changes have taken place since I arrived here almost a half century ago. I have witnessed the decline and fall of colonialism in Africa and the emergence of the new and struggling African states. I have survived civil wars, revolutions, and one of the greatest human tragedies of our time, the genocide of 1994. More than once my home has been occupied by soldiers—some of them welcome, others not. The names of towns and countries have changed, and friends have come and gone. I have experienced great happiness and unbearable heartache. I have known extraordinary people and been witness to extraordinary events. I have sailed up the Congo River and camped in pygmy villages. I have attended the coronation of a Tutsi king and been a guest at the Presidential Palace. Elephants have roamed across my land, and I have communed with the mountain gorillas. I have seen the end of an era and the beginning of a new Rwanda, a country struggling to reconcile its traditional way of life with a new Africa at the dawn of the twenty-first century.

Yet, with all the changes, much has remained the same. Rwanda is still the most beautiful place on earth. My vine-covered cottage still sits on a rise surrounded by English gardens and towering hedges of hydrangeas. I still have no electricity or telephone. Food is prepared on a wood-burning stove, and the only light in the evenings is candlelight and kerosene lanterns. The chairs are African-made, laced with cowhide strips, and straw mats and goatskin rugs cover the floors. The workers still come each day to work in the fields, and every morning at my back door mothers line up with their sick babies waiting for me to treat their fevers and runny noses. The rocky road to Mugongo has, if anything, become more difficult to travel. But tea is still served at four, and every evening the crested cranes come to roost in the tufted leaves of the dracaena trees. Mikeno and Karisimbi rise majestically out of the mist to cast shadows across my land, and Nyiragongo, an active volcano, lights up the sky to the west each evening. On a clear day, I can still see Lake Kivu in the distance. And there are still more stars in the African night sky than in any other place on earth.

Today, Mugongo is filled with the sound of children's laughter and singing. This country that I love has given me much. Rwanda is my home, and it is here that I intend to spend the rest of my days. Its beauty is my inspiration. Its struggles have been my struggles. Its grief has been my deepest sorrow. Its people are my strength, and its children are my greatest joy.

PART ONE

I

KENNETH

On July 9, 1949, my husband Kenneth and I sailed out of Brooklyn Harbor on a cargo ship bound for the west coast of Africa. We were leaving behind friends and family and seven years of unfulfilled married life in search of adventure and happiness in the land Kenneth dearly loved. We would find enough adventure to last several lifetimes, but the happiness and fulfillment I yearned for would continue to elude me for many years to come.

Little in my life to that point had prepared me for the rigors and hardships I would encounter in this strange and faraway land. I was born in South Orange, New Jersey, in 1912—the eldest of three children. My brother William is four years younger than I, and my sister Dorothy is six years younger. Although we are dear friends now, while we were growing up our age differences prevented any true intimacy in our sibling relationships and left me with a deep sense of isolation and insecurity. We led a very sheltered life, even for those times, but it was a happy childhood, and our home was the gathering place for an endless stream of aunts and uncles, cousins, grandparents, and friends.

My father, William Gurden Halsey, was a bond trader in New York. He was a man of uncompromising integrity and courtliness, a leader in the church and community, and a natural-born charmer with a gift for making everyone feel special. As children, we were endlessly captivated by his magic tricks and fanciful tales of make-believe. He was always very dignified and proper in demeanor, and he seldom left the house without his straw boater and a fresh pansy in his lapel. Above all, he was a devoted family man, and I believe that his happiest moments were spent indulging those he loved, particularly my mother. My mother, by contrast, was the pragmatist of the family. It was left to her to bring us all back down to earth when necessary—at times a bit too abruptly for my liking.

My mother was born Rosamond Howard, and until the day she died at the age of ninety-four, it was her affection and approbation which I desperately sought and which I never felt were received in full measure. Her father, Neil Howard, came from a family of southern aristocrats. They lived in Atlanta until Sherman's army swept through the South, leaving the city and my great-grandparents' home in smoldering ruins. The family retreated to their plantation near Macon, Georgia, to a life of poverty. Neil Howard married my grandmother, Julia Hamilton Otis, in 1882, and they produced seven daughters—two of whom died in infancy. My mother was the eldest of the surviving children. In time, my grandfather moved his family to New Jersey, where he became quite successful in real estate. Mother was born in Atlanta and was very proud of her southern roots. Throughout her life, whenever she was asked where she was born, she always responded in a southern accent, though she had lived in New Jersey since she was two years old.

I came from a life of some privilege. We lived in a substantial house on Turrell Avenue in South Orange, with a live-in maid and an English gardener. It was a life of boarding schools, country clubs, and debutante balls—an endless labyrinth of proprieties and prohibitions. But it was certainly a comfortable existence and one that provided every expectation of being able to fulfill my dreams. The problem was that I couldn't seem to define those dreams, and throughout my childhood and as a young adult, I continually strayed from the conventional path I was expected to follow.

Our lives took an unexpected and dramatic turn when I was seventeen years old. My father lost most of his money in the stock market crash of 1929, and the rest trickled away in the years that followed. Our financial downturn left a deep and lasting impact on our family. My father was devastated and felt obligated to reimburse many of his investors to the extent he was able from his own dwindling resources. My mother accepted our reversal of fortune with a remarkable degree of stoicism. Outwardly she maintained a brave and cheerful front, while secretly she sold pieces of silver and family heirlooms to pay the grocers and the laundry bills. Although it was primarily my mother's strength and good humor that kept us all going, even she had her limits. In 1934, we were forced to sell the house on Turrell Avenue, and she never quite recovered. When we traded in the Packard convertible for a Buick, she made up her mind never to drive an automobile again. And for many years, she never did.

My brother and sister were still quite young at the time and seemed to adapt to the change in our circumstances more readily, but those years instilled in me a deep-seated fear of poverty that has remained with me all my life.

Our financial misfortunes eliminated any possibility of my attending college, but I was determined to pursue a career in the field of art. I was accepted at the Traphagen School of Fashion Design in New York City and ultimately won a scholarship for "life drawing." After two years I was apprenticed at an artists' studio which specialized in fashion illustration and store window displays. My salary was ten dollars a month! I eventually left the studio and went into business for myself, doing fashion illustrations for New York department stores. I was finally on my own, but just barely self-sufficient.

I moved into a studio apartment at 35th Street and Madison Avenue in a building owned by Junius Morgan, son of J. P. Morgan. The Morgan residence was on 36th Street, and not wanting unsightly high-rise buildings in their backyard, they had bought up most of the brownstones in the block below. The house I lived in was rented to a woman who in turn sublet rooms to musicians and artists. I could look out my window into the Morgans' courtyard and watch afternoon tea being served from an elegant silver service. In the autumn, rows of pheasant, fresh from the hunt in the country, were hung on a clothesline to cure. The Morgans' two young sons, accompanied by their nanny and wearing little white gloves, rode their tricycles round and round the courtyard for hours, their squeaky wheels driving me to distraction.

New York at that time was teeming with eligible young men. I had my fair share of dates, but as often happens, those I took an interest in did not seem particularly interested in me, and vice versa. On Sunday afternoons, my sister Dorothy and I would go off to art exhibits or polo matches on what we called "husband hunting" excursions, but the results were typically disappointing.

While attending a class at the Art Students League, I met Dr. Charles Lowell Putnam, a surgeon whose son Patrick lived among the Bambutti pygmies in the Ituri Forest in the Belgian Congo. Dr. Putnam had retired at the age of seventy to pursue his lifelong interest in drawing. At the same time, I developed an interest in a talented artist named Robert Hale, and he and Dr. Putnam and I became great friends.

One evening in the fall of 1941, Dr. Putnam suggested that I accompany him to a showing of films on Africa by the famous African hunter and explorer Kenneth Carr. By the time I met Kenneth, he had lived in Africa for twenty-eight years, most of that time in Uganda. Over the years, he had explored most of the African continent and had worked as a tattoo artist, a coffee planter, and a miner of silver and tungsten. He had become world renowned as a big game hunter and was a member of the New York Explorers Club. Moreover, he was an accomplished filmmaker and photographer.

Kenneth was born and raised in England. Throughout his teenage years he had been a very serious musician, and hours of daily practice on the cello left him pale and delicate. This was not the son his father, an enthusiastic hunter and sportsman, had dreamed of. As a result, on his twenty-first birthday, Kenneth's father bought him a ticket on a Union Castle boat bound for Cape Town—in an effort to "toughen him up a bit." Kenneth spent several years exploring South Africa and Kenya in search of adventure and opportunity. In 1912, he bought a tract of land in the Masaka district of Uganda, where he built a house and planted coffee. He joined the British colonial army during World War I, and was engaged in minor skirmishes with the Germans along the southwestern Uganda frontier.

It was fifteen years before Kenneth returned to England, by which time his father was dead. He had become the hunter his father would have wished—a hunter of lions and elephants, rather than the deer and birds of England. He was so highly regarded that he was chosen as the guide for the great expedition in 1921 of Prince William of Sweden, who had come to Africa to collect specimens for the Stockholm Museum. Prince William's expedition killed scores of animals, among them fourteen of the now endangered mountain gorillas, which are still on display at the Stockholm Museum. At that time, gorillas were considered to be carnivorous, man-eating creatures and fair game for hunters and poachers. We now know, of course, that they are vegetarians and nonaggressive and are among the world's most endangered species.

Kenneth had come to the United States as a tourist in 1939. He had made a series of extraordinary color films of Africa taken during a yearlong safari from Uganda to the African west coast. Since he was well over military age when Great Britain entered World War II, the British Consulate in New York requested that he remain in America to show his films, with the proceeds benefiting Bundles for Britain. These were virtually the first color films of Africa to be shown in the United States. He had filmed the 1938 eruption of Nyamulagira volcano, the Bambutti pygmies, the Mangbetu (a tribe that binds its women's heads to elongate them and make them more beautiful), the "duck-billed" women of the Congolese Babira tribe, and Nigerian horsemen wearing medieval-style armor. Through the showing of his films, Kenneth became quite a celebrity.

That evening at the Art Students League, Dr. Putnam's son Patrick, who was home on leave, introduced me to Kenneth. I was instantly captivated by this handsome, worldly man. Kenneth was tall, slender, and permanently suntanned, with dark hair and brilliant blue eyes. His adventurous life was a stark contrast to the lives of the young lawyers and stockbrokers that made up my circle of friends. I was deeply drawn to Kenneth, but even more so to the exotic images on the screen.

A few weeks later, Bob Hale and I were invited to be the houseguests of

Dr. Putnam at his home in Bedford Village, New York. As we rode up together on the train, Bob began to tease me by saying that all the guests at the Putnams' party would be stuffy intellectuals with whom I would have nothing in common. I was painfully shy at the time and began to wish with all my heart that I had never accepted the invitation in the first place. Then, in an effort to reassure me, Bob said, "There will be one person there who is almost as shy as you are." I was strangely excited to learn that the person he referred to was the handsome British explorer Kenneth Carr.

Kenneth was a quiet and reserved man. Nevertheless, his charming British wit and riveting tales of explorations in the wilds of Africa attracted the attention of everyone he met. Whenever possible, the two of us would slip away quietly and go for long walks together in the countryside. We talked for hours about his adventurous life and my somewhat vague and unfulfilled aspirations. I felt I had found a true friend in Kenneth, and possibly a great deal more.

I was thrilled when he invited me to dinner in the city the following week. We saw each other often after that, and my attraction to him grew stronger with each passing day. When I brought him home to meet my family, he presented me with an exotic-looking pin made from an actual lion's claw that had been laminated in gold. It was clear that Kenneth was considerably older than I, but I found him to be more attractive and more exciting than any man I had ever known. We became engaged a few months later and were married in May of 1942. Looking back, I can see that I was wildly in love and had my head in the clouds, and I saw only what I wanted to see. It wasn't until after we were married that I discovered exactly how much older and how painfully inhibited Kenneth really was.

It was always expected that I would marry "well." I suppose that meant a successful husband and a house and family in the suburbs. I am certain that Kenneth was not what my family had envisioned for me. Although they were very fond of him, they were concerned that the age difference was too great and that I was entirely unprepared for the sort of life marriage to Kenneth would bring. But I was determined to marry him, and I was certain that I would make him happy and that our marriage would last forever.

My grandmother lived to see me married. I remember what she said to Kenneth the first time they met. She put her hand on his arm and said, "Oh, when I think of what those beautiful, blue eyes have seen!" I wanted to see everything that Kenneth had seen.

We lived together in my tiny apartment, subsisting mostly on my meager earnings and occasional assistance from my family. It was a shock for me to learn that Kenneth was practically penniless. When he had been asked to show his films in America, it was with the understanding that it would be at his own expense—his contribution to the war effort. Prior to our marriage, he was not permitted to work in the United States, since he had entered the country on a tourist visa. What little money he had disappeared quickly, and he was ultimately forced to pawn his cherished movie projector. It wasn't until after Pearl Harbor that "friendly aliens" with tourist visas, such as Kenneth, were legally allowed to work in the United States.

I continued to work as a fashion illustrator, specializing in ladies' clothing, hats, and accessories for major department stores. Kenneth did what he could to contribute by offering to pose for me. I still smile at the image of this tall, rugged, athletic, and very proper Brit standing in the middle of our crowded apartment sporting an elegant ladies' hat and smoking his pipe.

Once the United States entered the war, Kenneth was recommended for a post in Washington with the Board of Economic Warfare and we moved to Alexandria, Virginia. While the war raged on in North Africa, government and military officials feared that fighting would spread to Central Africa, and it was Kenneth's role to provide information and expertise on the region. For a time, he was quite content to sit in an office and talk endlessly about his favorite subject. After less than a year, it became apparent that the war would not reach Central Africa, and Kenneth's advice was no longer required. His knowledge of mining landed him a position as a field engineer for mica production with the U.S. Metals Reserve Project in western North Carolina, and we moved to Spruce Pine where we lived for three years. Eventually, we bought a little house of our own in Skyland, near Asheville.

Never in my adult life have I experienced the luxury of financial security, and those early years of marriage to Kenneth were no exception. We struggled constantly to make ends meet. There were adjustment problems as well. Kenneth had been a bachelor for a very long time, and he was accustomed to long safaris and a completely independent existence. Marriage must have been uncharted territory for him.

He once said to me, "Rosy, the trouble with marriage is that you lose all *privacy!*" This, he said in the British pronunciation. When I replied, "If it was *privacy* that you wanted, why did you get married?" he didn't respond.

I began to wonder why Kenneth did marry me. I was an innocent bride in every sense of the word and had wildly romantic notions of how married life was supposed to be. Kenneth, for all his worldliness and maturity, was as inexperienced as I when we married, and the physical act of love seemed to bring him more embarrassment than pleasure. My upbringing had in no way prepared me for this sort of dilemma, and I was far too modest and naive to even consider discussing such a delicate topic with Kenneth or anyone else. I concluded that it must be my own inadequacies that were to blame.

Although I had long since outgrown my shyness, Kenneth never did. His reserved nature, along with the differences in our ages and the lack of passion in our marriage, left me feeling both lonely and disillusioned. And then, I longed for children. But it just didn't happen.

Despite all of my high hopes and fierce determination, by 1949 our marriage was deteriorating and neither one of us was very happy. Unwilling to give up on the prospect of a happy future together, we decided that the solution was to move to Africa.

A friend from North Carolina said to me, "To follow a man to Africa, he must be *pure* gold." I wasn't entirely convinced of that, but I did feel certain that in the land Kenneth loved so much we would both discover the happiness and passion that had eluded us for so long. I did not realize at the time how completely dependent upon each other we would be for companionship and fulfillment in this strange new land.

2

The Journey

My poor family was aghast at the news that their dear girl was going off to the "Dark Continent," but nothing they could do or say would dissuade us. This was the great adventure I had been waiting for all of my life, and I embarked upon it with my usual steely determination and reckless abandon.

I bought four new cotton dresses at Lord & Taylor, a pith helmet at a New York outfitter's, and a lifetime supply of cold cream. I got my passport and visas and underwent all the required inoculations. We sold our house, packed up our most precious belongings, and booked passage on a Farrell Line cargo ship called the S.S. *African Glen*, bound for Matadi—the Atlantic seaport in the Belgian Congo. The ship had accommodations for just twelve passengers, and we shared our stateroom with our lovable but ungainly Irish terrier, Sheila. Our destination was Ruanda-Urundi (now the two separate countries of Rwanda and Burundi), where Kenneth hoped to prospect for tin and gold.

The transatlantic crossing was pure bliss. Friends and family came to see us off and celebrated our voyage with orchids and champagne. As the sun was setting, we slowly moved out of Brooklyn Harbor with our loved ones standing on the pier, and I wondered if and when I would ever see them again. The days and nights at sea were heavenly. This was the closest thing to a honeymoon we ever had, and the future seemed full of hope and promise.

We reached Matadi early in August of 1949, where we were to spend our first night in Africa. It was quite a shock to leave the confines of the big ocean liner for the smelly, dusty streets of this bustling West African seaport. The only hotel in town was booked solid, so we ended up spending the night in a shabby rooming house overrun with drunken sailors and cockroaches three inches long—complete with whiskers. A chamber pot under the bed served as the sanitary facilities, and the mosquito netting had holes in it the size of tennis balls.

The following day, we boarded a steam-powered locomotive passenger train and traveled the narrow-gauge railroad two hundred fifty miles inland to Léopoldville (now Kinshasa), the capital city of the Belgian Congo. We were practically the only passengers on board and were immediately surrounded by porters clamoring to carry our baggage—even my tiny camera case. The porters were enormous men dressed in ragged shorts and uniform jackets of thin gray cotton. They spoke Lingala, which Kenneth didn't understand. Suddenly, I was terrified. We were planning to live in a country where we couldn't speak the local language and where I was certain my rudimentary French would be insufficient to converse with the Europeans. Kenneth's years in Africa had been spent predominantly in English-speaking countries, and his French was almost as limited as mine. He spoke fluent Swahili and several of the Bantu languages of East Africa, but this was foreign territory to us both. Nevertheless, I could not take my eyes away from the exotic sights and scenery as we chugged along inland toward Léopoldville. The hilly terrain was lush with flowers and pineapple groves, and at each stop along the way, vendors crowded the platform selling papayas, avocados, and a variety of exotic fruits and vegetables.

We spent eleven days in the charming colonial town of Léopoldville while Kenneth visited with friends and business associates. From there, we boarded a wood-burning paddle-wheeled steamboat, called the *Berwinne*, and sailed up the Congo River twelve hundred and eighty miles through the great equatorial rain forest to Stanleyville. The *Berwinne* was a replacement boat for the regular passenger boat (which had run aground) and was in very poor condition. Our stateroom, which we shared with Sheila, was only seven feet square and contained just one narrow bed furnished with dirty linens. Six rusty nails on the door served as a closet, and there was no ventilation. Only one of us could stand up in the cabin at a time, and we eventually resorted to sleeping in shifts.

The *Berwinne* made stops periodically throughout the day to replenish the wood supply needed to keep it moving. There was no radar in those days, and consequently we could navigate only during daylight hours. At night we would tie up at small villages to take on more wood, and the local villagers would crowd the docks, clamoring to sell food and handicrafts.

The journey took fourteen long days. My fears surrounding our inability to communicate proved to be well-founded. The only passengers we were able to converse with were two British missionaries going only as far as Coquilhatville and a Flemish army adjutant who happened to speak a little English. We were repeatedly reminded to take our quinine and warned not to take tub baths on board because of the bilharzia (parasites) in the brown river water. The air was filled with mosquitoes and tsetse flies, and the food served in the dining room was appalling. I survived almost entirely on bread and the fruit we bought from river vendors. I confess that the tough meat we were served, which I suspected to be monkey, went into Sheila's dish.

It was unbearably hot and humid, and the steamy air was filled with frightening sounds. The Congo River at its western reaches is more than ten miles wide, but we never experienced a sense of great expanse, as we remained close to the river's edge, navigating around the many islands that dot its shores. The foliage was thick with trees and vines infested with chattering monkeys, which at first seemed exotic but soon became commonplace. We ran aground countless times, which invariably gave rise to momentary spurts of frenzied activity, followed by interminable delays.

As the days wore on, the mood on board became increasingly somber and apprehensive. There was a discernible reticence among the passengers to venture into the interior. Families huddled together. Some played cards for hours at a time. There was no music or entertainment of any sort to break the monotony. Kenneth immersed himself in books and walked Sheila back and forth across the deck. I passed the time leaning against the rail watching crocodiles sun themselves on small verdant islands. I feared that Kenneth's thoughts were as full of misgivings as my own, and I found myself wondering why I had ever agreed to leave America and come to this strange and terrifying place where I felt I had no right to be. I envied the third-class passengers below and listened to their laughter and merriment as they sprawled on the lower deck and cooked their own meals on charcoal-burning braziers. At night, they would sing and dance, cuddle with their children, and make love. This was their country and they knew how to live here. Would I ever be able to say the same?

The *Berwinne* finally docked at Stanleyville, a picturesque colonial outpost. We had come as far as the Congo River could take us. After a bath and a hearty meal, we made our way directly to the only used-car dealer in town and examined our options. Kenneth, in a rare moment of whimsy, had his heart set on a flashy red Fiat convertible with leather seats. Still dazed from our recent ordeal and only able to imagine what might lie ahead, I suggested that we consider something a bit more utilitarian. We had a bit of a row over this, but in the end I prevailed and we drove away in a dark blue, secondhand Ford pickup truck. The Ford turned out to be a godsend. It survived even the rocky roads to the Kivu and held up for many years after that.

With our baggage in the back of the truck and Sheila between us, we set out for the Ituri Forest to visit Kenneth's friend and noted anthropologist

Patrick Putnam and his wife Anne at their camp and guest house. As mentioned previously, Patrick was the son of my friend Dr. Charles Putnam from New York. After earning a degree from Harvard, Patrick had studied tropical medicine in Belgium and subsequently established a campsite on the banks of the Epulu River in the Ituri Forest with his first wife, Mary. Mary was a talented landscape gardener who had managed to create exquisite gardens out of the rain forest in this primeval wilderness. The exotic locale soon attracted some of the more adventurous and celebrated tourists, and eventually the Putnams converted their sprawling compound into a guest house.

Patrick was madly in love with Mary. Unfortunately, on a visit home one winter, Mary contracted pneumonia and died in New York. Patrick was devastated, but determined not to go back to Africa without a wife. He married Emily Baca, the daughter of the governor of New Mexico. I don't believe he ever really loved Emily, and it was said that he spent much of the first weeks of their marriage weeping over the grave of his first wife. Emily hated life in the Ituri Forest, and after several bouts with malaria, she left and never returned.

Patrick's third wife, Anne, was an artist who had grown up in New York City. This was not a very happy marriage either, and Patrick eventually took to living on an island a respectable distance from the guest house. From there, he would hurl insults at poor Anne, as she did her best to keep the guest house running and prevent the rain forest from completely taking over.

I recalled meeting Patrick in New York in 1941—a tall, distinguished-looking man with red hair and striking blue eyes. By the time Kenneth and I arrived at the Ituri Forest, Patrick was unrecognizable. At the time, he was confined to his bed with malaria. The room stank, and everything in the house, including the masks and curios that hung on the walls, were green with mildew. On the bed with Patrick were two furry bush babies and a small monkey. His red hair was graying, and he was so gaunt that we feared he wouldn't last another week. As it happened, Patrick lived until 1955, when he died of a combination of tropical illnesses.

The moisture and mildew were overwhelming. There was no shower, so I asked if I might take a bath. "Of course, Rosamond!" Patrick exclaimed. "Nothing like a hot soak to restore the weary traveler. We have *two* concrete bathtubs—both of them cleverly painted green to disguise the mold and mildew!"

I immediately determined that I didn't need a bath all that badly and began to suspect that Patrick had been living in the bush a bit too long. Aside from his shock at Patrick's appearance, Kenneth took it all pretty much in stride, but I was appalled. Was this the sort of life I had to look forward to?

Among his peculiar talents and hobbies, Patrick harvested and sold the venom from pit vipers which he collected in the forest, and he scared me half to death with a spontaneous demonstration of the venom extraction process—brandishing about one of the deadly snakes which he retrieved from a basket he kept beside his bed. On a brief excursion into the forest, I was startled to come upon a dead goat lying across the path with a baby forest pig suckling its teats. When I reported this bizarre encounter to Patrick, he dismissed it as not being all that peculiar, muttering, "The goat had probably not been dead all that long!" I began to feel like a spectator at a freak show.

When Patrick discovered that I had brought books with me, he became quite animated. "I haven't read a book in months," he said, and insisted that I leave them for him to read. He assured me he would send them on when he was finished with them. He did, but when they eventually arrived months later, they were completely ruined—covered with the same pervasive mildew that covered everything in the Ituri Forest.

At that time, Patrick was considered the world's leading authority on the Bambutti pygmies. These are true pygmies, rarely over four feet tall, as opposed to the slightly larger Batwa pygmies of Rwanda. They could pass under Kenneth's outstretched arms with many inches to spare. Anne Putnam became great friends with the pygmies as well, and spent many hours watching and sketching them. I found them utterly intriguing and was endlessly amused by their childlike antics and continual laughter. They performed their tribal dances for us and took me for a ride through the forest on a tipoy—a bamboo litter supported by two poles and carried on the shoulders of four pygmy men.

The Bambutti insisted that we accompany them on a net hunt in the forest, which was an altogether terrifying experience. A long thin net made of vines was unrolled and secured between two trees. Several pygmies slipped silently into the forest to lure game into the net, while others hid in the foliage with poisoned arrows waiting for their prey. The first of the tiny antelopes lured into the trap was running so swiftly it crashed right through the net and got away. I was secretly overjoyed, but my exhilaration was short-lived. Several antelope were not so fortunate that day and, after being snared in the net, were killed by the poisonous arrows of the pygmy hunters crouched in the bushes beside me.

Years later, Anne Putnam wrote a marvelous book about the Bambutti pygmies, called *Madami*. After Patrick's death, she remained in the Ituri Forest until the approach of Congo independence in 1960.

We left the Putnams, the pygmies, and my precious books and drove for two weeks through rain forests, over washed-out roads, and across the wide expanses of the Rwindi Plains. I watched in awe as we passed great herds of elephant, buffalo, antelope, and zebra. Since our arrival in Africa, we had traveled over two thousand miles by train, riverboat, and pickup truck. At last we reached our destination—the lush, mountainous region of "the Kivu." All my fears faded away as we approached civilization and the most beautiful place I have ever seen. A crystal-clear lake surrounded by mountain peaks and coffee plantations, Lake Kivu was the center of European culture in the Belgian colonies. This was to become my home, and although I would leave it from time to time, I would never leave it for very long.

3

THE KIVU

The Great Lakes region of east central Africa encompasses some of the most spectacular scenery in all of Africa. Lake Kivu is situated between Rwanda and Zaire (at that time Ruanda and the Belgian Congo), and prior to independence and the establishment of national borders, the lush mountainous region surrounding its crystal-clear waters was known as "the Kivu." The lake is sixty miles long, set among myriad mountain peaks at an altitude of 4,789 feet. Unlike many African waters, it is uninhabited by crocodiles, hippopotamus, or parasites, making it an ideal spot for swimming and recreation. The mountains that surround it contain much of the mineral wealth in the region, and it is considered one of the crown jewels of Central Africa.

In 1949, its western shores—on the Congo side—were bordered by great coffee plantations that gradually ascended the mountain slopes. Elaborate European villas, adorned with a profusion of hibiscus and oleander, lined the water's edge, and coffee factories were nestled behind groves of orange, lime, and grapefruit trees—their fragrant blossoms mingling with the intoxicating scent of the coffee when it flowered. On the eastern Ruanda side, the small coffee plantations belonged to the Banyaruanda. The steep hills were terraced with crops, and the valleys were pastures for the long-horned cattle of the Tutsi, the tribe of the feudal kings of Ruanda. Bougainvillea and climbing roses grew in abundance, and banana groves edged the sandy beaches and flourished on countless small fertile islands.

At the northern tip of Lake Kivu, lying side by side on the Ruanda-Congo border, were the twin towns and Belgian government posts of Kisenyi (in Ruanda) and Goma (in the Congo). Kisenyi was principally a residential town with large villas and several hotels fronting on white sandy beaches. Tourists and European residents would come here to swim in the lake or dine on French cuisine at a charming hotel. Goma was the commercial center for the North Kivu, and its streets were lined with shops, banks, and offices. The Virunga volcanoes—eight conical peaks towering more than ten thousand feet high—formed the backdrop for the two small towns. Goma sits in the shadow of Nyiragongo, an active volcano called the "burning mountain." By day, clouds of white smoke would rise from its crater, and at night, fiery red ashes spewed into the sky. The combined European population of Goma and Kisenyi in 1949 was about four hundred people. By 1954, it had increased to almost seven hundred, including the planters on outlying farms, such as myself, who traveled to town to collect their mail, shop, and socialize with friends.

At the southern end of the lake were the towns of Cyangugu (in Ruanda) and Bukavu (in the Congo). Bukavu was the capital of the Congolese province of the Kivu. Surrounded by water, it was built on five narrow promontories jutting out into the lake. At that time, Bukavu and Cyangugu had a combined European population of approximately two thousand people. In the middle of the lake at its southern end lies Ijwi Island, a large island that had been ceded to Prince de Ligne of Belgium by King Albert. The prince had engaged in an adulterous love affair with the queen and was subsequently banished from Belgium to a life of exile on this remote tropical island paradise.

Many of the Europeans in the Kivu were titled. There was no setting in the Belgian colonies more inviting than this region surrounding lovely Lake Kivu with its perfect climate and fertile volcanic soil. It was here that many of the great families of Belgium had land holdings of coffee and tea plantations. There were titled French, Italian, and Polish families as well. As a result, pâté de foie gras, caviar, and vintage wines stocked the shelves of the shops in Goma, and Paris imports were sold in a dress shop called Champs Elysées.

Following World War I, Ruanda was assigned to Belgium as a trusteeship territory by the League of Nations. For many centuries, however, Ruanda had been a kingdom of the Watutsi. The Belgians and the Tutsi kings ruled side by side until rebellion swept the land in 1959 and the Tutsi monarchy was abolished. During my early years in the Kivu, it was not uncommon to see Tutsi aristocrats, their tall slender bodies wrapped in immaculate white cloth, drinking beer on hotel terraces, regarding the Europeans and their social customs with quizzical expressions. There was no color ban in this part of Africa, but there was little social contact between the Africans and Europeans. On the other hand, many European men in the Kivu had African mistresses (and in some cases wives), and as a result, there were many beautiful children of mixed race growing up in Kisenyi, Goma, and Bukavu.

Kisenyi's finest villas fronted on the tree-lined Avenue of Palms, across which was a right-of-way for shepherds to lead their cattle to the water's edge. Fishermen navigated their pirogues in the sparkling waters of the lake, and bands of hunters with poison-tipped spears and basenji dogs roamed the lava plains on the outskirts of Goma. Cows and sheep grazed on the golf course fairways in the middle of the day, and along the roads a daily procession of Congolese women could be seen, bearing on their backs enormous loads of firewood to be sold in Goma. Men with filed teeth and tribal scars, or cicatrices, wandered about the marketplace knitting cable-stitched sweaters, and children raced metal hoops made from the rims of gasoline drums along Kisenyi's main boulevard.

In those days, the chiefs rode bicycles to town, while European farmers drove Land Rovers or heavy-duty pickup trucks. I never would have imagined that by 1958, the chiefs would be driving American cars and that a tarmac road would be laid across the lava plains from Goma to Saké, making way for the rugged trucks and Jeeps to be replaced by luxury automobiles.

In many African countries, European planters helped sow the seeds of foment and revolution. In Kenya, for example, the white settlers claimed the best farmland in the "white highlands" outside of Nairobi, and the Kikuyu, in what was known as the Mau Mau uprising, fought to reclaim their land.

This was not the case in Ruanda. Although the Belgian administration was eager to produce commodities that would bring hard currency into the little country, it recognized the great need for arable land for the burgeoning native population. Consequently, the amount of farmland allocated to foreigners was strictly regulated. In 1938, the Belgian administration designated a limited number of parcels of land for the growing of coffee and pyrethrum by foreign plantation owners. Pyrethrum is a daisy-like flower grown in the highlands of east central Africa that contains a powerful insecticide. Each plantation consisted of exactly ninety hectares (one hectare equals approximately two and a half acres). Once these plantations were established, there were to be no more. Existing farms could be sold, but no new European farms could be created. Each plantation employed scores of local workers, whose wages, though not high by Western standards, were considered quite good for the region at the time. On each plantation, half the acreage (forty-five hectares) was "freehold," or owned outright by the planter. The other half was leased to the planter for a period of thirty-five years.

Thus, the number of foreign-owned plantations in Ruanda was strictly limited. As a result, when Kenneth and I arrived in the Kivu in 1949, it was not possible for foreigners to purchase new land for farming. Today, I am the last of the foreign plantation owners in Rwanda. All of the others left at the time of Congo independence. Many had owned plantations in both

Ruanda and the Belgian Congo, and when the Congolese drove them from their land and seized and nationalized their property, they fled the region altogether.

As a rule, foreigners were perceived differently in Ruanda than in most African countries. Never in Ruanda have the Europeans *("wazungu")* or Asians been expelled or even harassed. At the time of Ruanda independence, leaflets were dropped from airplanes that read in Kinyaruanda, the local Bantu language, "Europeans and Asians will show us the way to economic prosperity."

Shortly after we arrived in the Kivu, Kenneth and I moved into a small plantation house called Kilelema in the Mutura district of Ruanda. It was a charming stone cottage offered at a reasonable rent. The only condition to our rental agreement was that we agree to retain the existing staff of fourteen servants—four water carriers for nonpotable water, two water carriers for drinking water, four woodcutters, two houseboys, a cook, and an assistant cook. That seemed a bit excessive for just the two of us! My initial perception in those early days was that Africans in general were not especially motivated, and these in particular seemed to require and expect explicit instructions from me before making a move. I was woefully unsure of myself in my new role as mistress of the house, and somewhat intimidated by their exacting expectations of me and my inability to speak their language. Inventing chores to keep them all occupied, and then communicating those assignments to them, became a daunting exercise, and one which I began to dread more and more with each passing day.

While living at Kilelema, we met an Italian pyrethrum planter named Gino Imeri. Gino owned two plantations—one in the Mutura district of Ruanda and the other in the Masisi territory of the Congo. Gino was short and stocky with light brown hair and dark Italian eyes. He was also warmhearted and generous. He had been born of poor parents in Busto Arsizio, near Milan, and had left school at the age of twelve to become an apprentice garage mechanic. His older brother, Aristide, seeking fortune and adventure, diligently saved every penny he earned, and the two brothers set sail from Genoa to Mombasa in the early 1930s. During the course of a year-long safari, they lived entirely off the land, trading meat for necessities, and hunted elephants for ivory.

Aristide sailed back to Italy to market the elephant tusks. While awaiting his brother's return, Gino found a job as a garage mechanic in Dar es Salaam in Tanganyika and learned to speak English. Aristide eventually did return—with something less than a fortune, but enough for them to venture overland into the interior. They wound up in Bukavu at the southern end of Lake Kivu. Aristide bought a motorboat and began transporting goods from Bukavu to Goma and Kisenyi. Though successful, the transport business could not support them both, so Gino opened a garage in Kisenyi, which was an instant success. He repaired all the cars and trucks in the region, often rescuing vehicles that had fallen over the steep escarpments or been badly damaged on the rugged roads.

Gino invested in a pyrethrum plantation in the Congo, called Buniole. He subsequently acquired another plantation in Ruanda, called Mugongo, through one of the Belgian administration land grants, and became one of the first pyrethrum planters in Ruanda. Mugongo was located just five miles from Kilelema, and Kenneth and I spent many happy afternoons visiting with Gino. He was always delighted to exchange our American traveler's checks for Belgian Congo francs, and was equally pleased to have neighbors. Gino became a dear friend, and in the years to follow would play a significant role in the charting of my future in Africa.

For six months, Kenneth tried without success to obtain permission from the Belgian authorities to prospect for minerals in Ruanda. We were fast running out of money and on the verge of giving up when Gino offered Kenneth a job as manager of Buniole, his pyrethrum plantation in the Congo.

For days, Kenneth and I agonized over the decision. Our future hung in the balance as we vacillated first one way, then the other. We finally decided to reject Gino's offer and return to a more normal life in America. Our plan was to take an extended safari along the southern route through the Belgian Congo and sail home from the west coast of Africa. We set out one windy afternoon to break the news to Gino.

I have often wondered how differently my life might have turned out if we hadn't stopped to give a man a lift, and if the man's bright red cap hadn't blown away in the wind. When Kenneth stopped the truck, so the man could jump out and retrieve his cap, the trusty old Ford came to a grinding halt and refused to start up again. Gino found us sometime later stranded on the road. Being the expert mechanic that he was, he diagnosed the problem at once and reported sadly that it would take at least two months for the new parts to arrive. All of our plans went out the window, and we gave in to the inevitable and started packing for the Congo.

4

BUNIOLE

In February of 1950, Kenneth and I left our well-staffed cottage in Mutura and set out for the rugged mountains of the Masisi territory in the Congo. Buniole was a pyrethrum plantation of twelve hundred acres, although only a hundred and fifty were under cultivation. The homes and fields of the Africans who worked the plantation encompassed approximately two hundred acres, and the rest was forest. Buniole was my first real home in Africa. I wish I could say that it was love at first sight, but it took some time and a lot of hard work before that came to pass.

The house was a sturdy bungalow built from planks cut from trees in the forest. It was square and low, and designed with taste and imagination. Gino had forewarned that the house might need some sprucing up, but we were completely unprepared for what we encountered when we arrived at our new home. To our utter dismay, the house had been previously occupied by squatters and was in shambles. Birds roosted on the stone mantel, the cement floors were riddled with holes, and you could see through the knotholes in the walls. The entire house was thick with filth and decay.

We immediately hired a carpenter and a mason and set out to make it habitable. The house was scrubbed and swept from top to bottom. The wooden planks that formed the walls were treated with linseed oil and polished to a warm chestnut hue. The carpenter repaired the furniture that was salvageable and built new pieces to our specifications from trees in the forest. I made curtains for the windows and cushions for the window seats. Kenneth hung framed photographs and mementos of his hunting expeditions on the walls, and woven grass mats covered the floors. In time, we managed to tame the overgrown gardens, and soon the rooms were brightened with brass and copper bowls filled with pink rambler roses, lemon lilies, and honeysuckle. Sunlight streamed in through the windows, making the house bright and cheery in the daytime, and the warm glow of firelight and oil lamps at night made it very cozy indeed.

The house was divided by a wide hallway that ran from front to back. It had a sunken living room with a large fieldstone fireplace and a spacious dining room with wide casement windows that framed the forest and pyrethrum fields. The two bedrooms were on opposite sides of the hallway, and a bathroom and large storeroom stood at the rear of the house. The kitchen was a separate building in the backyard, and, naturally, there was no electricity or refrigeration.

Indoor plumbing in Africa is a somewhat primitive affair, but quite efficient nonetheless. At Buniole, we had hot and cold running water in the bathtub, and the water closet was of the old-fashioned variety with a pull chain. Three large oil drums were connected to the bathroom fixtures and served as water tanks. The elevated drums were kept filled with water which was hand-carried from the river three hundred yards away. A brick fireplace was installed beneath one of the drums, and each afternoon a wood fire was built to heat the bathwater. The water closet had a separate tank set high above it, and every day Basinda, the water porter, would climb a ladder to fill it.

Buniole lies at an altitude of seven thousand feet. The sun is very strong in the middle of the day, but the early mornings and late afternoons are cool and fresh, and the temperature at night dips to the fifties. The forest surrounding the plantation was dense jungle. Giant trees held parasite clumps of ferns, their branches festooned with hanging Spanish moss, vines, and lianas. The undergrowth was so lush it was almost impenetrable, except for the trampled paths created by the elephant herds that inhabited it.

A pyrethrum plantation is a thing of great beauty. A profusion of white flowers blooming year-round, blowing in the soft breeze and standing erect even in the heaviest of rains, creates a carpet of white across the fields and up the steepest hillsides. In the early mornings the fields at Buniole were curtained in a heavy mist that hung low over the land until dispelled by the sunlight.

Pyrethrum is a plant of the chrysanthemum family, although its flowers closely resemble the common white field daisy. Its effectiveness as a pesticide was discovered during World War I, when a battalion of soldiers bedded down one night in a field of pollinating pyrethrum plants. The next morning they discovered, to their great surprise, that the body lice which had plagued them were all dead.

In Africa, pyrethrum is grown in the highlands of Rwanda, Zaire, Kenya, and Tanzania at altitudes above sixty-five hundred feet. The mature flower heads are picked and then dried by indirect heat on flat wire trays in a drying house. At that time, the dried flowers were baled and then shipped to Mombasa for export to the United States, Japan, and the Argentine, where pyrethrin—a powerful insecticide harmless to warm-blooded life—was extracted from the flowers. In 1956, the pyrethrum co-operative of the Kivu built an extraction plant in Goma, enabling the pyrethrin to be extracted locally and shipped directly to world markets.

Pyrethrum culture is similar to that of the chrysanthemum. The plants must be weeded regularly and the dead stems removed. For maximum production, the plants should be renewed every two or three years. But even without such careful tending, the plants are so hardy they will continue to produce for many years. At Buniole, while the flowers were being picked in one section, new blooms were maturing in other fields. There was rarely a time when we were not harvesting.

The flower picking was done mostly by children—both boys and girls. They picked only the flower heads, snapping them off neatly so as not to break the stems. Small baskets were fastened to their waists, which when filled were emptied into larger baskets. At the end of the working day, which was three o'clock in the afternoon, the baskets were taken to the drying house to be weighed. The children were paid for the number of kilos they had picked during the month.

While they worked, the children sang long ballads in Kinyaruanda. The older children sang the verses, while they all joined in the chorus. There was always a great deal of laughter and improvisation. Although I was unable to decipher the lyrics, the melodies and harmonies were lovely. If I stopped to listen, they would insert my name, "Madame" or "Rosa," into the song.

As a rule, we employed only children age fourteen or older, but this was sometimes difficult to enforce. Sitting in a classroom or herding goats were tedious pastimes compared to working on a plantation. At Buniole, the children laughed and sang and were well cared for. The men at the drying house roasted cobs of corn in the big fireplaces of the dryers for their midday meals, and the workers carefully watched over them as they worked contentedly in the fields.

The workers at Buniole were predominantly Banyaruanda, although the Masisi territory, where Buniole is located, is the center of the Bahunde tribe. The Bahunde, formerly a cannibalistic tribe, file their teeth and ornament their faces with cicatrices. They are not a prolific people, and therefore the great coffee, tea, and pyrethrum plantations of the North Kivu depended to a large extent on the sizable Hutu population from Ruanda for their labor forces.

One hundred and eighty men were under contract to work at Buniole. Each year when new contracts were issued, each worker received a woolen blanket, a coat, and a pair of trousers. The blankets and trousers were brand new, but the coats were secondhand—purchased in bale lots from

America. They ran the gamut from Western Union uniform jackets to ladies' fur-trimmed winter coats. Army and Navy overcoats were the most highly prized, and there were generally one or two fine tweed coats from upscale American stores in the lot.

Excitement abounded when the coats were distributed. There were no mirrors, so the men had no way of knowing how they looked in them. In fact, most of the men had never seen themselves in a looking glass. Consequently, they would choose a friend and put the coat they had selected on him to see how becoming it was. To my endless consternation, they insisted upon wearing their coats while they worked in the fields. The daytime temperature at Buniole was always in the seventies, and perspiration rolled down their faces as they proudly wore their coats designed for winter weather in America. One funny old man wore the same coat for years— a lady's coat made of black wool with a high collar and cuffs trimmed in Persian lamb. The workers never wore their new trousers in the fields. Instead, several yards of unbleached muslin or striped pillow ticking were wound around their waists, forming a sort of skirt, which was held in place with a leather belt. If it had been up to me, they would have worn khaki shorts and shirts, but these peculiar outfits clearly pleased them.

The Banyaruanda are generally easygoing people who prefer not to be tied down to a steady job. In those days, they required very little money to get by. Therefore, it was extremely rare for a man to work more than the twenty days a month required by the terms of his contract. Buniole also employed "volunteers" who worked when the spirit moved them. At that time in the Congo, men who were not under contract to work for a European were required to work a certain number of days each year for their chief (usually ninety days), for which they received no payment. The rest of the year they worked their own fields or did as they pleased. Many would work for a European one or two days a month just to earn enough money to pay their annual tax, which in the 1950s was 440 francs a year ($8.80).

Every plantation employed a clerk, called a *karani*, to keep the books, mark the work cards each day, and supervise the labor. The *karani* supervised the headmen, or *capitas*, who worked all day in the fields, each one in charge of thirty or forty men. The plantation clerk at Buniole was a great mountain of a man named Cleophas Musafiri. He was a member of the Bahunde tribe, and his face was scarred with elaborate cicatrices. A line ran down from the peak of his forehead to the tip of his nose, and double half-moons were carved above each eyebrow and on both cheeks. Cleophas explained that this was a ritual performed on Bahunde boys when they reached puberty. Witch doctors carved deep incisions into the facial flesh with unsterilized razors, then rubbed charcoal into the wounds to give them color.

Cleophas had a small, neatly trimmed mustache, and, in contrast to his flashy appearance, his expression was one of habitual censure. The workers were very much in awe of him, and those who had known him for any length of time addressed him as "Baba," which means father. To the others, he was "Bwana," which means sir.

Cleophas had been the clerk at Buniole for so many years he had attained almost the status of a chief, and he made every effort to live like one. He had a large house where he received visitors and took his meals. Surrounding the house were the three separate huts of his three wives and their children. Cleophas sported a one-and-a-half-inch-long fingernail on the little finger of his right hand. When I asked him why he had such a long fingernail, he replied, "I use it to get rid of the little bugs that fly into my eyes. You see, I have very large eyes, and in the fields I am often bothered by bugs and little flies, so I pull down the lower lid and scrape them out with this long fingernail."

To his deep dismay, however, Cleophas had very poor teeth. Unlike most Africans, he consumed enormous quantities of sugar and, as a result, only one of his front filed teeth remained. He longed for false teeth and assured me that they needn't be very fine ones. "I wouldn't expect to have human teeth," he explained quite reasonably. "Possibly goat's teeth could be bought cheaply and would be very strong." I would have happily outfitted Cleophas with a set of false teeth, but in those days the nearest dentist was in Bukavu, a six-hour drive away.

Cleophas was also very fond of banana beer, or *pombi*—the "national drink" of the Congo. To our enormous relief, he limited his binges for the most part to Sundays, when he would host raucous parties with music blaring from his windup gramophone. I purchased many records for that gramophone over the years, and replaced the mainspring more than once.

While Kenneth ran the plantation, I ran the household. My responsibilities included supervising the houseboys and the gardener and planning the day's menus with the cook. Although our household staff was less than half of what it was at Kilelema, the servants did all the cooking, serving, cleaning, and laundry. They kept the home fires burning and the water drums filled. I was terribly appreciative of every little thing they did to make our lives comfortable, and I often told them so. Too often, according to Kenneth. Although Kenneth was highly regarded by the Africans and many were deeply devoted to him, he was a product of the colonial culture and temperament and was frequently harsh with them. I tended to be a bit more lenient. Too lenient, he often criticized.

I found the Africans to be utterly guileless, yet at the same time possessed of an extraordinary sense of morality and wisdom. They were kind and gentle people, and I was endlessly intrigued by their simplistic notions and amused by their perpetual melodramatics. My initial curiosity and timidity toward a culture so different from my own quickly gave way to feelings of genuine affection and respect. Many of the dearest and most important friendships in my life have been among the African people.

My expectations of a happy home life in true partnership with my husband were dashed almost from the start. Kenneth was away much of the time—either off on safari or in search of adventure and new opportunities—leaving me alone for weeks at a stretch. I was frightened and lonely and spent long hours weeping inconsolably and feeling terribly sorry for myself. In time, though—and as a matter of necessity—I managed to pull myself together and began to accompany Cleophas on his daily tours of inspection. I so enjoyed those long walks across the fields and through the drying house, greeting the workers and playing games with the children. I gradually learned to speak Swahili, and as time went by, I learned a great deal about running a plantation.

One of my first acts of self-reliance was to open a small dispensary for the workers on the plantation. I was completely unprepared, however, for my first encounter with a patient shortly after we arrived at Buniole. Kenneth was off on one of his long safaris, when I was awakened in the middle of the night by an insistent banging on the door. To my surprise, it was one of the workers in a terrible state of alarm. I did not speak Kinyaruanda or Swahili at the time, but he spoke enough French for me to understand that his wife was very ill. He begged me to come and save her life. I thought for a moment that it was some sort of bizarre hoax, but it quickly became apparent that I was expected to follow this man into the dead of night and perform a medical miracle. In a panic, I ran to the medicine cabinet, which was stocked with such items as aspirin, bicarbonate of soda, Band-Aids, and Mercurochrome. I hastily grabbed some aspirin and a small box of spirits of ammonia capsules, which had been a parting gift from one of my aunts. I followed the man across the fields, stumbling on the rugged path in the flickering lamplight, dreading the ordeal that lay before me, convinced that this was all a terrible misunderstanding. Trembling with fear, I stepped into a smoke-filled hut. The patient lay moaning on a bamboo mat surrounded by a bedside vigil of ten or more family members and countless goats and chickens. A fire was burning inside the hut, and the heat was suffocating. The woman was quite young and quite fat—a sign of health and beauty in Central Africa—but her eyes were closed and she gave no indication that she was aware of our arrival.

I felt her forehead in my most professional manner, then thought to feel for a pulse. Her forehead was noticeably hot, but probably no hotter than my own. She didn't appear to be very sick, but the moaning and groaning continued. Every eye in the room was focused on me, expecting powerful *muzungu* (white) magic. In desperation, I produced a silk-covered spirits of ammonia capsule, and holding it directly under her nose, I broke it open. The acrid fumes filled the stuffy hut and pandemonium broke out. People and animals ran in all directions, scattering like frightened chickens, and the patient sat bolt upright, coughing and gasping for breath. I fled to my house as fast as my legs would carry me and crawled into my bed, praying that the woman wouldn't die.

Early the next morning the woman's husband appeared at the back door—beaming. "That was powerful medicine you gave my wife, Madame!" he said joyfully. "Her illness is finished and she is quite well again. *Merci! Merci beaucoup!*"

When word of my magic capsule spread, the plantation workers and their families started coming to me with their illnesses and injuries. And that was how my little dispensary began. From that day until the present, every morning, women with their sick babies and people of all ages line up outside my back door waiting for me to treat their wounds and ailments. They come to me with colds and fevers, ear and eye infections, burns, intestinal worms, sprains, headaches, skin irritations, toothaches, vomiting, diarrhea, lacerations, and hangovers. Mostly I bind wounds, dispense baby aspirin, and apply ointment to little eyes infected with conjunctivitis. Burns are a common affliction, as the Banyaruanda live in small huts with open fires inside, and children crawl into the fires, or a log will roll off and burn them. I treat the burns with a paste I concocted from Mercurochrome and sulfur powder, which, I must confess, has produced some quite spectacular results.

In the early 1950s there were still many elephants in the forests surrounding Buniole. When the rains were heavy, they would often wander down from the higher elevations of the dense bamboo rain forest to the open areas of the plantation. They trampled the gardens and were a great menace to both the Africans and the planters. A rogue elephant can be very threatening, and occasionally people were killed. Fences were useless, but sometimes banging on drums or tin cans would frighten them away. Never for very long, however.

Kenneth's safari work at that time was strictly photographic, but he was still a superb marksman. One afternoon while Gino Imeri was visiting, several frightened workers came running to the house, shouting, "Bwana! Bwana! There are elephants in the fields!" Kenneth grabbed his rifle, and we all raced to the scene of the disturbance. There were four elephants—one bull and three cows. They had trampled several acres of pyrethrum and had wandered into a narrow wooded ravine. It was unusual for elephants to come out into the open in broad daylight, and they appeared agitated and disoriented by the ruckus they had created.

Kenneth would never shoot a cow elephant, but at Gino's insistence, he did take aim at the bull and fired once. The bull remained standing. Unable to get another clear shot, we eventually returned to the house. Moments later, there was more shouting—"Bwana! Bwana!" It seemed that Kenneth had killed the elephant after all. When he was shot, the females had closed in around him and held him up to keep him from falling. When they could support him no longer, they retreated to the forest and the elephant dropped to the ground. He had been killed instantly with a single shot straight through the heart. Elephants are amazing, almost mystical creatures, but they bring a whole new dimension to the term "garden pest."

Before we left Kilelema, Chief Kamuzinzi, the grand chief of Bugoyi, had presented me with a tiny silver-backed monkey as a gift of friendship. We named her Snooks, after the popular radio character "Baby Snooks." Kamuzinzi was nearly seven feet tall and was a first cousin to the king, Rudahigwa. He had a long narrow face and a bristly handlebar mustache, and he dressed in the traditional long flowing robe knotted at one shoulder. Chief Kamuzinzi had traveled to Europe and spoke fluent French, and was greatly respected and feared by his subjects.

The monkey Snooks was a constant source of joy and amusement for the entire household, and Sheila was very protective of her. When she wasn't riding around on Sheila's back, Snooks was kept restrained on a long rag rope tied around her waist and attached to a pole with plenty of room to run.

One afternoon, we heard Sheila barking frantically and ran outside to discover a large African eagle hawk soaring high in the sky over the ravine with Snooks in its talons and several yards of rag rope trailing behind them. Kenneth reacted quickly and ordered the workers to run to the edge of the ravine and clap their hands in unison to simulate gunfire. The clapping sounds disoriented the eagle, and it began to circle wildly. It finally released Snooks, and she landed in the top of a tall tree. The eagle continued to circle and was closing in, when one of the workers bravely climbed the tree and rescued her. Snooks was rigid with shock. We carried the bleeding little monkey into the house, and Sheila licked her wounds and pampered her for days until she was fully recovered.

Tragically, several months later, Gino pulled up to the house with a carload of provisions and a Sealyham terrier, which jumped out of the car and attacked Snooks—killing her in seconds. I wept buckets, and even Kenneth had tears in his eyes.

Life at Buniole was full of adventure and drama, but it was also very hard work. We were forty miles from the nearest town, and there was little time for a social life. I was far too busy to be bored, but I yearned for friends and gaiety. We became acquainted with many of the planters and businessmen in the Kivu and would occasionally leave the isolation of Buniole and make the long drive into Goma or Kisenyi for a Saturday evening of socializing, watching old French films, or dancing to phonograph records. It appeared that we had a perfect life. It was exciting and exotic, and I was falling in love with this land and its people. We should have been very happy, but instead Kenneth and I were drifting further and further apart.

When Gino announced that he was taking a seven-month holiday in Europe and was looking for someone to manage Mugongo—his pyrethrum plantation in Ruanda—I applied for the job. Kenneth was livid that I would even consider such an idea. He said it was improper and unseemly, and that I was utterly incapable of handling such an enterprise on my own. But my mind was made up. Perhaps, I reasoned, a short separation would do us both some good.

5

THE OVERSEER

Africa has a rich history of strong, independent women, but I was not at all certain that I was among them. I began to have serious doubts as to whether I could run a plantation the size of Mugongo all by myself, or if the workers would accept a woman as their overseer. I was leaving my husband and my only true friend in Africa to do something I knew very little about in a place where I knew no one and could barely speak the language. Although we had agreed to write, and Kenneth planned to visit as often as possible, we would be sixty miles apart, separated by terrible roads, which at times during the rainy season were impassable. I would be truly on my own.

As Gino drove off, his arm waving out the window, I stood and watched until his car disappeared down the road in a cloud of dust. I looked around me at what was to be my new home and my entire responsibility. Mugongo, located in the Mutura district of Ruanda, was a welcome contrast to the rugged isolation of Buniole. Seven pyrethrum plantations lay side by side to form an endless field of white flowers as far as the eye could see. Mugongo sits at the base of Karisimbi, the tallest of the Virunga volcanoes. Beside it is Mikeno, and to the west are Nyiragongo and Nyamulagira, two active volcanoes. In the valley to the south lie the glistening waters of Lake Kivu.

The spectacular open vistas and busy communal life dispelled any sense of loneliness I might have felt. Mutura is home to the tall Tutsi shepherds with their great herds of long-horned cattle and the elusive Batwa pygmies, purveyors of clay pots and magic spells. Narrow well-trodden paths meandered among the clustered huts of the agriculturist Hutu and past fertile fields of beans climbing on dried cornstalks and tobacco growing five feet high.

As plantation manager, I had a salary of two hundred dollars a month. The plantation clerk was a kind, earnest man named Zacharia, without whom I never could have coped. He kept the books, estimated each man's wages for the month, determined who was entitled to holidays, and settled all disputes. He had none of Cleophas's gregariousness or flamboyancy, but he was extremely fair and competent. Zacharia had beautiful handwriting and was very skilled at numbers, which he had learned at a Catholic mission school, and I never found a mistake when I checked his figures at the end of each month. Mugongo employed seven headmen to supervise two hundred and eighty workers. The day began with roll call at the drying house where the workers were assigned their duties. Baskets and hoes were dispensed as they set out for the fields.

At midmorning, I began my daily tour of inspection, walking for miles across the rolling fields and overseeing the work. As I passed by, each worker would stop and lift his hat—sometimes a battered old felt hat, but more often a turban of unbleached muslin—and say, "Jambo, Madame," with a wide smile. Most of the men kept their heads shaved, and those who did not carried combs made from the quills of porcupines.

After lunch, there was more overseeing to do, work releases to sign, and the next day's work schedule to plan. Then it was back to the drying house to inspect the day's harvest. The pickers would slowly make their way back from the fields, walking in single file carrying baskets full of daisies on their heads, laughing and singing. The work day was done and everyone was happy. By day's end, there would be fifteen hundred kilos of pyrethrum flowers ready for the dryer. The fires at the drying house burned continuously and four men worked throughout the night.

As I slowly made my way back to the house at the end of the day, I would look up and marvel at the majestic beauty of Mikeno's jagged peaks and Karisimbi's snowcapped dome, overshadowed by occasional clouds, and my heart would fill with gladness as the setting sun shimmered on the bamboo forests. Tea was served by a cozy fire, and with Sheila and Gino's four dogs curled up at my feet, I would reflect on the day and wonder what the following days would bring.

Gino had left me with an automobile—an old, dilapidated 1938 sedan, complete with a "special starter" and a "boy chauffeur" named Ntawukiruwabo. The special starter was four or five strong men to give it a running jump start, and the boy chauffeur couldn't drive. Instead, he filled the gasoline tank, checked the tires, and rode along beside me in the passenger seat to attend to any difficulties we might encounter on the road.

Once a week I would drive into Kisenyi to buy groceries and supplies, visit the post office, and do my banking. The boy chauffeur always accompanied me on these jaunts. Once we were settled in the car and ready to leave, the boy chauffeur would shout, "Sukuma!"—the signal for the men to start pushing. It usually took three or four attempts, but eventually the car would sputter to life and off we would go. I was completely inexperienced at driving on these roads, as Kenneth had never allowed me to drive an automobile in the three years we had lived in Africa. It is twenty-three miles to Kisenyi, downhill all the way, on a narrow winding road with a sheer drop-off to the right. As we approached the hairpin turns, I prayed there would be no other motorists coming in the opposite direction. As we bounced along, children waved, women smiled shyly, and men tipped their hats and bowed.

As we neared Kisenyi, the road became increasingly congested with people making their way to the market. Women carried great loads of bananas or sweet potatoes on their heads, men carted chickens or bundles of firewood in crude wheelbarrows, and boys herded goats along the crowded dusty road. Elegant Tutsi women rode in tipoys carried on the shoulders of their Hutu servants. I drove with one foot on the brake, one hand on the horn, and my heart in my throat.

From Mugongo to Kisenyi, there is a drop in elevation of three thousand feet. Delighting in the sudden warmth, I would shed my sweater and do my errands while the boy chauffeur watched the car. Afterward, I might take a swim in the lake or picnic on the beach, feeding the crumbs to the herons and crested cranes that wade on its shores. I was usually alone, except for a few children playing in the sand, or hotel employees washing linens in the lake, pounding them clean on the rough lava rocks. By two o'clock it was time to start back to Mugongo. The boy chauffeur would round up the special starters—offering them bribes of Belgian Congo francs—and we would slowly make our way home, in low gear all the way.

Kenneth's visits were infrequent and brought us no closer to a rapprochement. The months flew by and I was far too busy to feel lonely. My weekly visits to Kisenyi brought new acquaintances, and gradually I established a small circle of friends. Occasionally I would have callers at Mugongo.

When Gino returned, he was quite pleased with what I had accomplished. It had been hard work but I had enjoyed it, and I believed I had earned the respect of the workers and the other planters in the district. But now it was over. I was sorry to be leaving Mugongo and the people I had grown to know so well. I was also homesick for America and my family and not at all certain that I wanted to go back to Kenneth—or even stay in Africa. So I said good-bye to Kenneth for the second time and sailed home by way of East Africa and Europe. I had no idea at the time if I would ever return.

I was overjoyed to see my family again, but the sights and sounds and colors of Africa filled my mind. I visited with friends and shopped at elegant department stores stocked with merchandise I hadn't seen in years. I went to museums and the theater, but all the things I thought I had missed held little attraction for me now. Even the happy, successful lives of my friends and family seemed commonplace indeed, compared to the life I had left behind.

Kenneth had written a flurry of impassioned letters, begging me to return. He had rented a small house in Mutura and was looking to buy a coffee plantation in the Congo. I was not ready to give up on our marriage, or on Africa, so I agreed to give it one more try.

I sailed from New York to London on the *Queen Mary*, and then on the Union Castle Line through the Mediterranean past Gibraltar and into the Indian Ocean by way of the Suez Canal. We docked at Mombasa, where I boarded a train for Nairobi, and from there to Uganda. When I stepped off the train at Jinja, Kenneth was there to greet me.

Our reunion was a happy one, but short-lived. We had missed each other terribly during our long separation, and we were both hopeful of recapturing the joy of our first years together. It is possible that our expectations were too high, or perhaps we each had different needs. While I was in the United States, one of Kenneth's friends, the writer Mary Hastings Bradley, had urged me to write about our life in Africa, and I sold a story to *The Saturday Evening Post*, which was illustrated with several of Kenneth's photographs. This led me to imagine that we might become a modern-day Osa–Martin Johnson team, writing about and photographing together the wonders of life in Africa. On the voyage back, I had spent hours writing stories and articles in the hope that Kenneth would see this as an opportunity to work together. Despite my enthusiasm, Kenneth showed not even a flicker of interest in the idea, and all of my efforts were summarily dismissed.

Our life together quickly slipped back into one of disappointment and sadness for us both. The house Kenneth had rented was dreary and crude and poorly furnished. He began to stay away for long periods at a time, and my unhappiness turned to deep despair. I could be found at all hours of the day or night sobbing uncontrollably. In those days, Europeans were expected to maintain a certain degree of decorum. When it became known that I had been seen crying openly in front of Africans, Gino stepped in and demanded that this behavior cease at once.

I was making a spectacle of myself, and something had to be done. Gino suggested that I return to Buniole to manage the plantation on my own. Kenneth reluctantly agreed that this was the only sensible solution to the problem of "what to do about Rosy." So I went back to Buniole, and

Kenneth invested in a coffee plantation called Kania in the Mokoto territory of the Congo. We never lived together after that, but our lives remained closely intertwined during the turbulent years that were to follow.

One of the greatest sources of my unhappiness was the absence of children in our marriage. I desperately wanted children and could not imagine a life without them. And perhaps my family had been right about our age differences. We had never actually discussed Kenneth's age during our courtship, and he was less than forthcoming on the subject. It came as a shock to me when, shortly after we were married, I overheard him tell one of the guests at a dinner party that he had shot his first lion in 1912—the year I was born. It wasn't until years later, when I happened to see his passport, that I learned that he was nearly the same age as my father. Many men, when they marry younger women, assume a more youthful disposition. I always felt that Kenneth expected me to assume a more retiring one.

I loved Kenneth deeply, but we were not suitable as marriage partners. Our divorce became final in 1956, but we remained close friends until he left Africa in 1961. He returned to England, which he found too cold, then moved to South Africa, where he ran into difficulties cashing pounds to sterling. He then moved to Sydney, Australia, which he found too hot, and finally settled on St. Helier in the Channel Islands. We kept up a correspondence until he died in 1981 at the age of ninety-three. His landlady wrote me that he always kept a picture of me by his bedside. It was Kenneth who brought me to Africa, and for that I will always be grateful.

PART TWO

6

RETURN TO BUNIOLE

In February of 1954, I packed up my belongings and set off on my own for the Congo. I was happy to be returning to the familiar surroundings of Buniole. This was a new beginning for me, and a wonderful opportunity. I was a woman on my own now, and I had to earn a living. Best of all, it allowed me to remain in Africa.

The heavily laden pickup truck rumbled through the streets of Goma, then rattled across the plains of solidified lava formed from volcanic eruptions over the centuries. Just before Saké, I made a right-hand turn onto a rutted dirt road and began the steep twenty-mile ascent into the mountains of the Masisi territory. My arms ached from maneuvering the clumsy truck around hairpin turns and over the rough terrain of the tortuous road. Sheila and my Siamese cat, Mia, rode in the back with all my possessions, and bouncing along beside me was my cook, Sentashya, dressed smartly in khaki shorts and shirt, with white knee socks and brown shoes. He was born in the Masisi territory just a few miles from Buniole and was happy to be returning to his homeland.

Sentashya was a tall boy, darker-skinned than most Banyaruanda, with a round face and firm jaw. He had come to work for Kenneth and me at Buniole in 1950 as cook's helper, and at that time he was so tiny we called him "Toto," the Swahili word for child. Sentashya had grown up since then—both in stature and experience. He had accompanied Kenneth on safaris in Tanganyika and Uganda, and had been to Usumbura and Bukavu. He had just returned from Kenya where he had learned of the Mau Mau uprising and had spoken to both Kikuyu and Masai. He had seen the world, and now he was ready to come home. When I asked him how old he was, he said, "I don't know my age, Madame, but I know I am a man."

I recalled how he used to dance on the lawn at Buniole, a joyful little boy with arms outstretched, doing a comical rendition of the Ruanda dance impersonating the crested crane. When a small plane flew low over the pyrethrum fields, he had thrown himself on the ground in terror, fearful that it would fall out of the sky. Now he sat beside me, erect and self-assured, certain that he was a man. My guess is that he was seventeen or eighteen years old.

As we approached a neighboring plantation, the road narrowed to a deeply rutted lane and I slowed to a crawl. A mile or so farther on we came to a complete standstill where a mud slide caused by heavy rains had closed the road entirely. Sentashya got out and retrieved a spade from the back of the truck and started shoveling the damp, heavy earth. Like magic, people began to appear from all directions to contemplate our predicament and offer advice. They smiled and shook my hand and welcomed me back to Buniole. As I continued on, negotiating my way through the slippery mud, Sheila jumped out of the truck and raced ahead, sensing that she was in familiar territory.

With a mile or more yet to go, the outlying pyrethrum fields of Buniole came into view. They were a disheartening sight—thick with weeds and almost devoid of blooms. The road cut through deep, tangled forest, and a cluster of vervet monkeys dived from the branches overhead, scolding me as I passed. Coming out of the thicket, I looked across a small valley and my heart lifted. Nestled on a grassy knoll in a clearing in the forest was the little bungalow I remembered so well. After many months of sadness and turmoil, I felt I was home at last.

As we passed the drying house, we heard shouts of "Madami, Madami! Jambo, Madami!" Children slid down the bank and raced along beside us, laughing and waving. Men followed, and as I shut off the engine and got stiffly out of the truck, tears filled my eyes at the sight of the friendly, smiling faces. As helpful hands began to unload my belongings, I overheard the men ask Sentashya, "Is she really here to stay forever?"

I unlocked the front door and let myself in to the cold, musty house. Overcome with emotion and fatigue, I ate an early supper and collapsed in bed with thoughts of uncertainty churning through my mind. Was I capable of managing Buniole on my own? And could I live in such seclusion—eight miles from the nearest neighbor?

I awoke before dawn to the screeching sound of chimpanzees in the trees overhead. After a few minutes they moved off, and by sunrise they would be far from the house. Outside my open bedroom window, birds began to sing in an almost forgotten birdsong concerto. A cock crowed, and I stretched out in my narrow bed and turned my thoughts to what lay ahead. Sentashya was building a fire in the living room, and the sweet smell of pinewood filled the air. When I went in to breakfast, Berina was standing beside a perfectly laid table—his hands outstretched and his filed teeth displayed in a wide grin. Berina was a young Muhunde I had trained as houseboy in 1950, and he had come back to work for me again, as promised. With Berina as houseboy and Sentashya as cook, my household was complete.

It was a busy day. Berina waxed and polished the cement floors and scrubbed the bedrooms and bathroom. Sentashya took over the kitchen, and I unpacked and rearranged the furniture and household items until I was more or less satisfied. The sun slanted across the bright new cushions on the window seats, and a little black-and-white wagtail bird walked confidently in through the open door and—after looking around with approval—walked back out again. Swallows that nested under the eaves darted in and out of the casement windows with a flutter of blue and bronze wings, making me feel welcome. The warble of wood pigeons resonated from the cypress trees, and hordes of magistrat monkeys chattered away in the forest across the ravine, making a sound like the click of a tongue followed by a short cough.

Throughout the day people came to welcome me, bringing me gifts of eggs and vegetables from their gardens. My old friend Cleophas stood at the front door holding a fat hen and a basket of potatoes, saying, "I've brought you a complete meal, Madame." My tea was served on a square table by the corner window seat, and women who passed by stopped and waved, just as I remembered. When darkness came and the curtains were drawn and a fire crackled hypnotically on the hearth, Berina and Sentashya bid me "*Kwa heri*"—good night. The soothing sound of music filled the evening air as the night watchman played a reed flute made from the stem of a giant lobelia, and an indescribable feeling of peace and contentment came over me as I sat gazing into the fire.

The following morning, I turned my attention to the task of overseeing the plantation. There was much to be done to restore the fields to full production. Cleophas and I planned the work schedules together, and he accompanied me on my daily tours of inspection. Since the plantation covered such a large area and most of the fields were accessible only by foot, we spent the better part of each day together. I relied greatly upon his judgment and often asked for his advice.

I wish I had listened to him when he suggested that we replace the support posts of the small garage where I parked the truck. The garage at Buniole resembled a poor farmer's tobacco shed and consisted of six upright posts with a frame roof covered with mounds of elephant grass lashed down with split bamboo. One afternoon I backed into it a bit too aggressively, and the rear bumper collided with one of the rotted posts. There was a loud crack, and the entire roof collapsed on top of the truck, burying me beneath a mound of fallen timbers and soaking-wet grass thatching. Sentashya heard the crash and was the first on the scene. From the damp darkness of the rubble, I could hear the frightened voices of the workers as they frantically removed the debris and dug me out of the wreckage. Their relief was almost as great as mine when I was finally extricated unharmed. The Ford sustained minor damage, but nothing critical. Soon a new and bigger garage was built with strong support posts, but I never dared to back all the way in again. Even during the heaviest of rains, the old Ford's radiator stuck halfway out the garage door.

It rained incessantly those first few months. Rain beat on the corrugated iron roof in such a mad staccato that Mia the cat was in a constant state of agitation. The fields were often flooded, and on several occasions a river of rain poured down from the mountain slopes behind the house in such a torrent that we had to dig a trench across the backyard to keep the water from entering the house.

Most of the Africans I have come to know well have been farmers, and like all people who live off the land, their preoccupation with the weather is all-consuming. Weather prophets and rainmakers are highly revered in Africa and can earn a goodly sum—a jug of banana beer, or even a goat or two—if their forecasts prove accurate. Cleophas told of a weather prophet from his tribe whose remarkable ability to predict hailstorms earned him an enviable salary on a nearby coffee plantation. I have no idea what purpose a weather prophet would have served, but if there had been some mystical means of stopping the rain, I surely would have considered it.

During my early years in the Kivu, I greatly missed the changes of the seasons. I would dream of the orange, yellow, and scarlet trees of autumn, icicles hanging from the eaves, and the first pale leaves of spring. In this part of Africa, the dry and rainy seasons provide the only contrast in climate, as the temperature remains constant year-round. Gradually, I began to adjust to the pattern of the African seasons, which revolve around the cycle of rainfall and the rotation of the crops.

The four seasons of Ruanda are Urugalyi, the short dry season in January and February; Itumba, the heavy rainy season in March and April; Ikyi, the long dry season from May through August; and Umuhindo, the long rainy season from September through December.

The Ruanda calendar is divided into ten months. Muturama corresponds to our January and February and is the time when the millet is planted. March is Weruwe, the time when insects attack the millet. April is called Mata and marks the drinking of the new season's millet beer. May and the first part of June are Gicurasi, a time of illness and sadness, for the change from heavy rains to cooler, dry weather often brings colds, bronchitis, and influenza. June is Kamena, when the millet is ground into flour. July and the early part of August are called Nyakanga, a period often fatal to old cows, as they become very thin during the drought when the grass is sparse and dry. Kanama is the end of August and September, when crops are scarce and everyone waits for the rains to begin. October is called Uk-wakira, the most important month of the year, for this is the time to begin planting beans. November is Ugushyingo, a month of harvesting, and December is Ukoboza, when the rains persist and can damage the crops.

Africans believe that the moon has great influence over events. Its clarity and transformations, the faithfulness with which it measures time, and the assistance it provides to travelers cause them to regard it as their friend. They believe that the stars are the children, servants, and soldiers of the moon.

As the weeks and months passed, I came to know all the families living at Buniole. The line outside my back door each morning grew longer and longer, but not all had come to visit the dispensary. Many came just to socialize or to solicit my opinion on some recent event, and often I was asked to settle disputes or referee endless squabbles. Women would sit on the lawn near the house to watch me—as curious about my way of life as I was about theirs. Men would linger to offer bits of advice, or to light their clay pipes from the coals on the kitchen stove.

There were times when I was lonely, but I was never completely alone. I had Sheila and Mia to keep me company, as well as all the workers and their families. There were occasional visitors and infrequent trips to town. Kenneth came by from time to time, and although his visits were always welcome, they were often tinged with a note of sadness and regret.

Goma and Kisenyi were too far away to make the trip with any regularity, but when the weather was clear and there was no danger of becoming stuck on the road, Sentashya and I would make a long shopping list and drive the forty miles into town. Once there, I would cash a check for the workers' salaries, visit the post office, and stock up on a six-week supply of flour, sugar, coffee, tea, kerosene, nails, and anything else I needed—if I could find it. Often I would have lunch with friends at the Hôtel des Grands Lacs in Goma and listen to colorful accounts of recent scandals and events. My provincial lifestyle seemed very dull indeed compared to the recreations and social activities of the landed gentry of the Kivu.

Medical facilities in this part of Africa were few and far between, and the scarcity of doctors and dentists was one of the hardships that we all learned to live with. I once drove more than three hundred miles with Gino to see a Baptist missionary dentist in the Lubero territory of the Congo. His name was Dr. Hurlbert, and he ran a school for mulatto children and practiced dentistry on the side. Dr. Hurlbert had a foot-powered drill, and his sole source of illumination was a flashlight held by his son aimed in the general direction of my mouth. If the technology was less than cutting edge, the long scenic drive across the Rwindi Plains, past cattle farms and through forests of giant tree ferns, more than compensated. As a rule, I traveled all the way to Kampala to see a dentist—a trip of more than four hundred miles each way.

For a time there was a woman dentist in Kisenyi, who once treated Kenneth for a broken crown. First, she dropped the crown on the floor and stepped on it and broke it. She then sent away to Brussels for a new one. When Kenneth returned several weeks later to have it fitted, she dropped the new crown and couldn't find it. After turning the office upside down, it was ultimately discovered in Kenneth's shirt pocket. When she told him to put his head back and open wide, she dropped it down his throat and he swallowed it. Finally, when she suggested that he might "recover" it, he left her office without uttering a word and drove directly to Kampala.

Although visitors to Buniole were infrequent and trips to town were rare, I had the workings of the plantation to fill my days and occupy my mind. This was perhaps the only time in my life that I was not plagued by financial worries. I was paid a salary of three hundred dollars a month, plus a bonus on the pyrethrum production. The house was provided, of course, and I had a large vegetable garden, a poultry yard, and fruit trees. I was able to save more than half my income.

Gino had instructed me to increase the acreage of pyrethrum at Buniole, which entailed cutting back forest, digging out enormous stumps, and clearing off the underbrush before a new field could be tilled and planted. It was extremely hard work, but I was surprised to find that the men preferred it to the less strenuous work in the established fields. Huge trees were felled and the trunks hauled to the road, where they were transported by truck to the fires at the drying house. It took eight men to carry each of the heavy tree trunks balanced on poles slung across their shoulders. Stripped to the waist, the men would sing and chant, "Will it defeat us? No! No!" I walked along beside them, the sun hot against my shoulders, and applauded each time a heavy log slammed down on the roadside and rolled into place beside the others.

I walked for miles each day on my tours of the plantation. Sometimes, when the fields were thick with mud, the workers would carry me on a tipoy, a large basket made of split bamboo supported by two long poles carried on the shoulders of four men—two in front and two in back. The porters would sing and jog along the flat stretches of the paths and, at a given signal, shift the poles from their left shoulders to their right, and then, at regular intervals, shift back again. I would bounce in the air each time they switched shoulders, and the men would laugh and say, "Madami is a *mwamikazi* (Tutsi queen) today!" The real queen and royal princesses always traveled in tipoys in the days before the king and the big chiefs drove automobiles.

Sheila was my constant companion in the fields, frolicking and sniffing. One day as we were returning to the house, I heard a sound coming from a deep ravine beside the road. It sounded like a sick or wounded man gasping for breath. It was late in the afternoon, and dark shadows were lengthening across the road. We should have been home long before then. As I hurried toward the sound, the panting intensified. The hair on Sheila's back stood straight up as she moved slowly and cautiously with all senses alert. We were almost upon it when the sound ceased abruptly, and I suddenly realized that it was not a human sound at all. A chill of terror ran up my spine, and I broke into a wild run with Sheila at my heels—realizing at that moment that it was a leopard!

We tore through the tangled brush along the narrow path that led away from the ravine. Only once did I dare to look over my shoulder, and it was then that I caught a glimpse of this wily predator, moving furtively across the rugged terrain, watching us with its fiery eyes. It kept its distance, though, and Sheila and I managed to reach the safety of the house unharmed.

Kenneth had warned me years earlier that leopards make a rasping, sawing sound, and that they hold their breath just before they attack. I also knew that dogs were commonly preyed upon by leopards. The following evening, a man from a neighboring plantation stopped by for a drink and to warn me that he had seen a large leopard on the road near the ravine. From that day on, I made sure that Sheila and I were both safely inside before sundown, for that is the time when leopards awake from their daylong sleep to begin their nocturnal hunt.

Madame Pessina lived on a farm ten miles from Buniole. She owned a large truck and would occasionally transport pyrethrum to Goma for me. One afternoon she and her driver arrived, and we visited while several tons of dried pyrethrum were loaded onto the truck. They left Buniole at four-thirty in the afternoon, but at five o'clock I received word that the truck had broken down and they were stuck on the road. Sentashya and I climbed into the pickup and found them about five miles down the road.

While the driver tinkered with the engine, Sentashya and I covered the sacks of pyrethrum with a tarpaulin, roping them down tightly, as any dampness would spoil the carefully dried flowers.

I drove Madame Pessina to her house just as darkness was falling. She thanked me for the lift and waved good-bye as we set out for Buniole. When I pulled the switch to turn on the headlights, to my horror, nothing happened. The headlights were broken, and we had ten miles to travel on the dark and desolate road. In the casual manner of those who are accustomed to such inconveniences, Madame Pessina handed me a small oil lantern to light our way home. In total darkness and with no moonlight to guide us, Sentashya walked bravely in front of the truck, carrying the little lantern and guiding me around deep ruts and over steep ledges. About two miles from home, we heard the chilling, rasping sound of a leopard coming from the dense forest that bordered the road. Sentashya scrambled into the truck with eyes wide as saucers, and we blindly inched our way back to Buniole, terrified and trembling with fear.

To this day, leopards are still one of the few creatures in Africa of which I am truly afraid. I have seen the damage a leopard can do—to both animals and humans—and there is every reason to fear them.

7

THE EUROPEANS

The European population in the Kivu at that time was an eclectic community made up of adventurers and aristocrats, and there was no shortage of colorful characters among its ranks. They came from Belgium, France, Italy, Poland, Austria, and England during the first half of the twentieth century and established large plantations along the fertile shores of Lake Kivu and throughout the surrounding mountainous region. The cultural and commercial centers of the Kivu were the twin towns of Goma and Kisenyi in the north and the provincial capital of Bukavu in the south, each boasting wide tree-lined boulevards with tasteful shops and hotels catering to their aristocratic clientele. The settlers built elaborate European-style villas and plantation houses staffed with many servants, and created a world of refinement and privilege in this picturesque paradise. Many came to make their fortunes, many left fortunes behind, and many fortunes were lost at Congo independence.

The term "European" in this part of Africa is used to describe all whites, regardless of where they originated; therefore, as an American, I am considered a European as well. The official Belgian attitude toward the Africans was one of paternalism, whereby they were to be cared for and treated as children, while acknowledging their traditional customs and indulging their tribal rulers. The African word for European is *"muzungu,"* and when I recall those glamorous years before Congo independence, I find it not surprising that the *"wazungu"* were often regarded by the Africans with a healthy dose of skepticism.

A great many of the white settlers in the Kivu were titled. The warm climate and open frontiers of East Africa became a land of opportunity for the second and third sons of the European aristocracy born into a system of primogeniture. Among them were displaced and disenfranchised members of the nobility from the great royal houses of Europe. There were an equal number of adventurers and fortune seekers who had migrated to this exotic locale in search of wealth and opportunity. For the most part, they were a stalwart and indomitable group of men and women, who worked hard and played hard, and relied entirely upon one another for camaraderie and entertainment. They threw lavish parties, engaged in rowdy competitions, and dabbled in fanciful hobbies.

One coffee planter lived in a magnificent house with an elaborate dovecote built to house his collection of exotic birds. At dinner parties, his guests would scatter bread crumbs on the polished black-and-white tiled floors to feed his pedigreed white doves which strutted freely about underfoot. Another planter raised hybrid tuberous begonias that flanked the wide terraces of his villa down to the lake shore and were the envy of many a horticulturist. Jack Poelaert drove a 1922 Rolls-Royce and lived with his mother and a domesticated golden monkey in a spectacular house surrounded by fragrant citrus groves. Peacocks and crested cranes strutted across many lawns, and one French planter had a small game preserve on his plantation. A baroness, best known for her bawdy stories and off-color jokes, was formerly the madam of a high-class brothel in Paris prior to marrying a French baron and settling in the Kivu.

They came from diverse backgrounds, and they all had colorful stories to tell. Sergio Bottazzi was a successful Italian businessman who lived in a villa on the lake in Kisenyi. His father had been governor of Somalia during the 1940s, and both Sergio and his father had been interned as Italian nationals in a prison camp in Kenya during World War II. Sergio came to Ruanda in the 1950s and developed an irresistible fondness for Tutsi women. When his mother came to visit some years later, she was dismayed to learn that Sergio had no wife and no expectations of acquiring one. She was further dismayed to discover that she was grandmother to three beautiful half-caste children who were growing up wild and spoke only Kinyaruanda. Madame Bottazzi took the situation well in hand and stayed on to raise her grandchildren. She taught them French and Italian and took them to Italy on holiday. Madame Bottazzi was highly regarded throughout the Kivu for her exquisite tropical gardens, and she remained in Ruanda until she died in 1980.

One of the most colorful characters of all was Oswald, the Marquis du Chasteleer. Although Oswald had inherited his Belgian title, his father had been penniless and he had come to the Congo to make his fortune. He used his title, he would say, only in America where he traveled periodically to sell pyrethrum. Oswald became very successful and did indeed make his fortune. He owned two coffee plantations in the Congo and a lakeside villa in Kisenyi. Terraced gardens and an intricate maze decorated the lawns of one of his plantations, and arcades of clipped cypress trees formed an outdoor dressing room for bathers with fragrant leafy green walls. A waterfall cascaded down the mountain slopes and emptied into a pool stocked with trout from Kenya.

Oswald was a large man with enormous energy—both physical and sexual. He was not particularly handsome, but he adored women and he had an irresistible sense of humor. His exploits with the ladies were legendary, and as a tribute to his prowess, a great many people in the Kivu named their prize roosters "Oswald." He had been married to a lovely Austrian countess, who eventually left him after enduring a succession of infidelities with a remarkable degree of fortitude.

Oswald and I became great friends, but he never missed an opportunity to suggest that we broaden that friendship into something of a more intimate nature. And I never missed an opportunity to graciously decline. The first time I saw Oswald, he was dining with a stunning woman in the Hôtel des Grands Lacs in Goma. She was a countess and his mistress, and the first of a succession of ravishingly beautiful women I would see with Oswald over the years.

The loveliest of all was Yvonne Mendel, an accomplished violinist and the young bride and protégé of Sir Charles Mendel, a well-known patron of the arts in Great Britain. Sir Charles's first wife had been the famous interior designer Elsie De Wolfe, the originator of blue-tinted hair rinses for elderly women. Sir Charles professed openly that his marriage to Yvonne was a *"mariage blanc,"* and it was with his full knowledge and consent that Yvonne accompanied Oswald to the Kivu. Yvonne was well received by the European community, and everyone, myself included, found her charming and radiant. I felt that we might have become good friends, but she died tragically of intestinal cancer within the year, after having undergone several operations in Europe.

Oswald's peccadilloes kept the people of the Kivu amused and entertained for years. One of my acquaintances was a French baroness, whose daughter was married to a lawyer in Bukavu. The daughter fell madly in love with Oswald, and her husband implored his mother-in-law to intervene on his behalf in order to save his marriage. The Baroness marched off to wrest her daughter from the arms of this Lothario and ended up becoming Oswald's mistress herself. They were together for years.

Being a woman alone in the remoteness of Buniole, I was considered a bit of an eccentric myself, but in this society dominated by unattached men, I was frequently in demand as a dinner partner. Since entertaining usually involved traveling great distances on very bad roads, often there were weekend house parties, which were always very gay and extravagant affairs. Vintage wines and champagne flowed. Pâté de foie gras, quail's eggs, and raw oysters shipped on ice from Europe were commonplace, and an evening wasn't complete without elaborate games and dancing to the sounds of American jazz. The days were filled with swimming and boating, shooting contests, rounds of golf on the six-hole golf course, and equestrian events at the Goma Riding Club—which boasted all of six horses.

There were many lavish entertainments up and down both shores of Lake Kivu, but the most elegant parties of all were given by Karin and Adam Bielski. Karin was tall and lovely, with light brown hair, a porcelain complexion, and a commanding presence. She was by all accounts the "first lady" of the Kivu. Although somewhat reserved, Adam was charming and very distinguished and an exceptionally fine dancer. Like most of the Europeans, their path to the Kivu was a circuitous one.

Adam was a Polish count who had fought with the Polish army during World War II. At the time, he had a young wife named Sophia and an infant daughter. When the Polish army was defeated, Adam took his wife and child to Lisbon, where he made a living at the gaming tables. Eventually they found passage to Scotland, where he rejoined his regiment under a Polish general and fought among the Allies. In Edinburgh, Sophia fell in love with another man (one of Adam's closest friends), and she divorced Adam and took their little girl to Canada.

Adam fought in France, where he was badly wounded and left for dead by the Red Cross. It was only after his own troops found him and realized he was still alive that he was rescued and brought to an army hospital. By the time he recuperated, the war was over. Knowing he could never return to a communist Poland, Adam sought out a distant relative who had an export business in Holland. It was there that he found a job and met Karin.

Karin's grandfather had been Keeper of the Keys for the Dutch royal family, and as a child, Karin was tutored with Queen Juliana, with whom she maintained a close friendship throughout her life. She had married a man named Boreel whom she divorced in the mid-1940s. Adam and Karin fell deeply in love, but being a devout Roman Catholic, Adam agonized over the legitimacy of their marrying—since they both were divorced. It was a true test of faith, but love won out and they eventually married.

Adam's brother Roman sought refuge in Great Britain during the war, where he met and married Anna, the Princess Sapieha of Poland. Anna's brother, Prince Michel Sapieha, had been a hunting companion to King Leopold III of Belgium, and the king had deeded him a tract of land for hunting big game in the Belgian Congo. None of the family had ever seen this land, but when the war ended, the entire Sapieha family—including Roman and Anna and their Polish housekeeper—migrated to the Congo to establish a new life for themselves there. They planted tea and prospered.

Karin decided that she and Adam and her three children should leave Holland and join Roman and other Polish families who had settled in this part of Africa. They came to the Kivu in 1952. Karin was quite well-to-do, and she bought two houses side by side on a hill in Kisenyi. One was used as the living quarters and housed their extensive library while the other was used as bedrooms. They invested in a coffee plantation near Saké and did extremely well.

Many of the planters and aristocracy of the Kivu became good friends, and I feel privileged and extremely fortunate to have had them in my life. They brought me great happiness and were always there to assist in times of trouble. They welcomed me into their world, and what a charmed and intoxicating world it was! That world came to an abrupt end with Congo independence. All of the Europeans were forced to flee the Congo in 1961, and most fled the region altogether. I was fortunate to be living on my own plantation in Ruanda at the time and was able to make the decision to stay.

Roman and Anna were among the very few who remained, often taking refuge in Ruanda, but always returning to their land holdings in the Congo. One afternoon in 1964, while driving in the Congo, their car was ambushed by Congolese soldiers, and Roman and Anna were killed by multiple blows from machetes.

Karin Bielska left the Congo in 1961, along with so many others. Oswald went to South Africa, and Jack Poelaert to Uganda. Adam remained in Kisenyi until he died in 1989. He remained one of my dearest friends until the end. We often reminisced about those glorious years of privilege and complacency, before the Africans reclaimed the land that was theirs and our world was forever changed.

8

CECIL

Cecil Bellwood came into my life at a time when my self-confidence as a woman was at an all-time low. I had received an invitation to a dinner party at Karin and Adam Bielski's house in Kisenyi. It had been almost seven weeks since I'd been off the plantation, and I was eagerly looking forward to an evening with friends. A few days earlier I had inadvertently over-heard Sentashya and Berina discussing the way I conducted myself as a woman on her own, and the conversation went something like this: "Well, you know, she acts just like a man. She's almost as tall as a man, and she wears trousers like a man. And have you seen her drive that truck? She drives just like a man!" For all I knew, those remarks might have been in-tended as high praise, but I was cut to the quick. I made up my mind that some changes were in order.

As I maneuvered the truck up the steep driveway to the Bielskis' twin houses (in as ladylike a manner as possible), Karin and Adam greeted me with open arms. With the words "just like a man" still rankling, I was de-termined to put an end to any similar sentiments. I had worn my best dress of lilac silk and had taken great care to scrub the plantation soil from my fingernails, artfully apply a modicum of makeup, and tame my flyaway hair. The night was charged with a festive atmosphere. Among the twenty or so guests, there were Dutch, Polish, Belgian, French, Swiss, Italian, and British. I was the only American. The house servants circulated among the guests with enormous trays of cocktails, looking quite smart, dressed in starched white trousers, white shirts with black ties, and wide red-and-yellow cummerbunds.

It was an enchanted evening with music and champagne. Silver cande-labras and wall sconces held dozens of flickering candles that reflected off the crystal goblets and cast a warm glow against the rose-colored walls. Once again, my limited language skills put me at a disadvantage, but I found myself seated beside a Brit with whom I felt quite at ease. His name was Cecil Bellwood, and he was about my age, of medium height and build, with dark wavy hair. He was attractive, charming, and a fascinating conversationalist, and I was more than a little flattered by his attentions. We flirted and made small talk and danced whirling waltzes across the veranda. Cecil made me feel attractive and desirable again, and I was sorry to see the evening end. When he suggested that he might stop by to see me sometime, I never really expected that he would. But my ears picked up each time I heard a car in the distance coming down the long road to Buniole.

Several weeks later, to my surprise and delight, he did come. We had tea, and I showed him around the plantation. We talked for hours about anything and everything. He brought me up to date on all the news from Bukavu to Kisenyi, and I told him about my life and how I happened to wind up managing a pyrethrum plantation in the Congo.

Cecil was divorced. He had graduated from Sandhurst and was stationed in North Africa during World War II, where he saw intense fighting and contracted amebic dysentery. The dysentery continued to cause him severe intestinal problems throughout his life. He had spent some time in Kenya, where he had established many contacts, and he was now selling insurance to Belgian planters in the Bukavu area, working for a firm called Colin Hood.

Love affairs and adulterous liaisons were de rigueur in the Kivu, but I was determined to be an exception to the rule. My divorce from Kenneth was not yet finalized, so when I invited Cecil to be my house guest for an entire weekend, I was faced with the dilemma of whom to invite as chaperons. Cecil was always very proper, but a single man under my roof for a weekend would have started tongues wagging all over the Kivu. I came up with who I felt were the ideal candidates as chaperons—a friend from Kisenyi, Jack Poelaert, and his mother, Madame Poelaert. To round out the party, I invited my neighbors, Jean-Marc and Christianne Syners, for dinner on Saturday evening.

Cecil arrived in a downpour, heavily laden with baskets full of wonderful treats and delicacies, including fresh trout, a selection of wines, fresh plums, and Belgian chocolates. I was overwhelmed. I was also a bit uneasy about the weather. We were well into the heavy rainy season, and storms such as this one could go on for days, deterring all but the most determined of travelers.

We got on famously. Sipping sherry by the fire, I told him about the other guests I had invited and he seemed delighted. At the appointed hour, there was a knock at the door. Expecting the Poelaerts or the Synerses, I was disheartened to find a very soggy porter with a message saying that Madame Poelaert was ill and they would be unable to come. My carefully laid plans were coming unraveled, but I calmly reasoned that perhaps the Synerses would agree to stay the night—or Cecil could spend the night at their house. Before long, another knock at the door revealed a second porter, as drenched as the first, bearing a note from the Synerses explaining that they had been detained in Goma and, regretfully, would be unable to join us for dinner as well.

"I'm afraid this is rather awkward," I said, returning to the living room where Cecil was comfortably settled in a chair by the fire.

"Nothing can be awkward between us, Rosamond," he said reassuringly.

"Well, I'm afraid it is. You see, Madame Poelaert is ill and the Snyerses are stuck in Goma. You can't possibly stay the night if we're alone!" I said as though stating the obvious.

Cecil was very quiet for a few moments, then he simply said, "This is so pleasant being here together. Let's not ruin the atmosphere. Shall we have some dinner?"

With the rain pummeling the roof and lashing against the windows, we managed to have a very pleasant dinner, but the moment Berina began clearing the table, I started in again on our predicament. I was unyielding in my determination that Cecil must not stay, and he was just as adamantly opposed to the idea of leaving in such a downpour. We were at an impasse. When he finally offered to sleep in the car, I came to my senses and conceded that I was being thoughtless and silly and that of course he must stay. In the end, out of sheer embarrassment, we both went to bed very early—in separate bedrooms with a wide hallway and two closed doors between us. The next morning, with the sun shining brightly, I felt thoroughly ashamed of myself.

Miraculously, Cecil did not give up that easily. He came to see me the following weekend and many weekends after that—sometimes bringing friends, and eventually he came alone. He was very amusing and entertaining and could talk for hours on almost any subject. He was endearingly British in his speech and mannerisms, and he always managed to do or say exactly the right thing. He was also incredibly romantic, and I counted the days until I would see him again. He was loving and tender, and I discovered with Cecil a passion I had never known.

I cannot say that I was truly in love with Cecil. I believe it was more a powerful and well-timed infatuation. Twelve passionless years of marriage to Kenneth had left me feeling lonely and unfulfilled, and Cecil was exactly what I needed in my life at that time. On the other hand, I was steadfastly dedicated to the preservation of my reputation. Cecil humored me in this regard—or perhaps he was every bit as circumspect as I. In any case, discretion was our watchword. We went to parties in Goma and Kisenyi together, but not often enough to cause comment. The house servants knew only that Bwana Bellwood came to visit and stayed the night. I must assume, however, that they drew their own conclusions.

Cecil often had business in Goma, and he would combine his business travels with a visit to our secluded hideaway at Buniole. The plantation work filled my days, but the nights were our own. Cecil not only banished my loneliness, but he helped me discover what a happy and beautiful place Buniole could be. Together we would walk to the waterfall in the late afternoons, making our way along the overgrown path, surprising monkeys high in the tangled vines of the forest trees, and coming upon the narrow torrent of crystal-clear water that cascaded down the mountain onto the boulders and lacy ferns at our feet. The waterfall was fifty feet high, and the air around it was cool and misty. Cecil always brought special treats from Bukavu, and in this primal wilderness we would picnic on smoked salmon, fresh fruit, and cheese from Belgium—and always a glass or two of sherry. I was truly happy for the first time in many years, and I felt incredibly blessed to have this wonderful man in my life.

Frequently, when Cecil was leaving Buniole, I would ride along with him as far as the outlying fields of the plantation. The fields at Buniole were very spread out, and I was working very hard to increase the pyrethrum production, walking many miles each day. I don't believe I have ever been as fit in my life as I was during that time at Buniole. Sheila, my constant companion, always came along on these little junkets. After saying our good-byes, Sheila and I would get out of the car and begin the long walk back to the plantation house. Sheila would roam the fields, bounding about joyfully, while I inspected the planting and the picking—missing Cecil already.

On one such afternoon, long after Cecil's car had disappeared from sight, I suddenly realized that Sheila was not with me. I couldn't even remember if she had been in the car. I was absolutely frantic. I loved that dog to distraction, and with the constant threat of leopards in the area I was always wary of her wandering too far off. Sheila was my one link with the past. She gave me a sense of continuity. She had been with me since before I came to Africa, and it would have broken my heart to lose her. I raced breathlessly back to the house, hoping she would be there to greet me with her happy bark. But she wasn't there. It finally dawned on me that she must be in Cecil's car on her way to Bukavu! I remembered that Cecil had to stop for gas in Saké, two hours away. Surely he would discover her there and bring her back home. The evening came and went—with no Cecil and no Sheila. Two more days passed, and still there was no sign of either of them. I was sick with worry. By the fourth day, I had resigned myself to the unthinkable: that she was hopelessly lost or dead. Suddenly, I heard the sound of Cecil's horn and heard his car pull up to the house. I threw open the door, and Sheila jumped out of the car and covered my face with wet kisses.

"Where have you been?" I cried impatiently.

Cecil got out of the car and gave me a big hug. "Hello, old girl," he said. "Let's have a cup of tea, and I'll tell you all about it."

He explained that Sheila had never stirred or given any indication of her presence when he stopped for gas in Saké. It wasn't until he was well on his way to Bukavu that he realized he was not alone in the car. By that time, it was too late to turn around. He sent me a wire from Bukavu (which I never received), then fed her a T-bone steak and settled her down for the night. The next morning she was gone. Cecil knew how much Sheila meant to me, and he frantically posted signs all over town: "Missing Irish Terrier!" But no one had seen her. Two days later, Sheila appeared at his back door—hungry and disheveled and looking very homesick.

I can only surmise that she set out to find her way back to Buniole, and when she was unable to do so, she retraced her steps all the way back to Cecil's house, knowing he was her only link to me.

Cecil fed her and cleaned her up, canceled all his appointments, and drove all the way from Bukavu to Buniole (a six-hour drive) to bring her back to me. That was Cecil. He was the most kind and thoughtful man I have ever known, always calm in a crisis, sensitive and caring, and eminently capable in any situation. We had known from the very beginning that he could not stay in Africa indefinitely, but we resolved to make the most of our time together, and that we did.

My birthday comes in August, and that birthday in 1954 was a particularly memorable one. Cleophas and I sometimes took a short cut to one of the far reaches of the plantation, which involved a balancing act on a fallen tree trunk across a rushing stream. This was a very difficult feat for me, and one day when my tennis shoes were slick with mud, I slipped and nearly fell into the churning water below. I panicked and refused to budge. Cleophas, who was exceptionally light on his feet and could run across the log with his arms outstretched, had to guide me across by extending his walking stick to me and pulling me to the other side.

The next day Cleophas asked if he could have four men for three days to do a special job. I mulled it over a bit, and then agreed. It was pure coincidence that his "special job" was finished on the morning of my birthday. He and the men had built a rustic bridge across the stream, made of two sturdy support beams and smaller logs nailed across them horizontally to form a walkway. It even had a handrail so I could never topple over the side. Moreover, this bridge was finer than any bridge in all of Africa because it was covered with deep, soft grass. The men had packed four inches of topsoil over the logs and planted great, thick tufts of grass in the soil. It was one of the most wonderful birthday presents I have ever received.

The bridge became my favorite picnic spot, and I would bring sandwiches and coffee and sit on the spongy green carpet with my legs dangling over the side while I watched the stream bubble merrily along below me. It was here that I often saw black-billed turacos, which are among the most beautiful birds in Africa. They are about the size of a raven, but sleek and streamlined. Their feathers are an iridescent black and parrot-green, and the undersides of their wings are bright scarlet. A pair of turacos had nested in the tangled branches of one of the trees overhead, and if I sat very quietly on my bridge, I could almost always spot one or two of those glorious birds.

Cleophas was thrilled when he learned that his presentation of the bridge had fallen on my birthday, and he organized a children's dance to be held on the lawn in my honor. When Cecil arrived that afternoon, he found a merry birthday party in full swing. A great crowd of children formed a wide circle on the lawn, singing and clapping to provide the music for the dancers. There were eight dancers in all—four little boys on one side and four little girls on the other. The girls bent and swayed to the tempo, while the boys arched their backs, held their heads high, and stomped their feet—twisting their bodies and leaping into the air. It was a glorious afternoon and a magical moment. Listening to the children's lilting voices and watching the young dancers' solemn concentration on the intricate movements of the dance—and with Cecil sitting there beside me—I was as happy as I've ever been.

Berina had lofty aspirations of becoming a maître d'hôtel. Regrettably, he was a long way from realizing his dream. One afternoon, Cecil arrived unexpectedly around midday and discovered Berina serving my lunch dressed in a khaki shirt and shorts and wearing a soiled white apron. Cecil was shocked at this unseemly display and scolded him harshly. "Berina, how dare you serve Madame in such a filthy state? Where is your *kanzu*?" A *kanzu* is the long white robe worn with a cummerbund and fez which was at that time the standard uniform for house servants in Africa.

Berina was not the least bit offended. Quite the contrary. He had finally found someone whose standards matched his own, and his admiration for Cecil knew no bounds. From that moment on, Berina never served the table except dressed in a clean white *kanzu* with all the proper accessories.

When Cecil dined at Buniole, only the best china and crystal goblets would do, and the silver candlesticks and platters were polished to a Tiffany shine.

Berina was always eager to learn new skills which he considered to be *"maradadi"*—meaning to have a touch of elegance. I once found some photographs in a British women's magazine demonstrating how to fold dinner napkins into the shapes of lilies and swans. This is very difficult to do, but Berina was determined to master the technique. He spent many hours puzzling over the diagrams and practicing by trial and error until he could do them perfectly. He then told me that I must never invite more than four people to dinner, since we had only four place settings of the best china; and if there were more than four people we would have to use plates of "different tribes"—something he simply could not bring himself to do.

Berina's wife, Elena, had not accompanied him to Buniole. Instead, she had remained at their own house some distance away to tend to the fields. Once the crops were harvested, Berina brought Elena to live at the plantation. She did not plant corn or beans that autumn, but waited quietly for the birth of their second child, weaving colorful grass mats in the sunshine outside their hut while three-year-old Faraha played nearby. I was very happy to have this gentle, soft-spoken woman living so close to me. It was planting time and I was working harder than ever, but there have been few times in my life when I have known such serenity.

In retrospect, those happy months at Buniole seem to have been only a brief respite between upheavals. I had come to Buniole seeking peace and refuge, but I had found a great deal more. I had come to love this land and its people, and I had discovered in myself a strength and passion I never knew I possessed. Finding Cecil was an unexpected bonus. But I have learned a hard lesson over the years: just when you believe that the African gods are smiling on you, you discover quite by surprise that they are only toying with you.

9

TURNING POINT

In the fall of 1954, Gino Imeri returned from Europe and announced that he was selling all of his holdings in Africa and retiring to Italy. He arrived at Buniole one bright November morning and said, to my complete astonishment, "Well, Rosy, you must decide what you want to do next, because I'm selling my share of Buniole in the spring."

This was the last thing I had expected to hear. The plantation was at its peak of production, and the fields were a profusion of white, healthy flowers. I knew that Gino's partner, Mr. Sharff, was completely satisfied with the job I had done, and I was certain that Gino would be pleased as well. I tried to hide my disappointment, but I could feel my whole world, once again, slipping out from under me. He said he wanted twenty-four thousand dollars for his half share of the plantation. I sighed and said, "Oh, if only I had enough money to buy it myself!"

"No, no!" he said emphatically. "This place is far too isolated. You couldn't possibly live here alone permanently."

Later that same day when I went into the kitchen to talk to Sentashya about supper, I received another shock when he announced, "Madami, I am leaving Buniole. I have worked for you now for four years, and it's time for a change." I was too stunned to respond, so he explained further. "I don't always want to stay in one place. When you were with Bwana there were long safaris and new places to see, but you never go on safari anymore." He concluded by saying that he planned to leave at the end of the month.

Sheila found me weeping between the rows of sweet peas and tried to comfort me. Sentashya's love of adventure had been a joy to me, and it was this same restless spirit that was sending him away. I knew how much I would miss him.

A week later in Goma, Berina arranged for me to meet a friend of his named Simon Bandu, a small, pale-skinned Muhunde, who was an experienced cook. His pretty wife was the sister of one of Cleophas's wives, and they both happily agreed to leave Goma and come to Buniole with their three young daughters.

I had lunch with Gino and told him again how much I wished I could buy his share of Buniole. "Perhaps I will keep Buniole after all and sell only Mugongo," he said. "I am asking fifty thousand."

I had managed Mugongo during one of Gino's extended holidays in 1953, and I knew its potential for pyrethrum production. Mugongo belonged solely to Gino and was located in the Mutura district of Ruanda, one of the best growing areas for pyrethrum in all of Africa. It sits at a higher elevation than Buniole, with a drier climate, and it was one of the finest plantations in the region. At fifty thousand, it was a bargain. Unfortunately, I did not have fifty thousand dollars.

Driving home with my new cook and his family, I felt more unsettled than ever. My divorce from Kenneth would soon be final, and I had to decide where I wanted to live and what I wanted to do with the rest of my life. It seemed to be the logical time to leave Africa and go home to America, but every time I considered leaving, I found that the moment had slipped by a long time ago. This land had taken hold of my heart and soul, and it would not let go. For too long now, I had been drifting from one place to another. If I was to make Africa my home, it was time to establish some roots.

Sentashya left on the day Simon arrived, shaking my hand and sauntering off without even a backward glance. I often wondered where his search for adventure led him during the turbulent years that followed. I never had news of him after that day, but I could easily imagine him joining up with Patrice Lumumba or one of the other radical leaders of the day and being swept away by the lure of militant nationalism and revolutionary propaganda.

Simon was an excellent cook, as well as quiet, efficient, and scrupulously clean. Berina was overjoyed with this change in the household, and he served with pride the elaborate dishes Simon prepared.

Berina's son was born at Buniole early in December and was named Noeli. He was a sturdy baby, born with an instinctive air of self-confidence. Swaddled in sheepskin, with his fat cheek pressed against his mother's strong back, his brown eyes regarded the world and the people around him with solemn interest and not a trace of timidity. No parents were ever more proud of their firstborn son than were Berina and Elena.

It was an easy birth for Elena. Banyaruanda women traditionally rest in their huts for four days following the birth of a girl and five days following the birth of a boy. Childbirth usually takes place on the ground, and there is often a midwife present. After the child is born, it is washed with warm water and then rubbed with grease. The umbilical cord is cut with a sliver of wood, which is kept as a charm. Elena, who was a Muhunde, had only her sister in attendance at the birth, and she left her hut to bathe Noeli in a polished gourd shell when he was only two days old. From that day on, she resumed all of her regular activities.

The rains began in the middle of December and continued for days. The plantation fields were flooded, and portions of the road were periodically closed due to washouts and mud slides. I had planned to spend New Year's Eve in Kisenyi with the Bielskis, and was looking forward to seeing Cecil there as well. The morning of December 31 dawned with the sun struggling to break through the billowing black clouds. It seemed like a propitious sign, so I set out for Kisenyi to welcome in the new year. I encountered only a few rough spots along the way and reached the Bielskis' house in just under three hours. By evening the storm had passed over and a full moon shone brightly amid the glistening stars. I stared at the moon over Cecil's shoulder as we danced and made a wish that 1955 would bring me as much happiness and good fortune as the previous year had brought.

To celebrate the New Year, a festive Intore dance was held in Kisenyi. This is a traditional dance of the Watutsi and is one of the most beautiful of all African dances. The dancers begin their training when they are small boys. Intore means "the chosen," and it was considered a great honor to have a son chosen to dance for his chief or a noble. The greatest honor of all was for a boy to be chosen to dance with the king's Intore. These were always the sons of chiefs or nobles.

Every chief had his own dancers, and each court had its own instructors to teach the dancers new interpretations and movements. The practice sessions were secretly held, for there was great rivalry between the chiefs and each hoped that his dancers would outperform the others. In the old days, the dancers dressed in the skins of the colobus monkey. Today, the colobus is a protected species and the dancers are no longer permitted to wear the beautiful furs. The musical instruments that accompanied the performances were horn flutes, a single-corded instrument called an *"iningiri,"* and small drums which the musicians beat with the tips of their fingers.

The dancers who performed for us that New Year's Day were the dancers of Kamuzinzi, the grand chief of Bugoyi. Each dancer wore a short underskirt of scarlet cotton draped with a piece of white cloth decorated with colorful designs and long bright fringe. The headdresses were flowing manes of sisal representing the lion's manes worn in days gone by. Their bare chests were ornamented with beads and bright strips of cotton and their ankles were encircled with bells. Each dancer held in his hands a lance and a shield.

They danced in groups of thirty or forty. During the war dances, each performer would simulate the joy of provoking and conquering his enemy. With chests protruding, fists clenching the lances and shields, and bare feet hammering the earth, they would leap into the air—tossing their heads and twisting their bodies, bounding higher and higher. They wore arrogant, exultant expressions signifying the triumph of victory and their contempt for death. Some of the dances lasted thirty minutes or more, and the dancers rested only for short periods between each sequence. Periodically they would present their weapons to the chief and sing of his great deeds, while posturing obsequiously before him.

The New Year's Day performance was attended with great enthusiasm by the Europeans, and all the spectators crowded into the small Kisenyi grandstand, which was flanked by colorful banks of red and yellow canna blossoms. When "The Unsurpassables" performed the grand finale, the Exit Dance, we all applauded wildly.

A week later, I was enjoying a late Sunday breakfast at home when I heard a car grinding its way through the muddy hollow near the drying house. I was surprised to have visitors at that hour, and even more surprised to hear two men speaking Italian. They were Mr. Lera and Mr. Meneghini, friends of Gino's. After I sent Berina for fresh coffee, Mr. Meneghini looked eagerly around the room and announced, "I have bought Mr. Imeri's half share of Buniole for my sons, and we are taking possession on February first."

Just like that. I was stunned. I had seen Gino on New Year's Day, and he had reassured me that he would most likely keep his share of Buniole. Nonetheless, Mr. Meneghini informed me with great authority that they had signed the papers the previous evening. He also told me that Gino and Mr. Sharff wanted to see me in Kisenyi right away.

In addition to his one-half ownership of Buniole, Mr. Sharff owned a pyrethrum plantation called Milindi, which adjoined Mugongo and which Gino, as his partner, had managed for many years. When I arrived in Kisenyi that afternoon, Mr. Sharff surprised me by offering me the job of managing Milindi. I was far too confused and upset by all of these recent revelations to give him an answer on the spot, so I asked for a week to think it over.

Before the week was out, I received another offer—this time from Gino, offering to sell me a one-third interest in Mugongo. The price was to be one-third of fifty thousand dollars, or $16,600. He agreed to accept a down payment of $3,500, with the balance to be paid out of profits, at seven percent interest. Gino planned to retain one-third ownership, and my other partner was to be Kenneth. I believe that this was Kenneth's way of saying how much he regretted that our marriage had not fulfilled all of my needs, but that he still cared for me and would always look out for me. Gino and Kenneth were to pay me a small salary for the management of the plantation. In addition, I would receive a salary from Mr. Sharff if I agreed to manage Milindi.

It seemed too good to be true. The management of Mugongo would be entirely my responsibility, as Gino intended to live in Italy and Kenneth now owned two coffee plantations in the Congo and rarely came to Ruanda. He did, however, maintain a small house on a farm in Mutura where he visited on occasion. I was over the moon with joy. At last, I would have a home of my own.

Gino and I agreed that I would leave Buniole in mid-February. Berina and Simon offered to come with me to Mugongo, but their wives resisted. They had planted new crops, and they did not speak the local language of Kinyaruanda. They were happy and settled, and they wanted to stay in the Congo near their families. Mr. Meneghini offered to keep them both on at Buniole.

Young Mr. Meneghini had already arrived by the time I was packed and ready to leave. Cleophas said a quick good-bye, then followed his new employer into the fields. Men came to shake my hand, and children lined the road shouting, "*Kwa heri*, Madami!" Sheila rode in the front seat with her head on my lap, and Mia bounced around in her traveling basket in the back among the suitcases and boxes. I drove that old pickup truck through the mud and over the ruts and around the twists and turns for the very last time with tears streaming down my face.

In the midst of all this turmoil, I received the most surprising offer of all and had to make one of the most difficult decisions of my life. Cecil was being sent back to London. This dear and loving man asked me to marry him and return with him to England, but I found I could not leave Africa. In a poignant reminder of our first evening together at Buniole, we had come to a heartbreaking impasse. I wouldn't leave, and he couldn't stay.

I loved Cecil very much, but I had come to realize that I loved Africa more, and I have never really regretted my decision. Although we corresponded for a number of years, I never saw Cecil again after I left Buniole.

A missionary once told me that whenever he drove up into the hills of the Masisi territory in the vicinity of Buniole, he felt that the mountains were closing in around him, taunting him with their dark mysteries and primal spirits. I always felt that those hills were sheltering me in their dark shadows, offering me a cloistered haven and embracing those that I held dear—keeping us all safe from harm.

10

MUGONGO

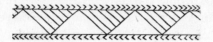

And so it was that I came to Mugongo as plantation owner—or at least part owner. I have no doubt that God was watching over me during this time, for had I remained in the Congo where troubles later broke out, I would have lost everything. Getting here had been a long and roundabout journey, but at last I had a home of my own. That was in February of 1955, and Mugongo has been my home ever since.

Mugongo is located in the Mutura district in northwestern Rwanda. Few places on earth can rival its panoramic vistas and bucolic splendor. The lofty peaks of Karisimbi and Mikeno dominate the landscape to the north. Nyiragongo and Nyamulagira, two active volcanoes, loom to the west, and Lake Kivu shimmers in the sunshine in the valley below. Towering dracaena trees, giant hagenias, and monkey puzzle trees frame the imposing vistas, and across the rolling terrain, fields of flowers sway gently in the breeze. Meandering footpaths in all directions wend their way through cool, dark cypress forests, leading to clusters of grass-roofed mud huts and neatly tended *shambas* (fields) of the Banyaruanda. Wood fires fill the air with a sweet, smoky fragrance.

In 1955, Mugongo Plantation consisted of ninety hectares, approximately half of which was planted in pyrethrum. The remainder contained the house and gardens, rolling hills, grottoes, and dense forests of cypress and eucalyptus trees. The plantation house was small and square, built of whitewashed brick and covered with a delicate vine called creeping fig, which gave it the appearance of being firmly anchored to the ground. It is a sturdy little bungalow and has always reminded me of the house the little pig built, which the wolf—though he huffed and he puffed—could not blow down. There has been a lot of huffing and puffing over the years, and my little house is still standing. A few modifications have been made since that time, but the house originally consisted of just two large rooms—a living room and bedroom. In addition, there was a kitchen, a storeroom, and bathroom in the rear. It was neat and cozy, and it suited me just fine.

By this time I was familiar with the workings of a pyrethrum plantation, and since I had managed Mugongo for a short time, I was acquainted with the people and the surrounding area. With its open expanses and busy communal life, Mutura was a lively contrast to the dark seclusion of Buniole. It was teeming with people traveling up and down the road or along the narrow paths that meandered through the fields. Bicycles flashed by with bells jingling, and cars drove slowly up and down the rocky road. Travel agents featured this picturesque spot as a main attraction on the "Circuit de Bugoyi," and tourists would drive by in big beautiful cars, consulting maps and taking pictures of the magnificent scenery. Little boys would leave their sheep and goats unattended and run to the side of the road to see the *wazungu* in their fancy automobiles. Occasionally, tourists would stop to photograph my garden and often would stay for tea. Many of these visitors were British or American, and I would question them eagerly for news from home.

We were hardly isolated, though. Mutura contained seven pyrethrum plantations, lying side by side, although only one other planter, a young Belgian with a Tutsi mistress, lived there. The others had villas in Kisenyi or Goma and visited their plantations once or twice a week. It was a relatively short distance (twenty-three miles) to Kisenyi, and friends would frequently stop by for lunch or tea, with no concern of being stranded for days, as often happened at Buniole.

Gino's cook, Sembibi, agreed to stay on to work for me, as did his houseboy, Edouard Rugamoka, although he was decidedly unenthusiastic about working for a woman. Edouard was an intelligent man whose abilities could have taken him far beyond the level of house servant; however, he seemed to have no greater aspirations. He led a very peculiar existence. His wife and three sons and three daughters lived in Rambura, thirty miles away, and the only time he visited them was during his two-week vacation twice a year. On rare occasions, one of his children would come to Mugongo to deliver a message, but he generally had no news of his family between visits.

Edouard lived in a grass-roofed hut under a massive cypress tree not more than twenty yards from my house. As far as I could ascertain, he lived a celibate life there, yet I have seldom known a man more placid and content than he. Edouard spent hours each day leaning against the sill of the open kitchen window, smoking his pipe. Often, when I entered the kitchen and he would turn to me with a smile, I had the distinct impression that he was smiling at the pleasant reveries I had interrupted, rather than at me. During the six years he worked for me, I never heard him raise his voice or saw him angry. He took very little interest in the dramas and activities that went on all around him, and although he listened to each tale with grave attention, he rarely commented.

Edouard was a devout Catholic. Although he attended Mass only once or twice a month, his greatest ambition was that his eldest son, Celestin Ntebebe, should become a priest. This was a lofty goal for a Hutu boy at that time, as more than ninety percent of the seminary students were Tutsi, and Hutu boys were rarely accepted. Celestin was an exceptional student, however, and his teachers intervened on his behalf. Miraculously, he was accepted at Nyundo Mission Seminary near Kisenyi. When it came time to enter the seminary, fourteen-year-old Celestin came to Mugongo to say good-bye to his father. I can still recall his eager, smiling face as he marched off to enter the mission and fulfill his father's dreams. Clutched in his hand was a small light-blue cardboard suitcase containing brand new khaki shorts and shirts, underwear, a towel, soap, pencils, and an exercise book. I took his picture as he waved good-bye to his proud father.

Less than two months later, Celestin was expelled. It was the only time I ever saw Edouard cry. Celestin had been accused of throwing scissors at another boy during a quarrel. A Belgian priest in Kisenyi attempted to intercede on his behalf, but to no avail. They refused to reinstate him. The priest told me privately, "If it had been a Tutsi boy, there would be no question of his reinstatement." Celestin did not become a priest. Soon afterward, he enrolled in an agricultural school near Bukavu and embarked on a successful career in agronomy and wildlife preservation, ultimately making his father extremely proud.

For two years, I managed both Mugongo and Milindi. My workday began at sunrise and ended at sundown. Luckily, I had Sembibi and Edouard to keep the household running smoothly. The plantations in Mutura were not large enough to provide homesteads for the workers and their families, but the region was so densely populated that there was an abundance of workers who lived on their own small plots of land nearby. The two plantations combined employed three hundred and fifty field hands and a hundred and twenty children to pick the flowers. The vast majority of the workers were Hutu—strong, thickset people of Bantu stock with open, smiling faces and friendly dispositions.

The plantation work was far more taxing than I was accustomed to and required five or six hours of walking each day. To reach the outermost fields at Milindi, I had to climb a long steep hill through the forest and hike across two miles of open fields. Once there, I was at the highest point, and the rest was all downhill. It was a beautiful walk. Herds of forty or fifty long-horned cattle would cross my path, urged on by young shepherds. On the ridge of a hill, I might see a woman standing alone—the scarlet cloth she wore tossing and blowing against the cobalt sky. Scattered across the landscape were countless thatch-roofed mud huts, encircled by *lapangos* (fences) of thorn trees or bamboo to protect the sheep and goats from leopards. The huts were surrounded by a patchwork of small *shambas* planted with corn or millet, beans, and potatoes.

I soon became engrossed in the lives of the people around me, and Mugongo became in every sense my home. Zacharia Rubungo had been the plantation clerk at Mugongo for sixteen years. His prominent position and high moral stature earned him the title of unofficial judge for local disputes considered not serious enough to take to the chief's court. Zacharia was a wise and deliberate mediator, and his opinions were highly regarded. He would call upon many witnesses and conduct hours—sometimes days— of discussion before reaching a verdict. It was fascinating to watch these tribunals in progress, and I was always impressed to see how willingly the people involved accepted and abided by his decisions.

These proceedings generally took on a very solemn atmosphere. One of the first cases I witnessed involved a worker who was brought to my house on a tipoy. He had been fighting with another man and the man had bitten him, leaving a deep, jagged wound in his leg. His assailant was also brought to the house and made to watch me dress the wound. Zacharia listened intently to both sides of the dispute, then asked me how long I thought it would be before Gahembe, the injured man, could return to work. I guessed two weeks. Zacharia ruled that the man who had bitten Gahembe's leg must work for two weeks, and each day's work would be entered in the payroll ledger under Gahembe's name. The man accepted his punishment willingly and worked every day until Gahembe's leg was healed.

Another morning, I was startled to find a sobbing woman in my living room. Her husband, Gasaza, had chased her to my house, still brandishing the stick with which he had beaten her. Her shoulders were ridged with welts. The man was in a murderous rage, and there was little that Zacharia or I could do to calm him down. The trouble had erupted over a small sum of money the wife had earned picking pyrethrum. Instead of turning the money over to her husband (as was the custom), she had spent it on a new piece of fabric for herself. Zacharia sent her to her father's house with an escort for protection, and I fired Gasaza on the spot. The woman never returned to her husband. Sadly, at the chief's tribunal, Gasaza was awarded custody of their two children.

Each case was unique, and very often the verdicts were based more on expediency than jurisprudence. In one such case, a man named Rwamay-

In 1929.

Me (age two) with my mother, Rosa-mond Howard Halsey, 1914.

Our wedding day, May 2, 1942.

Kenneth Carr, 1941.

With Kenneth and Sheila aboard the
S.S. *African Glen*, July 1949.

Kenneth with Bambutti pygmies, 1949.

Buniole plantation house.

At Buniole, 1951.

With Kenneth on safari, 1951.

Kenneth, me, a field hand, and Gino Imeri with elephant shot at Buniole.

With Snooks, 1950.   On "birthday bridge" at Buniole.

Cleophas Musafiri, plantation
clerk at Buniole, 1954.

With Cecil Bellwood at Buniole,
1954.

In a tipoy at
Mugongo, 1955.

Tutsi chief.

Children picking pyrethrum at Mugongo.

Picking pyrethrum at Mugongo.

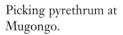

Pickup loaded with sacks of dried pyrethrum.

At Mugongo, 1956.

Hutu schoolchildren at Mugongo.

Shaking hands with pygmy chief Ruha-bura.

Treating a baby at the backdoor dispensary, 1950.

Sembibi cooking an omelet at Lake Ngondo.

Rudabeka on elephant watch.

Kayonga, beating a drum to ward off elephants, and me.

With Sembagare at Mugongo, 1957.

Betty with "surrogate mother" (fur jacket) and me, 1956.

Sembibi feeding Bahati, the bushbuck.

With Bahati, Terry, and Tisa, 1957.

Bahati at six months.

Rudahigwa and Queen
Mother at a Jubilee
celebration, 1957.

Tutsi nobles at Jubilee.

Hutu men dressed in
banana leaves to rep-
resent their humble
station in the realm,
at Jubilee.

ora had ordered his wife to go outside and round up the goats that were grazing on a distant hill. She was cooking supper and refused to obey. This led to a quarrel, and the woman stormed out of the house. When Rwamayora realized that she had not gone to fetch the goats, he lost his temper and picked up the pot of food she had been preparing and dumped it on the ground. In retaliation, the wife snatched up a piece of patterned cloth Rwamayora had bought for himself and announced that she was leaving him. She spent the night with neighbors.

The following morning, Zacharia called upon a number of the elders in the district to help him settle this weighty matter. The wife was a young beauty with lovely eyes and a flirtatious smile, and she was clearly relishing all the attention the incident had aroused. The verdict came down entirely in her favor. Zacharia solemnly decreed that it is a man's job to herd goats and a woman's job to do the cooking. Rwamayora, he said, had been bad-tempered and unreasonable. The wife was awarded the piece of patterned cloth and told to go home peacefully with her husband. She pouted prettily at the spectators, then dutifully followed her husband home. Later, one of the men on the council confided to me that they hadn't really believed that Rwamayora was entirely to blame, but they knew that this young wife was very headstrong and would probably have left her husband if they had ruled in his favor.

A Batwa village lay between Mugongo and Milindi, and I passed by it every day as I made my way from one plantation to the other. The Batwa pygmies were the original inhabitants of Ruanda. With the arrival of the agriculturist Hutu many hundreds of years ago, the Batwa were forced from the plains into the forests. Centuries later, the Tutsi overpowered the Hutu, forcing *them* into the forests, and the Batwa were driven into the mountains, where they have remained. The Batwa are hunters and potters and artisans of witchcraft. They plant no crops at all. Occasionally, the women and children are sent out at night to steal peas or beans from the fields of the Hutu, but for the most part they are content to live off the meat of the wild animals they kill. They consider their pursuit of hunting to be far superior to that of farming—the occupation of the Hutu.

The children of the Batwa are funny little creatures, unlike any children I have ever known. Their tiny faces are drawn and thin, their eyes are wild and staring, and their voices are very harsh. I found their whimsical behavior and capriciousness immensely appealing. They always knew when I was approaching and would dash from their huts and stand near the path just to watch me go by. Sometimes, daring little girls would reach out to touch me, and I was always startled to discover that their hands were as rough as tree bark. One morning, a group of pygmy children called out for me to wait at the end of the path. Moments later they appeared carrying a tiny baby. The idea was not so much for me to see the baby; rather, they wanted the baby to have its first glimpse of a white woman. The pygmy men usually vanished at my approach, but I could often detect their presence by the clap-clap of the wooden bells worn by their hunting dogs.

One Sunday afternoon as I was walking with the dogs across a distant field, there suddenly appeared before me a small group of pygmies—three women and two children. They bashfully greeted me, and then a small boy began to play a harplike instrument. With a tiny rod he tapped out a tune on the metal bowstring of a longbow, such as hunters used. A gourd fastened to the bow served as the sounding box. He tapped out a thin, plaintive tune and swayed to the rhythm, watching me intently with eyes very bright. The others began to dance and sing to the music, as bees hummed overhead in the golden sunshine. One last clear note rang out, and they stopped dancing, burst into giggles and vanished just as suddenly as they had appeared.

This particular pygmy village was ruled by Chief Ruhabura. The wealth of Ruhabura and his family was represented by the large herd of goats they possessed. Ruhabura was four-and-a-half feet tall, with a deeply lined face, and was said to be terribly wicked. He was reputed to have killed more than a hundred men in his lifetime. It was said that during a famine in 1943, Ruhabura and a band of pygmies ambushed three men returning from the market with baskets of grain. Ruhabura killed one of the men with his spear and was then attacked by the other two. One of them slashed him with a machete, cutting off the last two fingers of his right hand. When his mutilated hand eventually healed, the remaining fingers stiffened and permanently curled inward, adding to his savage appearance. I shook Ruhabura's hand many times, and although I detected none of the alleged cruelty or wickedness in his demeanor, I shuddered every time I touched his deformed, clawlike hand.

One of the most beautiful places in all of Mutura was Lake Ngondo, a small picturesque lake situated on the lower slopes of Karisimbi. It was here that shepherds brought their cattle to drink at the end of the day. During the dry season, when the streams and water holes had dried up, thousands of head of cattle were led to this lake each day. In the evening, elephants came to drink and bathe beneath the stars.

Often, after a long day in the fields, I would come to Lake Ngondo to picnic, or simply to observe the activity at this busy gathering place. Occasionally, I was accompanied by my cook, Sembibi, and my gardener,

Batandarana. Sembibi would carry a teakettle and picnic basket, while Batandarana sauntered along with a basket of dry kindling and a car blanket on his head.

It was nearly an hour's walk through the bush along a wide cow path banked by closely cropped emerald grass. The pungent smell of cattle and elephant dung mingled with the spicy scent of wild thyme and other herbs. Uprooted or broken thorn trees lay scattered where elephants had passed. Tiny forest birds darted about in quick flashes of scarlet, green, and blue, and balanced on the wobbly heads of spiky crimson flowers called red-hot pokers and immortelles, the white strawflowers that abound in the lower regions of the volcanoes. Occasionally, people would pass by carrying large baskets of potatoes, corn, or millet on their heads, or shepherds would appear carrying wooden jugs of fresh milk. Women could be seen gathering firewood in the forest, and I would sometimes stop to play with their babies while the women tied the branches and saplings they had collected into great bundles, which they effortlessly balanced on their heads. The babies would ride home on their mothers' backs, content and protected under the shade of the long branches.

When the lake came into view, hundreds of small brown ducks, called grebes, could be seen bobbing up and down on the surface, appearing more like wooden decoys than live birds. Sometimes a pair of crested cranes—the stately, elegant birds sacred to the Banyaruanda—would spread their great wings and dance on a sandy cove. Crested cranes are graceful terrestrial birds with pale gray feathers and wings of black and white. Their heads are capped in black and crowned with a fan-shaped crest resembling spun silk the color of champagne. When they fly away, their call is a repeated, vibrant, bell-like note that can be heard from great distances.

My picnic spot was a narrow grassy point jutting out into the lake. Sembibi would build a fire and cook an omelet, which he served from the sizzling pan. Shepherds would come to greet me, and their servants would take embers from our fire to light their masters' black clay pipes. Salt licks edged the shore. These were long troughs made from hollowed tree trunks and filled with brown, coarse-grained salt. Shepherds sat in scattered groups endlessly discussing their herds, while cows jostled each other for position at the water's edge. The shepherds accepted my presence with equanimity, and whenever they sensed that elephants were close by they hastily warned me to leave. One afternoon when I was alone and had lingered on long past their warning, an old Tutsi shepherd stood watch from a distance until he was satisfied that I was safely on my way home.

Ngondo was situated in the forest reserve. As such, its trees remained untouched, and the ducks and Egyptian geese that inhabited it were protected. It was also inaccessible by automobile. One afternoon, I received a visitor at Mugongo. His name was John Oxley, and he was the South African consul to the Belgian Congo, stationed in Elizabethville. He had heard of Lake Ngondo and asked if I might take him to see it. It was a particularly lovely day, and the idyllic setting of sparkling water, aquatic birds, and shepherds with their cows was so extraordinarily beautiful that John was moved to quote Wordsworth: "Earth has not anything to show more fair: / Dull would he be of soul who could pass by / A sight so touching in its majesty."

The lake became my special place at Mugongo, a place where I could sit quietly and commune with the wilderness and the people and animals that inhabited it. Ngondo remained one of the most beautiful unspoiled treasures in all of Ruanda until 1970, when a government development project allocated the surrounding land to homesteaders. Much of the forest was cut down, and houses were built and crops were planted where cattle and elephant once roamed. It is believed that an earthquake created a crack in the bottom of the lake, for suddenly the water drained away. And like a perfect, fleeting moment, Lake Ngondo disappeared forever.

II

BANYARUANDA

One of the great joys of living in Mutura with its diverse population and busy communal life has always been my close interaction with the Ruandan people and the generosity and openness with which they welcomed me into their world. Hundreds of people passed by my house each day, traveling up and down the road or meandering along the footpaths that crisscross through the fields. Dozens would line up at my back door dispensary each morning, and others would come by to tell me their troubles or to report some dramatic or newsworthy event. Hutu farmers brought fresh fruits and vegetables, and Tutsi shepherds delivered fresh milk in large wooden jugs. Pygmies peddled fanciful clay pots in all shapes and sizes. Their world became my world, and my life became deeply immersed in their culture, customs, and traditions.

In the 1950s, Ruanda's three ethnic groups—Tutsi, Hutu, and Batwa—were easily distinguishable by their notable physical characteristics, their mode of dress, and their station in the realm. Despite the rigid caste system which existed at the time, the vast majority of the Banyaruanda lived a simple life in harmony with the land and shared in common many of the ancient rituals of their heritage.

The Tutsi were the tribe of the feudal kings of Ruanda and represented a relatively small percentage of the population. They were the aristocratic minority who ruled Ruanda in a tenuous partnership with the Belgian administration. As a rule, only the Tutsi held positions in government, education, and the priesthood. Tall and slender, with small heads, slightly tilted eyes, aquiline noses, and delicate lips, they towered above the rest of their countrymen in both stature and rank. Adult males often reach heights of seven feet or more. Many of the Tutsi women were exceptionally beautiful and the epitome of elegance, wrapped in many yards of immaculate white cloth, accented by a piece of scarlet, yellow, or purple fabric fastened at the shoulder. The wives and daughters of the nobles rarely ventured forth on foot, but were carried from place to place on tipoys borne upon the shoulders of their Hutu servants. Tutsi men wore long flowing togas of white or yellow cloth, and many at that time still adhered to the picturesque tribal custom of combing their hair into an elaborate cockscomb.

The Hutu made up the vast majority of Ruanda's population and were predominantly agriculturists. It was the Hutu farmers who cleared the land, planted the fields, and harvested the crops to sustain Ruanda's agrarian economy. Short and thickset with irregular features, they were cheerful, hardworking peasants with high moral standards and an endearing propensity for melodramatics. All of my house servants and field workers were Hutu, and they preferred to dress in a curious blend of traditional African garb and the tattered remnants of cast-off European clothing.

By the 1950s there remained only several thousand pygmies in Ruanda. The Batwa had no tribal organization to speak of, and their lives were devoted largely to hunting. They lived a primitive existence in the mountainous regions, far removed from their longtime oppressors—the Hutu and Tutsi. Their only possessions were their bows and arrows, their hunting dogs, and the untanned skins they wore. Adult Batwa men averaged four feet, ten inches in height, and the women rarely exceeded four feet, six inches. They were fiercely independent and shunned all forms of physical labor. They raised no crops at all and subsisted primarily on the meat of the animals they hunted. Pygmies were not required to pay taxes in those days, and indeed it would have been difficult to extract payment from these peculiar little people who had no money and no intention of earning any.

Despite the physical differences and social distinctions, all Banyaruanda shared similar cultural customs with respect to courtship, marriage, family structure, and how they conducted their lives. There were very few unmarried adults in Ruanda, as it was every man's desire to have a wife and children and to live in a house of his own. For many centuries, the Banyaruanda practiced polygamy. A Tutsi man with large herds of cattle in distant regions found it advantageous to have a wife in each location. If his herd was small, a second wife was considered an extravagance. A Hutu man with large fields to cultivate often took a second wife as a practical necessity. Several wives meant many children—a sign of wealth and prestige. And in the case of a highborn Tutsi, a second or third marriage established connections with other notable families.

It has always been the custom in Ruanda that a marriage dowry be paid to the father of the bride (or to the head of the bride's family). The official dowry at that time was one cow or eight goats and was the same for all Banyaruanda. There was no open discrimination based upon the wealth or status of the family, or the beauty of the young girl. There is no denying, however, that a father took these matters into account when determining the suitability of a husband for his daughter. A Hutu rarely married a Tutsi, and the daughter of a chief often married the son of another chief. A man with great herds of cattle hoped to find a son-in-law whose father was as wealthy as he. Once the dowry was paid, the chief of the district was notified of the couple's intent to marry. The chief then recorded the marriage with the district tribunal.

Banyaruanda weddings begin with prolonged lamenting. The bride, who is heavily veiled, is taken from her home and from her weeping mother by a large procession of female attendants. This procession, which may consist of as many as twenty or thirty young girls and two older female family members, accompanies the bride to the village of the bridegroom, where he is waiting with family and friends. No matter how long the journey, the young bride is expected to cry and resist every step of the way, demonstrating her grief and sorrow at the impending loss of her virginity. Her attendants lament with her—moaning and crying and singing sad songs. When the mournful procession reaches the exultant bridegroom, the bride is immediately whisked away into the fine new hut he has built for her and takes no part in the festivities and gaiety enjoyed by the wedding guests.

The traditional Ruandan wedding ceremony is pagan, but it is bindingly legal. The festivities are centered around the drinking of *pombi*, or banana beer, served from numerous clay pots. Most of the drinking is done from one immense clay pot—four or five feet high—placed in the center of the yard. Each guest brings his own gourd to dip into the pot. When the last drop of *pombi* has been consumed, the groom ushers his bride to the house of his parents, which is usually in close proximity to his own new house. They are greeted at the threshold by his mother, who is holding a baby boy—borrowed for the occasion. The baby is placed on the young bride's back to signify her wish that the marriage will be blessed with many children. The groom places his bare right foot on his bride's left foot and embraces her. Then they enter his parents' house. Inside, his mother offers the bride a pot of *pombi*, which they all drink together, and the father of the groom gives the young couple a gift of money. The groom's friends traditionally give gifts of money as well, and the bride's attendants give the couple a woven grass mat for their bed. After drinking *pombi* with her new in-laws, the bride and her husband retire to their own hut.

The bride wears a garland of leaves made from a special plant called *"umwishywa,"* which her mother had placed around her throat in the morning. The groom removes the garland and arranges it in a girdle around her hips. He then takes a small amount of milk in his mouth, mixed with grass, and spits it on the head of his bride to promote fertility. These are the central rites of the marriage. It is customary on their wedding night for the bride to try to resist her husband.

Four days after the wedding, the bride is allowed to return to her home to visit her mother. With the exception of this prearranged visit, only her husband and her bridal attendants are permitted to see her for a period of one month. At the end of thirty days, a dance is held in celebration of the young couple. During the honeymoon period, all of their food is prepared by the mother or sisters of the groom. After the celebration marking the end of the bride's seclusion, the bride begins to prepare food for herself and her husband.

The only notable distinction between Hutu and Tutsi weddings is that, in the old days, Tutsi weddings were always held at night and Tutsi girls were not told beforehand of the date of their marriage. Their attendants would arrive unannounced to dress the bride and take her to her bridegroom. As a result, the element of surprise was added to her fear and resistance, and her cries were apt to be quite genuine. In one such wedding procession that passed by my house, the young Tutsi girl being carried to her bridegroom on a tipoy called out to me, weeping and wailing, "Save me, Madame! Save me!" It might be inferred that Ruandan girls are forced into loveless marriages, but this is rarely so. In most cases, the young couples choose each other. Marriages are occasionally arranged by the parents, but if either the bride or the groom is opposed to the match, the engagement is called off.

In Batwa marriages, the dowry is paid in goats—sometimes as many as sixteen—in addition to many pots of *pombi*. Years ago, the dowry was paid in elephant tusks, and it is said that at one wedding, six tusks were paid to the father of the bride. As for the wedding ceremony itself, the young couple, the guests, and the family members start out running. The bride is given a head start, while the groom counts to ten. The groom then chases her, followed by the guests. The wedding takes place on the spot where the groom catches the bride.

After marriage, the young couple resides close to the parents of the bridegroom and is guided by them for as long as they are alive. This extended family, which may include first and second cousins and the servants of the household, takes the name *umulyango*, which means family. Throughout his life, a father keeps his sons close to him. He designates among his sons which one will succeed him as head of the family upon his death. This son collects the taxes of his brothers and manages any affairs of the family which would require the attention of the chief or other officials.

Daughters do not inherit. Sons alone divide their father's estate—the eldest son receiving slightly more than the others. When a man dies leaving no heirs, his wealth is given to the chief. If a small child is orphaned, its paternal grandfather becomes its legal guardian. If this grandfather is dead, a paternal uncle or cousin becomes the child's guardian.

Every child in Ruanda is given three names at birth—one chosen by the parents, another by the paternal grandparents, and a third by the maternal grandparents. The child's full name includes all three names, although it is the parents who decide which name the child will be called while it is small. When the child is older, he or she may be baptized and may choose a Christian name as a first name, using one of the Ruandan names as a last name.

All Ruandan names have a meaning—usually pertaining to the circumstances of the infant's birth. For example: Sekabanza means "one who begins life laughing"; Nsengiyumva means "we prayed and our prayers were answered"; Banyamwabo means "a child whose parents are alienated from their families"; and Hakizimana means "only God can save."

Divorce has always existed in Ruanda. It is usually preceded by several temporary separations. The wife will go home to her parents' house with complaints that her husband has insulted her, beaten her, neglected her, or was lazy. Her parents try to smooth things over and persuade her to return to her husband. It is always the wife who leaves the husband. She is never sent away. If a husband is unhappy with his wife, he will demonstrate by his behavior that he does not want her, and then she will leave him. Both sets of parents make every effort to save the marriage, for they wish to prevent a rift between the families.

A woman may be granted a divorce if she has been abused by her husband or if he is impotent. A man may divorce his wife if she neglects her domestic duties or commits adultery. In those days, a woman's inability to bear children was not considered grounds for divorce, as a man could always take a second wife. A divorced woman takes with her only the clothes on her back when she leaves her husband. She returns to the house of her father, who must then return the cow or goats which had been paid as the dowry, plus any offspring of the animals. The young children of divorced parents are sent to live with their maternal grandparents. Traditionally, children remain with their mother and her parents until they are seven or eight years old, at which time they are sent to live with their father and may be permitted to visit their mother from time to time.

Before the arrival of Europeans, the punishment for adultery in Ruanda was very severe. Adulterers were often pursued by their chief and forced to drown themselves in a river, or were banished to a barren island in the middle of Lake Kivu where they starved to death. Fortunately, such transgressions were extremely rare.

In the old days, there were very few spinsters in Ruanda, as polygamy was the accepted custom and every maiden was a treasure—no matter how plain. But in 1950 the Belgian government enacted a law refusing to recognize the legality of second or third wives, or the legitimacy of children born to them. This was deeply distressing to the Banyaruanda, as it was their belief that babies considered to be illegitimate (those born out of wedlock) must be put to death.

Since the 1960s, modern influences, social and economic advances, and intermarriage among the ethnic groups have resulted in a gradual breakdown of many of the old customs and traditions. Tribal custom forbade a man to sleep with his wife until after a child was weaned—usually a period of two years. This prohibition acted as a natural birth control, and if a man had several wives, it was not considered a hardship. Today a man is allowed only one wife. The more observant Ruandans still adhere to the two-year abstention period, and their children are spaced several years apart. But most are gradually breaking away from the old customs, and this is reflected in the escalating birthrate. To compound the problem, the bride price in many parts of Africa has risen very high, and immorality and promiscuity have resulted, as the men often cannot afford to pay the bride price.

Banyaruanda conduct their lives according to many deeply rooted superstitions and taboos. For instance, Ruandan women are forbidden to eat the meat of goats. Years ago I asked a Tutsi chief why this was so, and he explained quite rationally that goats have all the characteristics they dislike in a woman. They have long beards, harsh voices, and are stubborn and feisty, whereas a cow has all the characteristics they desire in a woman. Cows have soft voices and gentle dispositions. Ruandans worship their cows as they would worship their women.

Ruandan women may not pass under a spear, cut the grass, roof a hut, or imitate a cock's crow. No one must ever sit on a basket of grain. When it thunders, one must never light a pipe, sit on a chair, or lie on a sheepskin. A traveler who knocks his left foot against an obstacle, or encounters a light-colored striped rat on a path, should return to his home immediately to avoid bad luck. A woman kneading bread must be silent. Even if she is summoned, she must not answer. If a woman should become so angry as to hit her husband with a long wooden spoon used for mixing bread, he will leave her. His pride would prevent him from remaining with her after such an affront.

It is very bad luck to kill a crow, a black-and-white wagtail bird, a lizard, a frog, a toad, or a hippopotamus. If a glossy ibis alights on a house, it is a sure sign that someone will die. Young girls must never follow a path where cows have been mating. They must take another path to avoid sterility. Banyaruanda believe that if your heart beats rapidly, someone is saying bad things about you. To leave a walking stick in another man's house is to become his enemy. And the king must never bend his knees, for fear that Ruanda will shrink.

Ruandan women wear a skin belt called *"unweko,"* which is presented to them by their husbands on their wedding day. If a woman wishes to prevent a man from approaching her, she places this belt on the ground in front of him. No man will dare to step over it. It is believed that menstrual blood can have a bad influence, and a woman who is menstruating is forbidden to attend a sick child. Women never milk cows. Young girls are milkmaids only until their breasts mature.

Anyone who looks at a puppy before its eyes are opened risks having a blind child born to them or a child with an eye injury. This superstition is shared by the Bahunde tribe in the Congo. At Buniole, Berina refused to enter the guest room where Sheila had given birth to a litter of puppies, as Elena was pregnant and he was certain that something terrible would happen to the unborn child if he saw the newborn puppies.

A pending marriage will be called off if the cow given as the marriage dowry should die, or if it should run away twice from the father-in-law to be. To go through with the marriage after such a bad omen would be far too risky. Years ago it was believed that if a man pursued a young girl carrying a jug of water on her head and the girl became so rattled or frightened that she dropped the water jug and broke it, she could not return to her father's house. She would be so compromised at that point that she would have to marry her pursuer.

These are some of the taboos and superstitions that were related to me by an old man from Mutura. When I expressed a certain amount of incredulity, he said, "Do you mean that Europeans don't believe that someone is saying bad things about them if their hearts beat rapidly?"

"No," I replied, "but we do believe that someone is talking about us if our ears are burning, and we are about to receive some money if the palm of our left hand itches. There must never be thirteen at a table or three on a match, and to break a mirror is to have seven years of bad luck."

12

ELEPHANTS

One of my greatest trials during those early years at Mugongo was coming to terms with the large elephant population in the region. I was alternately stirred by their grandeur and annoyed by the havoc they generated. Protecting the fields from their feeding frenzies and keeping them at bay became an all-consuming occupation. It was not uncommon for elephants to wander out of the forests and onto the open fields in search of peas, sweet potatoes, or corn, but the real trouble started the day they discovered that the roots of the pyrethrum plants were a particularly tasty treat.

It is believed that elephants communicate through low-frequency sound waves inaudible to the human ear and that these sound waves can travel great distances. It seemed to be the case that one elephant (somewhere in the region) sampled the root of a pyrethrum plant, pronounced it delicious, and spread the word. Throughout the Kivu, from the mountains of the Congo to the highlands of Ruanda, elephants suddenly began uprooting pyrethrum plants, devouring the roots, and leaving the flowered stems scattered on the ground.

At Buniole we encountered elephants only on rare occasions when they came down from the mountains during the heaviest of rains. Here at Mugongo, the elephants were far more bold and much more prevalent. At night, they would leave the shelter of the forests and wander onto the open expanses of the plantation, churning up the fields and feasting on the plentiful vegetation. Their nightly raids began to take a toll on both the pyrethrum production and my forbearance. In frustration, I abandoned planting on twenty-five acres of the most fertile land closest to the forest. The elephants had won the battle, but I was determined to win the war.

It was Kenneth who came up with a scheme to dig a trench six feet deep and four feet wide along the mile or more that bordered the forest. It was a tremendous undertaking and took many months to complete. The digging was done entirely by hand and involved a great deal of maneuvering around the shelves of lava rock in areas where the soil was shallow. The trench was reinforced with a sturdy fence built along the perimeter, made of eucalyptus posts and secured by two layers of barbed wire. It looked formidable.

From our perspective the trench was a complete failure, but the elephants loved it. They waited until it was completely finished, then proceeded to dig open tunnels under the lowest rungs of the barbed wire so they could slide down into it. From there, they would climb up the perpendicular sides and onto the fields. On most mornings, the fields were rampant with the spoor of baby elephants. I began to wonder if they regarded our great barrier project as nothing more than an enormous playpen for their young. The females would herd their babies onto the fields for safekeeping and then wander off on their own to feast on pyrethrum. Other mornings, we would find the large, round spoor of bulls and discover that a half acre or more of young healthy pyrethrum plants had been destroyed. It was becoming very aggravating and very costly.

We built a night watchmen's hut in the middle of a large field in a section of the plantation called Bihungwe, the area closest to the forest. The men were given plenty of firewood to burn, high-powered flashlights, and noisemakers, including drums, two empty gasoline barrels, and blank cartridges to fire from an old shotgun. It was some distance from the house, so I wasn't disturbed in the least by the noise they made. In fact, I wasn't at all certain that the men actually remained there throughout the night. Nevertheless, their tales of repelling marauding elephants became increasingly more daring and heroic as each morning came around. To satisfy my curiosity, I decided to pay a surprise visit to Bihungwe to find out exactly what was going on.

A hazy half-moon hung low in the sky that night as I set off for the watchmen's hut at the edge of the forest. I was dressed warmly against the cool night air and carried a thermos of coffee and a small hurricane lamp to light my way. First, I stopped at the drying house to ask one of the men to go with me. When I asked for a volunteer, they all looked at me blankly.

"Go now to Bihungwe?" they asked incredulously. "But we have no spears, Madame!"

I insisted that one of them must accompany me, and after a good bit of prodding, a man named Machumbi reluctantly stepped forward. He tucked my small thermos into the pocket of his overcoat. Then, with the lantern in one hand and a machete in the other, he slowly started up the path toward the forest, as though headed for the gallows.

The narrow uphill paths were slippery that night. The earth had been packed hard from the trampling of many bare feet, and was now slick with mud after two months of rain. As we stumbled our way across the rugged terrain, we could hear the beat of the watchmen's drum grow stronger and stronger. In the murky shadows, every hillock and outcropping resembled the rounded form of an elephant's back. Machumbi was visibly trembling, and I was beginning to wonder if this had been such a good idea after all. We were suddenly overcome by the strong, pungent odor of fresh elephant dung.

"Machumbi," I said, "what would you do if we saw an elephant right now?"

"I'd run!" he responded without hesitation.

"You would leave me?" I asked, knowing full well that he would.

His reply was typically Ruandan. He said, "I wouldn't want to leave you, Madame, but what happens to us now is the will of God."

We could see that pyrethrum plants had been uprooted on both sides of the path. I stepped on some dried dung, and then into a hole nearly two feet across where a single spoor had sunk into a particularly soft patch of earth. By the time we spotted the watchmen's fire burning up ahead, I was considerably the worse for wear. They must have seen our lantern as well, for they immediately began to beat the drums and bang on the oil barrels with renewed exuberance. I raced toward the tiny enclave, comforted and relieved to see the brave, smiling faces of the three night watchmen.

They hooted with laughter when I told them how frightened I had been and teased Machumbi relentlessly when he admitted that he was afraid to go back to the drying house alone. He stayed with us for an hour; then, with eyes large with fright and a look of sheer terror on his face, he set off across the ominous landscape and vanished into the darkness.

The hut was made from bent branches and roofed with grass, and was not much bigger than an overturned basket. It could barely accommodate two people sitting close together on the grass mat that covered the ground. A fire blazed in the open doorway, filling the hut with smoke and stinging my eyes. I sat down beside Rudabeka, the head watchman, and waited to see what surprises the night would bring. It was moments such as these that I particularly relished, spending time with the men and getting to know them on a more individual basis.

I discovered that evening that Kayonga, the second night watchman, was a talented drummer. He told me that he had been trained at a mission school and had become the mission's finest drummer. At that time, few Hutu had the opportunity to learn the art of drumming, as drums were a symbol of sovereignty, and the possession of a drum was generally prohibited to all but the king and the provincial chiefs for their use on special occasions.

Kayonga's drumming was truly spectacular. He had taught the third watchman, Patani, a chubby boy of seventeen or eighteen, to play in accompaniment, and together they made a great deal of noise, which was, of course, the whole point. Clearly, they were playing for my entertainment and admiration as well, and they ran through Kayonga's entire repertoire with unrestrained gusto. For added showmanship, they tossed their drumsticks into the air and caught them without missing a beat.

When they tired of drumming, Kayonga and Patani picked up their spears and a flashlight and walked off across the fields in search of elephants. They returned a short time later with news that two elephants had broken through the barrier and were in a field nearby. Rudabeka went out alone to investigate and was back almost immediately.

"Madami!" he cried excitedly. "They are here! Right here! Come quickly to see them!"

My heart was pounding as I stepped away from the hut and stared uncertainly at the dark peaks of Mikeno and Karisimbi, half expecting to see a mad charge of elephants emerge from the shadows.

"Don't be afraid, Madami," Rudabeka said reassuringly. "I will protect you with my life."

Those were comforting words, in light of Machumbi's fatalistic sentiments earlier in the evening. I stayed close to Rudabeka as we made our way quietly to a spot downwind from where two elephants were happily munching on pyrethrum—the commodity upon which all of our livelihoods depended. They were an awesome sight. They appeared to be either completely oblivious of our presence or not unduly alarmed. Apart from the rumblings their stomachs made, they moved quietly for their lumbering size. They would raise their massive heads and trunks just long enough to chew great mouthfuls of the tender plants.

Kayonga and Patani took up their machetes and beat fiercely on the oil drums, while Rudabeka fired two blank cartridges into the air. The elephants took notice and decided that the party was over. From behind an outcropping, we watched as they loped across the field, leaving a trail of crushed pyrethrum in their wake, and stepped down into the deep trench with an agility I would not have believed possible, then awkwardly slithered under the barbed wire fence and disappeared into the forest.

When we returned to the hut, the moon had disappeared and it was very dark and cold. Patani added more logs to the fire, and I poured myself a steaming cup of coffee. Rudabeka chuckled as he knelt down beside me, slapping his knee to the rhythm of the drum. He knew he had put on a very good show, and he felt quite pleased with himself.

From deep in the forest we could hear faint voices crying, "Wa hoo, wa hoo oo!" Tutsi shepherds watching over their cows asleep in the open called out to ward off leopards and hyenas. Rudabeka, who was half pygmy and half Hutu, began to talk about the Tutsi. "Only the Tutsi in Ruanda know the secrets of *uburozi* (poison)," he said. "You must be very careful, Madami, for you have enemies among the Tutsi here who would like to kill you."

I laughed at the absurdity of this notion, for the Tutsi who lived near Mugongo came to my door each day to receive medicine, to show me their newborn babies, and to tell me their troubles. Even so, Rudabeka reminded me of a time when cows had come onto the fields to graze on pyrethrum. In anger, I had fined the shepherd a hundred francs (one dollar) for each of the six cows that were grazing in the fields. He begged for leniency, but I refused to give in, and he eventually paid the fine.

Now, Rudabeka was saying that afterward the shepherd told his friends that one day he would bring me a bottle of poisoned milk, and my death would be his revenge. To my astonishment, Kayonga and Patani agreed that this was so. I thought apprehensively of the five bottles of milk I bought each day from three different shepherds, but I was feeling far too contented at that moment to worry about enemies and revenge and poisoned milk.

As the night wore on, the talk turned to gentler topics and Rudabeka spoke of his philosophy on women. "I am not a man who wants a woman to say 'yes, yes, yes' all the time," he said. "God gave woman a voice, so let her use it. Let her say what she wants and thinks and feels. Some men believe it is good food that makes a woman happy. But that is not so! A woman's happiness depends upon the kindness and gentleness of her husband. If a woman is content, she can be given the toughest piece of meat to eat and it will taste to her like sugar." Rudabeka had three wives, so he spoke with some authority.

It was close to three in the morning when I said good night to the men and headed for home. Kayonga was my fearless escort, armed with a six-foot spear and listening intently for any sound or movement nearby. This was not false caution, as many of the elephants that wandered onto the plantation were cows accompanied by their young, and there was always the danger of a charge should a female become frightened for the safety of her baby. Moreover, we had no way of knowing where the elephants might have roamed during the course of the night. On one occasion, they had wandered into the small vegetable garden less than fifty yards from my house.

The next morning, I walked back to Bihungwe to see how much damage had been done. Giant elephant spoor lay within six yards of the little hut, and there were tracks all around it. The earth was churned by enormous footprints, indicating where the elephants had turned and retreated from the drums and the fire.

I never did win the war with the elephants, and quite honestly, I would not have had it any other way. They are cunning and crafty, and they continued to exasperate and outfox me for as long as they existed in this part of Ruanda. Tragically, as the need for arable land and grazing pastures increased, more and more of the trees in the forest were cut down. Herds of long-horned cattle grazed where tall cypress trees had once stood, and cultivated fields ascended the steep slopes of the vanishing forest. By the mid-1970s, most of the herds had been decimated by poachers or had migrated to the other side of the volcanoes into Zaire. By 1980, all but a few of the elephants had vanished from Rwanda entirely.

13

LIFE IN MUTURA

Early in the spring of 1956, it was rumored that young King Baudouin of Belgium was coming to Ruanda to visit his colony. Excitement mounted as preparations got underway for the royal visit. From Kisenyi to Rutshuru, and all along the "Circuit de Bugoyi," workers planted festive flowers called "spice pinks" along the roadside. Bulldozers miraculously appeared to smooth the road (for the first and last time ever), grinding the machinery against the lava rock and sending showers of pebbles into the ditches—to the joy and delight of every little boy. Finally, after weeks of anticipation, the residents along the route received official orders to tidy up their grounds for the king's visit on the third Sunday in June.

It was announced that King Baudouin would attend the nine o'clock Mass at Nyundo Mission, then travel along the Mutura road en route to Rutshuru and Rwindi Park. At ten o'clock that morning, a crowd of people dressed in their finest clothes stood near my garden gate waiting for the royal procession. The Belgian flag we had prominently displayed in honor of the king's visit wrapped itself limply around the bamboo flagpole, rather than waving proudly as we had envisioned. But the garden was at its loveliest, and we were all poised to make a ceremonial impression.

We had a long wait. The royal limousine left Nyundo at ten-thirty, but the road was so thronged with the king's impassioned subjects that progress was slowed to a crawl. It was noon before we heard the distant cheers, followed by the sound of an automobile approaching. For many months, King Baudouin's photograph had been displayed on posters all over the Congo and Ruanda-Urundi announcing his pending arrival. In the photograph, he was splendidly attired in a military uniform adorned with medals and braids. The open touring car that slowly approached our waiting entourage held three passengers—a uniformed driver; a handsome young man in the front seat with thick wavy hair, dressed casually in a white shirt and slacks; and a heavy-set middle-aged man sitting alone in the back seat, wearing a uniform with rows of medals and a gold-braided cap. The car stopped briefly at the garden gate, and the three men acknowledged our cheers with smiles and waves before they drove on. When they disappeared from sight, I turned to the enraptured faces of the people in the crowd and realized only then that none of them had recognized that the handsome young man waving from the front seat of the car was actually the king, and that the uniformed man in the back seat was only his bodyguard. They all seemed so impressed with what they thought they had seen, I didn't have the heart to disillusion them.

As time went by, most of the spice pinks that had been planted along the roadside were eaten by goats, but in several places right in front of Mugongo there are still a few clumps of these sweet little flowers to remind us that young King Baudouin came to visit his colony in 1956.

My two-year contract to manage Milindi ran out in 1957, and although my income would be reduced by almost half, it was with little hesitation that I decided not to renew it. By this time, my dream of a real home at Mugongo was beginning to take shape, and it was there that I wanted to devote all of my time and concentrate all of my energy.

My first major project was to enlarge the garden, which was laid out between the front of the house and the road. An abundance of tropical plants and flowers thrive in the lower altitudes of Ruanda, but the temperate climate and high elevation of Mugongo make it ideally suitable for growing flowers indigenous to Europe all year round. I redesigned the layout in the style of a formal English garden, creating geometric-shaped beds with an intricate network of paths running through it. Along the road and bordering the edges of the front yard and drive we planted hundreds of hydrangeas, which eventually grew into massive flowering hedges surrounding the property. The tall cypress trees that grew along the road were cut back to create "Madame's Window"—an unobstructed view of the valley and Lake Kivu beyond.

We transplanted many of the existing flowers and planted a variety of seeds and bulbs that Gino sent from San Remo. Hundreds of agapanthus bulbs—also called blue or white Nile lilies—were separated and replanted. Borders of tall fragrant lavender edged the walkways, and narcissus, foxglove, and digitalis were carefully interspersed among the roses and calla lilies. That autumn I began to sell cut flowers to the hotels in Goma and Kisenyi. Each week, I delivered enormous bouquets of agapanthus, iris, gladiolas, and alstroemeria (Peruvian lilies) to my growing number of clients.

Banyaruanda, for the most part, have little or no interest in flowers and consider gardening to be the most menial of labors. Consequently, it was difficult to find good workers who were willing and eager to spend their days digging in the flower beds. Batandarana was an exception. Right from the start, he demonstrated an instinctive knack for tending and nurturing flowers, and he has been devoted to the development and success of the gardens at Mugongo for more than forty years. Batandarana became my head gardener in 1957—a position he still holds today. He was determined to master the English names for all the flowers, and it was a proud day for us both when he learned to say the word "delphinium." Batandarana has a particular fondness for freesias and has always referred to sweet William as "sweeties."

All temperate-zone flowers flourish at Mugongo, with the exception of peonies and tulips. Few temperate-zone flowers will survive at Ruanda's lower altitudes, and it was therefore a novelty for the residents of Goma and Kisenyi to receive bouquets of violets, roses, and sweet peas from Mugongo. Carnations, on the other hand, do very well near Lake Kivu, and several planters grew them commercially at that time and shipped them by air to Léopoldville, Stanleyville, and Elizabethville. Carnations flourish at Mugongo during the dry months, but they must be covered and protected from the heavy rains that sweep down from Karisimbi during the rainy seasons.

I soon had so many primulas and giant Oregon pansies that I decided to pot them. I sent for pygmy potters from a nearby village and gave them an ordinary flower pot to duplicate. The first pots they brought me were perfect, so I ordered some more. Perhaps the assignment was too mundane for their quirky natures, or perhaps they simply could not leave well enough alone. In any case, each batch of pots they produced became increasingly more elaborate, and I wound up with the most extraordinary collection of fluted, tiered, and bottle-shaped red clay pots imaginable. They were utterly delightful.

The pygmy women and children brought the pots to the house for my inspection, and they never seemed to mind when I rejected one or two on account of their being lopsided or misshapen. Each child would receive a cookie, and the women were handed articles of clothing or empty bottles, which they prized. They barely acknowledged the money I paid them. And before they left, they always danced for me. There was one very old woman who, in spite of her distorted face and bare withered breasts, danced with extraordinary grace. She would lift her arms high above her head and move slowly with a sensuous rhythm, which I imagined must have been quite captivating when she was young.

Prior to 1960, public elementary schools in Ruanda were almost exclusively for Tutsi children. Very few Hutu children received any education at all. I made up my mind that all the children who worked as flower pickers at Mugongo would be taught to read and write. I hired a teacher, bought books and supplies, and converted one of my outbuildings into a schoolroom. I knew that the families relied on the money the children earned, so I established a combination work/school day wherein the children worked the fields in the mornings and attended school in the afternoons. There were some skeptics who believed that the children would lose interest and quit once the novelty wore off, but the majority came to class eager to learn, and many far preferred their classroom studies to the work in the fields.

Sundays were very special days at Mugongo. The road below the garden saw a constant stream of people passing by from early morning until sunset. On Sundays, the people of Mutura attended church services, visited with friends and neighbors, and engaged in various forms of entertainment. This was their day of leisure and groups of families strolled together up and down the busy road. The women moved slowly and gracefully, wrapped in many yards of colorful cloth, their heads held straight and high. Little girls wore their best dresses, and little boys raced along beside them on wooden scooters. Teachers, clerks, and shopkeepers rode by on bicycles with bells jingling, resplendent in crisp white shirts, neckties, and shoes polished to a spit shine. Groups of children would wander into the garden to dance for me, and I would think how remarkably blessed I was to live among such beauty and richness.

Living at Mugongo afforded me the opportunity to participate more fully in the social activities of the Kivu. For a time I missed Cecil terribly, but being an unattached woman, I received many invitations to dinners and parties given by friends throughout the region. Moreover, the proximity to Kisenyi and Goma made it possible for me to reciprocate with social get-togethers of my own. When Kenneth and I divorced, I had hoped that I might remarry, but it was several years before I met a man who interested me sufficiently to turn my thoughts toward romance.

Per Moller was Swedish, with eyes as blue as the African sky. He was raised near the Swedish archipelagos and had settled first in Kenya with his German wife. It was said that he and his wife had quarreled a great deal and that she would periodically leave him—riding off to Nairobi on one of her thoroughbred horses. Nearby planters would watch her gallop away in a cloud of dust and say, "There goes Mrs. Moller again, leaving her husband." She would stay away in Nairobi for a while, then eventually reappear—riding her horse slowly back home.

Eventually they divorced, and Per came to the Kivu to buy a coffee plantation. We met in the summer of 1957, and I felt from the moment I saw him that Per Moller had been brought to the Kivu especially for me. While he searched for property to buy, he and his mother and sister rented a large, rambling villa on the lake in Kisenyi where Per kept a small motorboat. On weekends, we would motor across the lake to visit friends or picnic on small islands, returning in the late afternoon to bathe and dress for an evening of dinner and dancing at the Bugoyi Guest House. It was glorious and exciting and romantic, and I became deeply enamored with Per.

Per was tall and handsome, with a strong build and the natural grace of a fine athlete. He was also a marvelous conversationalist and an accomplished linguist. He was fluent in both French and English, and spoke flawless Swahili from his years in Kenya. Per had traveled extensively throughout Europe, Africa, and Asia, and could entertain for hours with a limitless repertory of fascinating stories and thrilling adventures. His effortless charm and startling good looks attracted him to men and women alike. Men were drawn to him as a friend and companion, and half the women in the Kivu fancied themselves in love with him—myself included. One woman, a Swedish missionary, was so smitten with Per that she spent hours each week preparing his favorite Swedish dishes on the off chance that he might drop by.

Per set his sights on a coffee plantation in the Congo called Kania, which, by odd coincidence, was owned by Kenneth. Kenneth was reluctant to sell the property, but after months of unrelenting pressure from Per, he finally gave in. Per took possession of Kania in the spring of 1958, with big plans and high expectations. He began at once to remodel and enlarge the plantation house and hired many new field hands to increase the coffee production. None of us could have imagined that only two years later he would lose Kania and everything he owned, when the Congo erupted into violence and anarchy and even the bravest and most established European landowners were forced to flee.

In the aftermath of Congo independence, both Kenneth and Per sought refuge in Ruanda. Fortunately for Kenneth, he had invested the money from the sale of Kania safely in a bank in England, for he lost his remaining Congolese holdings as well. Kenneth was deeply sympathetic toward Per's loss of Kania and offered him a place to stay in a small house in Mutura near Mugongo.

When Per returned to Ruanda he was destitute. He came to my house almost every evening for dinner and worked alongside me each day on the plantation. This was a dream come true for me, and I was hopeful that he and I might build a life together at Mugongo. But these were difficult times for everyone in the Kivu. Most of our friends had lost everything, and some had lost their lives. Per's desolation over the loss of Kania and the tumultuous events taking place on the other side of the border turned to grief and despair, and our happy future together never did materialize.

Although our relationship developed into one of deep friendship and heartfelt love, it soon became apparent that it could never be anything more. Per suffered from a darker torment—one that haunted him with severe bouts of anguish and frequent thoughts of suicide. Homosexuality was little understood in those days, and rarely discussed openly. It was some years before I was able to accept the fact that Per could never fulfill my needs as a woman and that there was nothing I could do to change that, no matter how hard I tried. But now I'm getting ahead of my story.

14

SEMBAGARE

By 1957, Edouard began to have a change of heart regarding his solitary existence and asked for more and more time off to visit his family. One of his daughters was engaged to be married, and there were arrangements to be made for the wedding and dowry. It became apparent that Edouard would soon want to retire, so I began to look for another houseboy to replace him.

In April of that year, I engaged a seventeen-year-old boy named Sembagare Munyamboneza. Although he was hired as houseboy, it was clear from the start that Sembagare's true ambition was to be a chauffeur, and he rarely missed an opportunity to remind me of that fact. The old Ford had finally run its last mile, and I had recently purchased a brand new GMC pickup that was less than a year old. I was decidedly unenthusiastic about giving Sembagare driving lessons in the new truck, but he was persistent in his pleading, and his arguments did hold a certain amount of logic.

"Suppose you were ill?" he would ask. "I could drive to Kisenyi to get the doctor. I could deliver the pyrethrum to Goma and do all the transporting—which really isn't a woman's job, anyway . . ." And so it went, until I finally gave in.

The driving lessons took place every afternoon for exactly fifteen minutes. That was the most I could endure. After three months, Sembagare had mastered the basics, but he still couldn't steer. He seemed to think that the steering wheel had to be in constant motion, and he swerved uncontrollably all over the road. Help arrived in the form of a visitor named Jean Neyrinck, who volunteered to give Sembagare steering lessons. Jean found an assortment of empty kerosene cans, which he set up on the road to form a driving course. Watching this enterprise from the bedroom window, I was astounded to see Sembagare effortlessly maneuvering the truck between the oil cans. He even managed to make a U-turn without hitting a single tree or damaging a fender. When the lesson was finished, a jubilant

Sembagare marched into the house and announced that he had learned more about driving in two hours with Jean than he had learned from me in three months.

And with that, Sembagare became my chauffeur and his status in the community was elevated immeasurably. He was the first Ruandan in all of Mutura to learn to drive an automobile. I'll never forget how proud he was the day he drove back from Kisenyi with his *permis de conduire*. Friends stood along the roadside, applauding and shouting their congratulations when he called out that he had received his driver's license. From that moment on, Sembagare did all the driving that entailed transporting pyrethrum, or anything else that was considered "man's work"—and most of the other driving as well.

One morning, Sembagare's father rode along with us on our weekly trip to Kisenyi. It was the first time the older man had ever ridden in an automobile, and Sembagare drove very slowly and cautiously, mindful of his father's apprehension. When we returned home and dropped his father off near the path leading to his house, I asked him if he was proud of Sembagare and if he had enjoyed the drive. "Oh, yes, Madame," he said. "I am very proud of my son, but I did not enjoy the drive, and I think I will never ride in an automobile again."

Although automobiles were commonplace in those days and people frequently rode buses or taxies to the larger towns, they were still viewed by many Ruandans with a certain degree of skepticism. One day, Sembagare came into the house chuckling. He had given a lift to an old man who had asked him if he had eyes on the bottom of his feet. "If you don't have eyes in your feet," the old man said, "how do they know what to do?"

When we drove to Kisenyi, Sembagare always wore his khaki driver's uniform and his face maintained an expression of dignified correctness. Each time I got in or out of the truck, he would hold the door for me with such a deferential flair that you would have thought we were riding in a Bentley town car. On the way home, he would usually relax a bit and entertain me with comments on everything he had seen or heard in town. One morning, a very attractive Belgian woman was playing Ping-Pong on the hotel terrace, wearing the first bikini ever to appear in Kisenyi. I had noticed Sembagare stealing glances at her when we delivered the flowers to the hotel. Driving home, he remarked, "Madame Van Dycke is very beautiful. She has a nose just like a bushbuck."

Sembagare is a devout Seventh-Day Adventist, and I have always felt that it is his Christian faith and deep belief in the teachings of his church that have formed his fine character. In fact, he was seriously concerned for a time because I was not an Adventist as well. While serving the soup one day, he asked, "Madame, have you ever heard of Moses?" When I assured him that I had, he continued with, "Well, have you ever heard the story of David?" This went on for some time until he became reasonably convinced that my soul was not doomed to eternal damnation. In those days, his Bible was the only book he possessed in Kinyaruanda, and when he was not working, it was always close at hand.

In 1960, Sembagare became engaged to a Seventh-Day Adventist girl named Esther Nyirahuku. Esther's father and brothers were categorically opposed to the match and raised many objections. Sembagare's father opposed the marriage as well, and was very slow to pay the dowry and carry out the required formalities. It was two years before the wedding took place. During that time, Sembagare never saw Esther, although they wrote to one another occasionally. Sembagare waited patiently and faithfully, certain in the knowledge that he and Esther would eventually have a happy future together.

Finally, a date was set and a large wedding took place at the Rwankeri Mission Church, which Per and I attended. Sembagare had borrowed the pickup for the occasion and drove off looking very handsome and happy in a pair of dark trousers, a new white shirt, and a stunning necktie—a gift from Per. He had hinted to Per that it was his most fervent wish that my gift to the bride might be a bottle of French perfume. Naturally, I obliged with a bottle of Houbigant *eau de toilette* which I found in a shop in Goma and which was duly presented to Esther, with Sembagare's undying gratitude.

As was customary, the wedding ceremony was followed by a reception at the house of Sembagare's father. Winding our way along a narrow path between rows of tasseled corn, Per and I trailed behind a procession of twenty bridesmaids dressed in long skirts of pastel colors, singing sweetly in the soft morning air. The family compound was neatly tended and decked out in a festive atmosphere. The men gathered around an enormous pot of *pombi*, while the women surveyed the wedding gifts laid out on a long table. Per and I were the only *wazungu* present.

I was immediately ushered into Sembagare's new house to meet the bride for the first time. Several women were in attendance, and I was motioned to a chair beside Esther. It was dark in the windowless hut after the bright sunlight outside. Esther unexpectedly lowered her head onto my shoulder and trembled like a wounded bird. I took her hands in mine and tried to comfort her, whispering reassurances she didn't understand and for what I did not know. I could see that she had a sweet face and enormous dark eyes and looked lovely in her wedding dress—a filmy cloud of white lacy fabric. But this was not a happy bride. Before I could begin to determine the cause of Esther's sorrow, I was summoned outside to toast the bride and groom and watch the dancing begin. As I looked into Sembagare's blissful, smiling face, my heart ached for him.

I never did learn why both families had opposed the marriage, but perhaps their instincts had been correct. Sembagare and Esther were never very happy together, and the disappointments and unfulfilled expectations were a source of great anguish for them both. They had three daughters born two years apart, but their unhappiness became so great that they finally agreed to separate. They never did divorce, but several years later Sembagare married a girl named Nyiramagedede, and I believe they have been very happy together. They have two sons and five daughters. Sembagare continues to support Esther and their three daughters, in addition to his aunt, her seven children, their families, and countless foster children.

A few months after the wedding, Sembagare and I took our first long motor excursion together to the small town of Kabale in southern Uganda. This was Sembagare's first trip outside of Ruanda, and he considered it to be "the most exciting event of his life." Kabale is only a hundred miles from Mugongo, but it takes four or five hours to drive across the steep mountain roads—plus a half hour or more delay at the border crossing. The drive through the Kanapa Gap is breathtaking, with its panoramic vistas of the volcanoes and the many fingers of Lake Bulera. I had to remind Sembagare more than once to keep his eyes on the narrow, twisting road. The route wends its way through a magnificent stretch that cuts through one of the most dense bamboo forests in central Africa.

We arrived in Uganda on Election Day, and as we approached Kabale, nearly everyone we passed held up their fingers in the "V" for victory sign and shouted, "D.P.!" (for Democratic Party). This meant absolutely nothing to Sembagare, but he shouted back "D.P.!" in response, assuming that this was some sort of colloquial salutation intended especially for him. As we drove through the streets, he said happily, "I've never been here before, but everyone greets me!"

At that time, Kabale was a small town with a well-known inn called the White Horse, with wide lawns shaded by enormous eucalyptus trees in the front and a fine nine-hole golf course in the back. Situated at an elevation of six thousand feet, it was a favorite holiday spot for British government officials and their families, as well as tourists traveling from Kenya to

Ruanda or the Belgian Congo. The inn was run by an Englishwoman named Gytha Calder, and I had written ahead to let her know we were coming.

Sembagare slept in accommodations reserved for drivers and quickly struck up an acquaintance with a worldly Kikuyu from Nairobi, who took it upon himself to introduce Sembagare to the wonders of the outside world. Sembagare saw his first motion-picture film that evening at the White Horse—a Shell Oil production on the history of motor racing. Being a driver himself, this film was made to order for Sembagare, and his exuberance and laughter became infectious and spilled over onto the rest of the guests at the inn. He also picked up a few new words in English, and on the way home, he said, "From now on, Madame, you must not call me your 'chauffeur.' I am your 'dreever.' "

Uganda in those days was considered the "Pearl of Africa," to quote Winston Churchill, and we frequently took excursions to its beautiful national parks and game reserves. One of Sembagare's favorite places of all was Queen Elizabeth Park in western Uganda. Never at a loss for a biblical parallel, he likened it to the Garden of Eden. Twice a year we traveled all the way to Kampala (a trip of four hundred miles each way), and to this day it is simply inconceivable for Sembagare to imagine a larger or more prosperous city than Kampala in the early 1960s.

Sembagare has worked for me now for more than forty years. Or have I worked for him? It is sometimes difficult to tell. He has been my closest friend and the source of my strength throughout all these years. Through the many changes and ups and downs, he has resolutely stood beside me, saying, "God will help you, Madame." Countless times, when I have been on the verge of bankruptcy or frightened by political events, it has been Sembagare's quiet courage, gentle wisdom, and effortless faith that have sustained me.

The young boy I hired so many years ago is now my business partner and the manager of Mugongo. In all the years we have worked together, we have never had a serious dispute. Mugongo couldn't run without him, and neither could I.

15

A WELL-INHABITED GARDEN

My dreams of a house full of children were not to be, but there has been no shortage of the pitter-patter of little feet at Mugongo. My home has been filled with an assortment of pets over the years—both big and small, wild and domesticated. I have loved them like my own children, and, like children, they have brought me enormous joy and delight, comfort and companionship, and many moments of frustration and anxiety. There was, of course, Sheila, the beloved Irish terrier that Kenneth and I brought with us to Africa in 1949. Over the years, however, my menagerie has included countless dogs and cats, several monkeys, a goat, a burro, three African gray parrots, an antelope, and two bushbucks. One of my most memorable and unusual pets was a little gray duiker named Betty.

She was given to me by American tourists, Hale and Betty Huggins, who were traveling on safari through the Congo and Ruanda. Along the way, they had acquired a three-week-old gray duiker from a child offering it for sale by the roadside. A gray duiker is a small antelope native to the open plains of eastern Ruanda. The Hugginses were leaving Africa and traveling on to Bombay, and since the fawn was not yet weaned, it would never have survived the trip. Their travel guide suggested that they bring her to me. When I saw the delicate fawn, I felt that her chances for survival were very slim, but I agreed to take her and promised to name her Betty, after Mrs. Huggins.

When she came to us, Betty was no more than fifteen inches long. She had a sandy-colored coat with darker shading on her back and a dusky mark on her face that stretched from her forehead to her shiny nose. She had beautiful long eyelashes and tiny matchstick legs with shiny pointed hoofs. She looked like a little toy on wheels. Her wobbly legs skidded out from under her on the polished cement floors, until she learned that the rugs were islands of safety where she could walk without fear.

And what a nuisance she was! For the first few days, she bleated like a lamb incessantly and refused the baby bottle of diluted milk we offered her. She was terribly frightened and unhappy and made repeated attempts to run away. We could not release her, though, for she wouldn't have survived ten minutes on her own. On the third morning, I found Betty butting and rubbing up against the sleeve of my old fur jacket, which had been left hanging on the back of a chair. Willing to try anything at that point, I slipped the bottle of milk inside the coat sleeve with only the nipple protruding. Betty seized it eagerly and suckled the nipple until the bottle was empty. The feeding problem was temporarily solved, and for the next several weeks, my poor battered jacket became Betty's surrogate mother.

She refused to go near the bottle unless it was hidden inside the coat sleeve. Her attachment to it became neurotic. We tried everything we could think of to wean her from the coat, but she would have no part of it. If I held the bottle a few feet away, she would dart back and forth from one to the other—sucking on the bottle, then nuzzling with the coat. She kept this up until the bottle was empty. The coat had to be kept out of sight between feedings, or she would have destroyed it completely. As it was, she butted her head against it, licked the fur, and sucked on the sleeves whenever she saw it.

Betty was so beautiful and graceful that the entire household found her utterly irresistible. Sembibi insisted that her bed be moved to the kitchen where he could look after her. One morning, I entered the kitchen to find Betty and our new gray kitten, Bonnie, sleeping together in the little basket made from woven strips of bamboo. Betty was curled up on her blanket, and the kitten was sprawled across her with her head snuggled up against her silky neck. Betty opened her liquid brown eyes, and Bonnie acknowledged my presence with an outstretched paw—then they both drifted contentedly back to sleep.

After those first few weeks, Betty was never confined. She had complete run of the plantation and was free to come and go as she pleased. During the sunniest hours of the day, she would stay in the house or retreat to a little nest she had made under the honeysuckle vines that trailed over a stone wall in the garden. Visitors were always surprised when she appeared at the front door to greet them. She would look them over from a careful distance, then turn and walk sedately into the house. Like a perfect hostess, she would glance over her shoulder, inviting them to follow her inside. She would wait until everyone was seated, then settle herself down on the floor at my feet, gracefully lowering her front knees first, then folding her hind legs delicately underneath her.

Late afternoon was her playtime, and this was when she became quite animated and gay. Next to the house was a large square of lawn bordered by tall cypress trees that cast lovely shadows across the grass on sunny afternoons. This became Betty's playground, and it was here that she was joined by her playmates—Sheila, Sheila's son Brill, Bonnie the cat, and a goat named Bella. Bella was a male goat that had belonged to Gino, and when I acquired Mugongo he was part of the package. Bella had been castrated and was completely housebroken. He would butt his head against the door when he wanted to go out, and he slept curled up on the hearth at night. Every afternoon the animals would romp and play and chase each other around the lawn. They loved to play to an audience, and often Per would come by to watch what he referred to as my "well-inhabited garden."

It was impossible not to respond to Betty's irresistible high spirits. Running like the wind with the dogs in pursuit, she would come to a sudden halt and they would crash into her, sending her tumbling. She would startle Sheila by taking a graceful leap over her back, or Bonnie would jump down from a tree and pounce on her. The most comical of all was Bella, who lumbered around after the tiny antelope, trying for all the world to act like a rambunctious young kid instead of the fat old goat that he was. It was Bella who led Betty farther and farther from the house in search of special grasses and who introduced her to the delectable taste of flowers.

Bella had always been a nuisance in the garden, but whereas he ate only the leaves of the roses and delphiniums, Betty ate the blossoms. Left unattended, the two of them could decimate a section of the garden in a single afternoon. Bella would munch on rose leaves while Betty waited demurely by his side. When he was finished, she would move in and select the finest rose bud and nip it off neatly. I must confess that I was not entirely consistent in my disiplinary measures. When I found Bella eating the sweet peas, I whacked him across the nose with a calla lily stalk. When I saw Betty with a Countess Vandal rose in her mouth, I took her picture.

When Betty was about four months old, she began to resist sleeping in her bed, and eventually she refused to remain indoors at night. From the beginning, I had determined that I would not hold her captive, despite the risks of letting her run free. She found herself a hiding place close to the house where she could watch with enormous unblinking eyes the little creatures of the night—field mice and rock hyrax, porcupines, bats, and owls. She seemed to enjoy these forays into the mysterious nocturnal realm, but usually around midnight she would slip into her bed in the kitchen and remain there until morning. Like the anxious mother of a teenager, I tossed restlessly in my bed and was unable to fall asleep until I heard the tap-tap of her little hoofs on the kitchen floor.

As Betty grew older, she grew even more lovely. At six months, she was approximately the size of a goat—Bella excepted. Her coat was a lustrous, velvety sheen, and she was slim and sinewy and exquisitely formed. We would watch her in the early mornings, far across the fields, where the air was still cold and the vivid pink rays of sunlight were just beginning to widen to a clear golden haze. That was when she was her most spirited—bounding and leaping higher and higher in wide circles, adding an extra spark of beauty to the day. Bella, standing on a hillock soaking up the first warm rays of sunlight, nodded like a fat duenna chaperoning a frisky debutante.

The children in the neighborhood all loved her and would call out, "Bet-tee! Bet-tee!" One of the headmen on the plantation had a terrible habit of swearing at the workers, calling them "*sale bête*" (dirty beast), which he pronounced "sa-le bet-tee." He simply could not understand why I had given such a cruel name to such a beautiful creature.

Underlying all the joy that Betty brought to Mugongo was the growing concern of what was to become of her. She would never find a mate in Mutura, for only the red duiker and bushbuck lived in the surrounding forests. She was eighty miles or more from the warm plains where gray duiker bucks might have locked horns and competed for her attentions. She had been roaming farther and farther from home, and I knew that every moment she was out of sight, she was in certain danger. A leopard could take her down in seconds, and the pygmies, with their spears and hunting dogs, would not hesitate to kill a beautiful antelope running free. I began to think that it had been a terrible mistake to take her from her own environment and teach her to trust humans and play with dogs—her natural enemies.

I was awakened one night by Sheila's frenzied barking, followed by the hoarse cry of an antelope. I reached for a flashlight and ran outside just in time to see Betty come streaking across the driveway with a pack of wild dogs close on her heels. She was at the end of her strength and crying with fear. Sheila and I made a desperate lunge for the dogs, separating them from the terrified little duiker. My sharp cries and the bright flashlight, combined with Sheila's fearless attack on the leader of the pack, stopped them in their tracks, and they fled with their hackles raised and their tails between their legs. Betty vanished, but in the morning she was safely in her bed, and for almost a week she never strayed far from the house.

Another day, I was in the garden when I happened to see three men advancing slowly toward an object in the bushes by the roadside. One of the men held a club raised in the air, and I yelled "Stop!" just in time to prevent him from striking Betty. They were strangers who did not know she was our pet and thought it was their good fortune to come upon a young antelope grazing outside the forest.

For ten months, Betty's beauty and blithe spirit brought joy and happiness to everyone at Mugongo. One day, she did not appear on the fields in the morning or come to the kitchen for her bowl of milk. By afternoon, we began a long search, but she never was found. People said that she had gone into the forest to find a mate, but I don't believe she could have survived in the wilderness. We never saw another trace of her.

That was the beginning of a run of bad luck with my pets. Two weeks after Betty's disappearance, Sheila was struck by a Belgian military Jeep and killed instantly. It happened right before my eyes on the road in front of the house, and it thoroughly broke my heart. Sheila had been with me for eleven years and was rarely more than an arm's length away. She was just a puppy when Kenneth and I got her and brought her with us to North Carolina. She had shared our stateroom when we sailed from New York to the Belgian Congo in 1949, and traveled with us by train, riverboat, and pickup truck more than two thousand miles to the Kivu. She never allowed a stranger to approach me without issuing a sharp, warning bark, and she was always protective of those I loved. It was Sheila who had come to the rescue when the little monkey Snooks was being carried away by an eagle and when Betty was being pursued by wild dogs. When she accidentally ended up in Bukavu with Cecil, she had wandered for days trying to find her way back to me. It was into her thick, wiry coat that I sometimes cried, and it was her wet kisses and warm presence that brought me so much comfort. I have had many beloved dogs since that time, but none has ever taken the place of Sheila.

After Sheila's death, the house was lonely and silent. Brill (Sheila's son) grieved for his mother. I tried to keep him close to me, but barely two months later he was attacked and killed by a leopard. The houseboys said, "Your luck with animals is gone, Madame. A bad spirit is working against you now." I began to believe that they were right, and I was inconsolable.

That autumn, Jean-Marc Syners gave me a black-and-white spaniel puppy, which I named Tisa. Around the same time, I answered an advertisement in the *East African Standard* offering Irish terrier puppies for sale, and a few days before Christmas in 1957, two little terriers arrived from Kenya, which I named Katy and Terry.

One day the following summer, Sembibi called me into the courtyard where I found a man holding a frightened baby bushbuck whose mother had been killed. An adult bushbuck is about the size of a fallow deer. They have thick chestnut coats patterned with vertical lines of white spots down their sides and a narrow black stripe, speckled with flecks of white, along their spines. At the base of the neck is a small saddle of gray, and the undersides of their legs are pure white. Male bushbucks have beautifully turned horns.

I took her from the man and set her down. She stood on trembling legs, then began to walk stiffly about like a child on stilts, cautiously placing one foot down at a time. I thought to myself, Perhaps my luck has changed, and I named her Bahati—the Swahili word for "luck."

Bahati was very adaptable and easy to care for. She drank from a baby bottle right from the start, and when there was no bottle in sight, she sucked on our fingers. The day she arrived, Bonnie the cat came bounding toward her with a joyful leap of recognition, only to make a hasty retreat when she realized that this scrawny creature was not Betty after all. Bonnie never did accept Bahati completely, but the three young puppies adored her. They would lick the milk off her face and grab her spindly legs playfully in their mouths, toppling her over. We placed a big silver bell around her neck so we could hear where she was as she bounded through the fields and played with the dogs.

Despite the fact that she ate cornflakes for breakfast and sipped tea from a china cup, Bahati remained essentially a creature of the outdoors. I made no attempts to domesticate her as I had with Betty. I believed that if we could protect her while she was still a fawn, she would one day find her way back into the forest where she would live her life as it was meant to be lived. When I had tea in the garden, I could see her smoky eyes watching me from under the hydrangeas, but I felt no sense of guilt when I faced her unwavering stare.

Her ears moved with every sound. She began to go off on her own for a few days at a time, always returning to the safety of Mugongo. As time went by, her absences grew longer and longer, and eventually we rarely saw her. Finally, the day came when she went off into the forest and never returned. But for a year and a half, Bahati brought us joy and happiness and was a symbol of good luck to everyone at Mugongo.

PART THREE

16

A Feudal Kingdom

In retrospect, the 1950s in Ruanda were the waning years of a great kingdom. Its manifestations were as florid and baroque in their own way as were those preceding the dissolution of the Hapsburg Empire prior to World War I. It is undeniable that many of us heard faintly in the distance the rumblings of dissent, but none of us would have predicted that life as we had known it was about to change irrevocably.

Ruanda has a long history of colonial domination. The first colonizers were the Hutu, who overpowered the Batwa many hundreds of years ago. The second wave of colonization began sometime during the fifteenth century when the Tutsi migrated to the region and overpowered the Hutu. The third wave of colonizers were the Europeans, who arrived at the end of the nineteenth century. They are all but gone now, having left behind remnants of Western influence in the form of their language, their religion, and certain of their institutions. The true legacy of Ruanda's colonization, however, is the ancient enmity which exists between the Tutsi and the Hutu, which goes back more than four hundred years.

The agriculturist Hutu lived a relatively peaceful, simple life in the fertile hills and valleys of the region, until the warriorlike Tutsi descended upon the land. Although their arrival was met with fierce resistance, the keen intellect and superior military prowess of the Tutsi warriors, in addition to their imposing stature, led to the swift defeat and total subjugation of the large Hutu populace. The Tutsi established a feudal kingdom and consolidated their hold on the land and its people for many centuries.

Well into the twentieth century, there existed in Ruanda a civilization as archaic and enslaving as the feudal kingdoms which dominated Europe throughout the Middle Ages. Until abolished by the Belgians in 1957, Ruanda's political and social structure was a firmly entrenched feudal caste system, called *"l'ubu-hake,"* based on the rights and obligations of lords and vassals and the ownership of cows. The Tutsi were the lords, the Hutu were the vassals, and the cows were the great long-horned cattle which represented a man's wealth and stature in the realm. The people were born into this system and knew no other way.

A man who accepted the gift of a cow or several cows as a fief became the vassal of his lord and swore eternal allegiance to him, accepting the vassalage as a family obligation which his sons would inherit upon his death. The lord, in return, accepted the vassal as his protégé and promised to protect him, to represent him in all matters to his chief or to the king, and to assist him in times of misfortune or illness.

When a man wished to possess a cow and become the vassal of a lord, he would petition with the words, "Make me rich, and I will be your child and you will be my parent." Once a man was accepted as a vassal, he was required to pay homage to his master by bringing him offerings of beer or baskets of grain several times each year. If a vassal was granted six or more cows, he was obliged to offer his master his choice of one or more cows from his herd several times during his lifetime. A vassal was allowed to retain one cow as a marriage dowry for each of his sons.

The Tutsi dynasty claimed a celestial origin, as did the pharaohs of Egypt and the emperors of the Orient. The first ruler, King Landa, is said to have lived in the sky and given birth to the first Tutsi. It is not known precisely when they began to emigrate toward Central Africa, or if they came from Egypt or from Abyssinia. The Tutsi are believed to be of Nilotic descent and bear a close resemblance to the Bahima tribe of Uganda, the Banyambo of Ndorwa and Karagwe, and the Peuls of the Sudan—both in physical stature and in their pastoral customs and political organization.

Of their earliest kings, who may have been entirely legendary, nothing remains. Their tombs, if they ever existed, were not marked or have been lost in the passage of time. The reign of Gihanga, the tenth king, or *mwami*, appears to have been authentic. It was during his reign that the long-horned cattle are said to have first appeared in Ruanda. Gihanga is also credited with the discovery of fire. At the royal court, in a special hut maintained in his memory, a fire burned night and day in an immense clay pot. Guardians watched over it to make certain it was never extinguished, and only the reigning king was permitted to light his pipe from this fire.

The funeral rites of the Tutsi are another indication of their Nilotic ancestry, in that their kings were mummified. The corpse was carried to a sacred forest reserved for royal funerals, where a large hut had been erected as a tomb. The body of the king was placed inside the hut and laid out on a screened litter four or five feet above the ground. A fire was built under the litter to dry the body and prevent its decomposition. The corpse was continuously turned by attendants so that all sides were evenly exposed to the heat. When the body was completely dried, the royal remains were placed on a bed of herbs and covered with lion and leopard skins.

The official mourning period lasted four months and was a time of great misery. During this period, cohabitation between husbands and wives was forbidden. Even the bulls were separated from the cows. Men and children shaved their heads as a sign of mourning, and all work in the fields ceased. If the crops were ready for harvest, it was permissible to harvest the minimum amount required to sustain the population, but even then it had to be done discreetly.

When I first came to Ruanda in 1949, the *mwami*, or Tutsi king, was Charles Mutara Rudahigwa, who—at six feet, nine inches tall—was, during his reign, the tallest monarch on earth. Rudahigwa's reign had not been an easy one, though. He had succeeded his father, Yuhi Musinga, who was deposed by the Belgian administration after a thirty-five-year reign on account of his contempt for Christianity and his fanatical adherence to the past. Musinga was said to have been a brutal ruler, exercising his supreme power over the life and death of his subjects with extreme cruelty.

Rudahigwa's mother had been Musinga's first wife. Although Rudahigwa was the eldest son, Musinga had numerous wives and many children. Traditionally, the successor to the throne was one of the king's younger sons, as the strength of Ruanda was symbolized by the virility of the king. According to legend, the true heir to the throne must be a child born holding in his tiny hands the seeds of millet, squash, or other plants indigenous to Ruanda—an indication from their god, Imana, that he was destined to rule. The identity of this infant who was to become the successor was confided by the king to three trusted courtiers—members of the royal council, called "Abiru"—who revealed it publicly only after the king's death. After giving birth to the royal heir, the young queen never bore another child. She lived apart from the *mwami* and dedicated her life to the nurturing and protection of the young heir to the throne.

At the time of Musinga's deposal in 1931, Rudahigwa had already attained considerable recognition and prominence as a subchief. He was fluent in French (which endeared him to the Belgians) and acquiesced to the Belgian demand that Ruanda adopt Catholicism as its national religion. Accordingly, the Belgians chose Rudahigwa over his many brothers as Musinga's successor and proclaimed him *mwami*. Throughout his reign, Rudahigwa struggled to maintain the delicate balance necessary to appease the Belgian administration and, at the same time, preserve the supremacy and omnipotence of the *mwami* over his subjects.

* * *

My first introduction to the *mwami* and his royal court was in 1956, when the Hollywood film *King Solomon's Mines*, based on H. Rider Haggard's adventure classic, was shown to the king and queen and the royal courtiers. The movie, which was partially filmed on location in Ruanda and starred Stewart Granger and Deborah Kerr, contains some of the most authentic African dance sequences on film, including a dazzling depiction of the dance of the Intore, such as I had seen performed in Kisenyi on New Year's Day of 1955.

The showing of *King Solomon's Mines* had been arranged by the American Consulate in Léopoldville and took place in the royal city of Nyanza. Many of the European residents of Ruanda were invited, myself included. The *mwami* and his queen, their courtiers, and the Tutsi nobles who took part in the film were all present, as were a number of Belgian officials and priests from a nearby mission. It was a mild, clear night, charged with an air of excitement and wonder. A large screen was erected in the middle of a wide dirt road. On one side of the screen, chairs had been set up for the invited guests. On the other side (the back side), a huge crowd of Banyaruanda sat with expectant faces waiting for the movie to begin.

The king and his entourage made a ceremonial entrance. One would be hard-pressed to find a more majestic figure than this giant of a monarch who could trace his family dynasty back more than four hundred years. Rudahigwa and his courtiers were dressed in traditional white robes with flowing togas knotted at their shoulders, and his queen, Rosalie Gicanda, was wrapped in billowing layers of pale pink.

A disheveled young American arrived with the movie reels just before sundown and began to set up the projector. I looked around for the American consul general or some U.S. official to preside over this auspicious event, but saw only the young projectionist in his rumpled raincoat. He never approached the king or queen or acknowledged them in any way. Although royal etiquette prohibited any show of emotion, diplomatic protocol required that they be formally recognized and greeted by an American official, and they were rightfully offended.

The soundtrack for the film was in English, and as a result, the Africans were unable to understand the dialogue. Restlessness and murmurs of disappointment rippled through the crowd until the action sequences progressed to the familiar landscape of Ruanda. From that point on, the spectators provided their own soundtrack with cheers and improvisional dialogue, as they followed the safari adventure across the desert to the royal city of Nyanza, shouting with glee each time they recognized friends—and in some instances themselves—on the big movie screen.

The city of Nyanza was almost entirely devoid of Western influence, as the Belgian administration had refrained from intruding upon the royal seat of the Tutsi monarchy. There were no hotels, and outside visitors were discouraged. When the movie ended, the king and his entourage and most of the invited guests assembled at the one small restaurant in town for sandwiches and drinks. The rumpled young American sat as far from his royal hosts as possible and spoke to no one. I longed to speak to Mwami Rudahigwa and the queen; however, unsolicited conversations were frowned upon. Accordingly, my overtures were limited to smiles from across the room, for which I received the briefest nod of acknowledgment.

The Tutsi population in my commune of Mutura was made up primarily of shepherds living the nomadic existence of their ancestors. They were considered the country cousins of the educated Tutsi who were employed in the towns or the nobles who formed the retinue of the *mwami* at Nyanza. Tutsi shepherds were often away from their homes for months at a time, moving from place to place in search of richer grazing land for their herds. They slept in the open and subsisted almost entirely on milk.

The long-horned cattle of Ruanda are similar to those depicted in Egyptian carvings and have large lyre-shaped horns with a span of five feet or more. As the result of a veterinary inoculation program implemented by the Belgians, the cattle population in Ruanda had increased so dramatically that by the mid-1950s experts estimated that the herds should be reduced by at least half. This would have been a difficult undertaking, since in Ruanda a man's wealth and stature were symbolized by the size of his herd of cattle, and it was every man's ambition to own as many cows as possible. To the Banyaruanda, the loss of a cow can be as traumatic as the loss of a family member, and there were frequent suicides among the Tutsi when their herds were lost or significantly diminished.

One of the most enduring legacies of the European colonists was the proliferation of Christianity throughout Africa. With the succession of Rudahigwa, and at the insistence of the Belgian administration, Catholicism was adopted as the official religion of Ruanda in the early 1930s. It is now estimated that as much as seventy-five percent of Banyaruanda are Christians. Their deeply ingrained culture has instilled in their Christian faith a distinct African quality, and it is undoubtedly that quality that has contributed to its endurance. Although many have adopted the Christian deity as their own, the Banyaruanda have not turned against their pagan god, Imana. They are a deeply religious people and believe that their lives are in the hands of God every moment of every day. Imana is the supreme being and creator of all things, and he is so kind and beneficent that there is no reason to fear him. The Banyaruanda do not pray directly to Imana, for he is so high above them that it would be considered an act of vanity. Rather, they pray to the spirits of certain demigods who are their patron saints.

Conversely, the Banyaruanda greatly fear the spirits of the dead. All bad luck is believed to have come from these spirits, who are always close at hand but cannot be seen. If there is famine or illness, it is the result of an evil spirit at work. Banyaruanda believe in reincarnation and that they exchange their spiritual soul for the spirit which returns to earth. This spirit is both weak and strong and requires their help and intervention. It will not leave them in peace if it is refused assistance.

The leaves of plants containing magical properties, or a bit of lamb's wool, are placed in the right hand of the dead. The symbolism is expressed by the words "Return among us without thorns, as these plants sweet to the touch we have given you," or "Return among us with the gentleness of a lamb." Banyaruanda build a tiny hut close to their own huts to shelter the spirits of the dead, and each day several kernels of grain or a few drops of beer are placed inside it. At family gatherings and special occasions, these spirits are always remembered. A small fire is built near the tiny hut, and a receptacle of beer is placed beside it as an offering to the spirits.

17

JUBILEE

In June of 1957, I had the opportunity to witness the royal court in all its splendor when I journeyed to Nyanza to attend the three-day Jubilee celebration marking the twenty-fifth anniversary of the reign of Mwami Rudahigwa. Thousands of spectators came on foot from great distances to pay homage to the king. Others came packed like sardines in the back of trucks, singing joyfully as they bounced along in billowing clouds of dust over the winding roads that led from all corners of the realm to the royal city of Nyanza.

I was accompanied by Karin Bielska's three children, their Dutch housekeeper, and my houseboy, Edouard. We brought along tents and hampers of food and pitched a campsite in one of the lovely groves of eucalyptus trees outside the royal village. We had departed Kisenyi long before sunup and arrived in Nyanza just as the royal procession was beginning to make its way slowly toward the stadium. The scene was as colorful and majestic in its own way as was the pageantry of the royal courts of Europe. The long cortege was made up entirely of Tutsi nobles—their imposing height accentuated by the white togas they wore fastened at their shoulders and the long white robes wrapped around their slender bodies.

Rudahigwa, the queen, and the queen mother were carried into the stadium on ornate tipoys borne upon the shoulders of Hutu servants. The king was dressed in white and wore a long cape of royal blue draped about his shoulders. His headdress was a cascading plumage of white sisal attached to a wide band of blue and white beads, with long beaded fringe that parted over his face and fell to his shoulders. The queen, Rosalie Gicanda, was dressed in a white gown wrapped in a cloud of white tulle. The queen mother, Kankaza Nyiraruvugo, wore a headdress similar to that worn by the king and was dressed in a pink tunic and a voluminous skirt of soft white fabric. Her shoulders were draped in a shawl of white organdy banded with gray silk. The queen mother ruled the kingdom in partnership with her son, and was therefore almost as revered as he. She closely resembled the king in physical appearance and was so youthful-looking she could easily have been mistaken for the queen. The three monarchs maintained expressions of solemn dignity—neither smiling nor acknowledging the enthusiastic greetings of the cheering crowd.

The ceremonies opened with a Catholic Mass conducted by Monseigneur Bigirumwami, the first ordained African bishop in the Belgian territories of the Congo and Ruanda-Urundi. A choir of one hundred boys dressed in black robes sang traditional hymns, their earnest faces framed in wide white collars. The princesses of the realm sat together with shining upturned faces, dressed as delicate butterflies. Headbands of white sorghum stubble were worn across their narrow foreheads to symbolize fertility. The sheer white fabric draped about their shoulders lifted gently in the breeze, remindful of butterfly wings. Otherwise, they were as still and lifeless as the figures on an Egyptian bas-relief—in contrast to the pampered, capricious young women they undoubtedly were.

At the conclusion of the Mass, the entire assemblage made its way to the royal palace through a wood of eucalyptus trees. I marveled at the specter of the tall figures dressed in white who seemed to float gracefully beneath the trees in the filtered sunlight. Their towering height and regal bearing evoked a feeling of wonder and awe. The men walked in pairs, often holding hands, as is the custom in Ruanda. Women, in groups of four or five, chattered animatedly among themselves in hushed voices as they approached the palace.

At the edge of the wood, we joined the crowd on a small square of lawn in front of the palace to witness one of the most solemn rituals of the festival—the presentation of the royal drum, Kalinga, the sacred symbol of sovereignty. Kalinga itself was never beaten. Rather, other drums were beaten in its honor. It was said that the sacred drum was ornamented with the genital organs of enemies killed in battle. Kalinga was always kept well guarded from public view, and I was therefore surprised to learn that its presentation was to be one of the events at the Jubilee. The presentation did take place; however, the drum was so heavily swathed in layers of white cloth that its shape and size were completely obscured. It was borne upon a litter carried by Batwa men, followed by Hutu women singing a symbolic song. At the end of each verse, the women would raise their arms in gestures of subservience to Kalinga.

The palace was a large brick residence with a wide veranda in the style of a European villa. Following the ceremony, Batwa men presented their offerings to the king. Among the gifts were cows with newborn calves, ornate pots of honey, drums, leopard skins, and carved stools—all of which

Rudahigwa received with cool indifference as he sat impassively on the veranda with the royal family and Belgian officials.

The afternoon festivities reconvened at the stadium. Awaiting the king
was a glittering array of gifts that stretched from one end of the stadium to
the other. Many were presented in pantomime or ancient tribal ritual.
Among the gifts were a grandfather clock, a motorboat, and a Mercedes
Benz. The early kings of Ruanda toured their kingdom in small, beautifully thatched grass huts attached to long horizontal poles, which were
carried on the shoulders of servants. A perfect replica of one of these
"touring huts" was presented to Rudahigwa, who in fact toured his kingdom in a Lincoln convertible. Again, the extravagant gifts were accepted
with indifference, and I was shocked to see that many of the gifts and their
presenters were not acknowledged at all.

When I expressed my thoughts to Edouard, who was standing right beside me, he looked at me in stunned disbelief. "But, Madame," he said,
"everything in Ruanda *belongs* to the *mwami!* The land, the crops, the people, and the animals are all his!" Why, indeed, would a person be grateful
for a gift that already belongs to him?

The most beautiful cows in the land, called *"inyambo,"* were ushered
into the stadium by royal attendants. These sacred cows were kept solely
for the pleasure of the king and for exhibit on holidays and special occasions. They were magnificent beasts, adorned with beaded necklaces and
tiny antelope horns. Their great lyre-shaped horns were ornately decorated. Their hoofs were brightly polished, and their udders were painted
white.

All of Ruanda's traditional tribal ceremonies were enacted during the
festival, making it a truly historical pageant. Tutsi women, dressed in skins
of brightly dyed cowhide, represented the queens of the early kings. Attached to their headbands were two fifteen-inch-long antennae covered
with tiny red and white beads, and their ankles were encircled with hundreds of bands of a special grass called *"ubutega."* A group of twenty or
more Hutu men appeared as part of the pageant draped only in banana
leaves—a reminder of their humble station in the realm. They played their
parts with little enthusiasm, and I wondered to myself how much resentment had accumulated over four centuries of Tutsi domination.

The highlight of the festival was the dance of the Intore. One hundred
dancers with brilliant, multicolored sisal headdresses streaming about
their faces tossed their heads and pounded the earth with their feet in perfect rhythm to the beating drums, leaping higher and higher into the air.
We left the field amid the ceaseless roar of the spectators. It had been a
dazzling spectacle, and although we did not know it at the time, it was to be
one of the last such celebrations of the great Tutsi dynasty.

* * *

Soon afterward, there began to be indications of open dissension between the Tutsi monarchy and the Belgian administration. Rudahigwa feared the newly enacted Belgian reforms were undermining his power and that the democratic principles advocated by the Europeans threatened the supremacy of the Tutsi race and the continuation of their rigid caste system. Rudahigwa deliberately incited hostility toward the Belgian authorities among his chiefs and courtiers.

On the morning of July 27, 1959, a rumor began to circulate throughout Mutura that the *mwami* was dead. The workmen gathered at the drying house and begged me to tell them if this was true. I went to the house and turned on the radio—dialing station after station. I finally picked up a frequency from Brazzaville in the French Congo that reported: "The Mwami of Ruanda died on July 25 at Usumbura. The cause of his death has not been announced." I immediately returned to the drying house and told the men what I had heard. They received the news in stunned silence, then left the plantation and returned to their homes.

I was left alone to ponder what the true circumstances were and what the repercussions would be. I was shocked to learn that Rudahigwa was dead and felt apprehensive about the future. The official explanation of Rudahigwa's death was announced the following day. It was reported that on July 25, while in Usumbura, Rudahigwa had complained of a severe headache. He was taken to the hospital where he was treated by his Belgian physician. As he was leaving the hospital, he suddenly grasped his head in his hands and crumpled to the floor in a lifeless heap. The forty-eight-year-old monarch was pronounced dead of a cerebral hemorrhage.

Almost immediately, speculation was rampant throughout the land that the *mwami* had been assassinated. Indeed, many of us feared that he had been murdered by the Belgians, perhaps by lethal injection. Two independent European doctors were called in, and both concurred with the original diagnosis. Due to mounting tension within the country, an autopsy was advised. The queen mother flatly rejected the idea, and the autopsy was never performed. Months later, I spoke personally to one of the doctors who had examined the body—Dr. David Stewart of Louisville, Kentucky—and he assured me that the king had indeed died of a cerebral hemorrhage.

It was later learned that Rudahigwa had been plotting to overthrow the Belgian administration in Ruanda. An actual date for the coup d'état had been set, and the only reason it did not take place was that Rudahigwa died before the plan could be carried out. It was said that his body had become weakened by excessive drinking and other overindulgences and that he had been undergoing medical treatment for some time. Rudahigwa's true physical condition had been known only to his trusted courtiers and had been carefully concealed from the public.

The funeral services were held in the royal city of Nyanza on July 28, 1959, in the presence of Monsieur Harroy, vice governor of Ruanda-Urundi; Monsieur Lafontaine, vice governor of the Belgian Congo; Monsieur Tordeur, the provincial commissioner; Mwami Mwambutsa of Urundi; Bishop Bigirumwami; and other dignitaries of the Catholic Church. I did not attend, as I had been advised that, with the widespread suspicion that the *mwami* had been assassinated, the attitude toward Belgians in particular and foreigners in general was very antagonistic.

The funeral was, in effect, the last great manifestation of the Tutsi dynasty in Ruanda. Friends later described the event as being fraught with tension. Vice Governor Harroy read a message of condolence from King Baudouin of Belgium, followed by a eulogy to the *mwami*, but the words of tribute were obscured in the clamor, as rumors of assassination circulated among the tense and angry crowd. An atmosphere of menace and hostility was directed toward all the Europeans present.

A long procession carried Rudahigwa's body to the sacred burial ground. Grand Chief Kayihura of Kisenyi stepped forward and shouted in a voice strained with emotion that the *mwami* could not be buried until the royal council, Abiru, had designated his successor. Complete silence fell upon the crowd as a member of the royal council came forward and announced that the childless Rudahigwa had chosen as his successor his young half-brother, Jean Ndahindurwa, who had taken the name of Kigeri V.

A wild roar erupted as a young man—seven feet tall and astonishingly thin—stepped forward to greet his subjects. Instantly, all hostility was forgotten as the people cheered their new sovereign. The power of the absolute monarchs of Ruanda was nearing extinction, however, and the reign of Mwami Kigeri V would last less than two years.

18
REVOLT

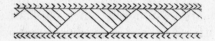

The death of Rudahigwa was the pivotal point in Ruanda's social and political modern destiny. With the succession of Kigeri V, a mood of discontent swept through the land and consumed the people of both ethnic groups. Tutsi nobles conspired to oust the Belgian administration, and Hutu leaders sought equality in business and education and emancipation from their longtime oppressors. Throughout the land there was an undercurrent of uneasiness and a clamoring for change.

For the first time in Ruanda's history, political parties were established. The UNAR (United National Ruandaise), made up of Tutsi nobles and chiefs, openly voiced its opposition toward the Belgian administration. This was followed by the establishment of Aprosoma, a political movement promoting the interests of the Hutu. Rudahigwa had ruled under the guise of a benevolent patriarch, but the young and inexperienced Kigeri regarded the new Hutu leaders with fear and open contempt. He received only members of his own party at his court and turned a deaf ear toward those who urged tolerance and cooperation. Whereas Rudahigwa had been a symbol of national unity, Mwami Kigeri split the country into two distinct political and ethnic factions.

On November 1, 1959, a Hutu subchief, Dominique Mbonyumutwa, was attacked and wounded by a band of young Tutsi assailants. The assault on the Hutu leader ignited a wave of arson and violence that spread throughout the district of Ndiza, destroying nearly every Tutsi-owned house or building. The incident rapidly escalated into a full-scale rebellion, as bands of Hutu insurgents swept across the countryside, enlisting recruits as they went from village to village, attacking Tutsi and burning their homes. In some cases, their Hutu servants were targeted as well.

The only weapons available to the Banyaruanda at that time were spears, bows and arrows, clubs, and flaming faggots. Desperately outnumbered and generations removed from their warrior ancestors, the Tutsi coerced the Batwa into defending them against the Hutu insurgents and sent the fearless little archers on reprisal raids.

The country was soon ablaze. Small grass-roofed huts became infernos, and sturdy brick and tile-roofed houses were demolished by machetes and clubs. Bricks and mortar were torn apart by hand, and the doors and window frames were ripped from the walls and set on fire. Hundreds of cattle were killed or maimed. The official death toll during the first ten days of the revolt was one hundred and twenty-four; although many bodies were abandoned between rows of corn or in banana groves by fleeing, panic-stricken families and were therefore not included in the preliminary count. Fifty people were killed at Kibuye alone, an area thirty miles south of Kisenyi.

The vast rural areas of Ruanda were not made up of towns or villages. Rather, the people lived in family compounds. Throughout the hills and valleys of the countryside, the huts of the Hutu were nestled alongside those of the Tutsi. In areas where the Tutsi outnumbered the Hutu, the Hutu huts were destroyed as well. As hillside after hillside was devastated by fire, the people fled by the thousands, seeking sanctuary in the towns and missions.

The Belgian government moved swiftly to crush the rebellion. Fifteen hundred Belgian troops were transferred from the Congo into Ruanda. Roadblocks were set up, and small planes circled above the trouble areas to spot conflagrations and fighting. There was no official response from the *mwami* until the revolt was in its twelfth day. That morning, yellow leaflets were dropped from spotter planes and fluttered through the air to the anxious people in the fields and villages below. The leaflets were an appeal to stop the fighting and live in peace, and bore the photograph and signature of Mwami Kigeri. They were received with skepticism and bitterness by the frightened men at Mugongo.

"Why doesn't the *mwami* do something?" they asked. "If he would speak to us, we would know what to do. Only the *mwami* can stop this war."

Kigeri remained at the royal palace under the protection of Belgian troops. His first secretary, Kimenyi, was arrested for instigating the deaths of many Hutu. The genital organs of the Hutu that were killed were said to have been added to those that adorned the royal drum, Kalinga.

Leaders on both sides of the conflict were killed. The UNAR devised lists of Hutu antagonists whom they swore to eliminate. Thousands of Tutsi—mainly women and children—fled to Uganda during the first days of the rebellion, after which the border was closed. The small prison in Kisenyi was crammed with two hundred and fifty prisoners—both Hutu and Tutsi. Kisenyi was overrun with bewildered, homeless people, carrying what few possessions they had been able to salvage. Weary women with babies strapped to their backs were trailed by older children clutching their mothers' skirts, gazing at the unfamiliar surroundings with eyes wide with fright.

Hutu leaders claimed that the insurrection had been initiated, in part, to avenge the attempt by the Tutsi to overthrow the Belgian administration in Ruanda. Consequently, they felt betrayed that the Belgians had not supported their actions. They considered the arrest of hundreds of Hutu grossly unjust. At the same time, Tutsi leaders complained bitterly that the Belgians had not sufficiently intervened in their behalf during the crisis. The Belgians found themselves in a difficult position, embroiled in an ethnic and class struggle that had been simmering for centuries.

I remained at Mugongo throughout those turbulent weeks while the inferno and bloodshed raged all around me. From my front lawn, I could look out over the valley and see the flames of hundreds of fires scattered across the landscape. Almost all of the field hands at Mugongo were Hutu, as were most of the house servants and gardeners. Conversely, all the shepherds in Mutura were Tutsi. Many of my Tutsi neighbors feared for their lives and moved their cherished cattle deep into the forest where they were concealed on the lower slopes of Karisimbi. Their most valued possessions were packed in baskets or wooden crates and hidden in caves. Hutu workers at Mugongo sheltered many Tutsi men, women, and children in the drying house to protect them from the marauders.

Among the Tutsi shepherds who lived near Mugongo was a man named Gahereri, whose cattle herd was estimated to be in excess of five hundred head. Gahereri was six feet, eight inches tall and remarkably slender. He had a long, narrow face, deep-set eyes, and a large, prominent aquiline nose. He dressed in the traditional long white robe, which was usually covered with dust, and wore a long red woolen scarf tied around his neck. To complete the outfit, he sported a well-worn trench coat and an elegant black felt hat, which somehow never seemed out of place with his large, callused bare feet. When I shook his hand, I was always surprised to find that his slender hand was ice-cold to the touch. Gahereri had five grown sons, each as tall as he, and their combined families constituted a formidable clan. One of Gahereri's granddaughters was named after me. She was called "Madame."

At fifty years of age, Gahereri was still incredibly strong and was held in high esteem as a great *kurwana* fighter. *Kurwana* is a duel between two men, each armed with a four-foot cane of very sturdy wood, traditionally cut from a tree called *"umunzemze."* The combatants would thrust and parry with the canes until one of them had broken the arm of his opponent.

For years, I bought one calabash of milk from Gahereri's family every day. At the end of each month, Gahereri himself would come by to collect payment. The only dispute we ever had was over the number of days in any given month. I maintained that I should pay for thirty calabashes of milk in those months that have only thirty days. Gahereri insisted that all months had thirty-*one* days, and he bellowed and carried on, saying that the house-boys and I were trying to cheat him. I showed him the days of the month on a large calendar, but he could not read and would not accept my expla-nation. In frustration, I gave up and paid him for thirty-one calabashes of milk every month—even in February.

After I paid Gahereri, he would invariably make his way to the nearest drinking establishment and spend all of the money on banana beer. Later in the afternoon, this tall, spindly man could usually be seen swaying and staggering slightly on the road, as he slowly made his way back home. If he happened to catch sight of me as he passed by the house, he would ceremo-niously tip his hat and bow.

At the outbreak of the rebellion, Gahereri declared that he would never leave Mutura. "I will die on my own land," he said to me. "I will not be dri-ven off!" Most of his cattle remained hidden in the forest for a very long time. A month or two after the revolt, it was learned that Gahereri had of-fered the pygmies several head of cattle in return for killing Hutu. Early one evening, I was alarmed to see fifteen or twenty Hutu men running across the pyrethrum fields toward Gahereri's family compound. The houseboys shouted, in a mixture of excitement and dread, "Madami, they will kill him now—and all of his sons!"

I stood on a bench in the garden and was horrified to see dozens of Hutu men, armed with spears, running from all directions and surrounding the huts of Gahereri's family. There was much shouting and posturing, but no blood was shed that night. It seemed that Gahereri had been able to pacify his antagonists, and I began to feel confident that he and his family would not be frightened away easily. They must have been sufficiently fright-ened, however, for soon afterward, Gahereri and his family left Mutura in the middle of the night, driving their cattle up the road and into the Congo, where they resettled.

Ruanda's Tutsi leaders had sealed their fate by openly denouncing the Belgian administration. As a result, the Belgians reversed their allegiance in support of the Hutu. Many of the Tutsi chiefs fled the country, and those who did not were either in hiding or in prison. Many thousands of

Tutsi families were homeless and wandered aimlessly about in the larger towns or took up temporary residence in churches, missions, and universities. The Belgian authorities provided them with food and shelter for many months until they could be persuaded to return to their old homesites.

The aftereffects of the rebellion were immediate and profound. Hundreds of thousands of Tutsi ultimately fled Ruanda for Uganda, Urundi, and the Congo. From Mutura to Kisenyi, the hillsides and valleys were scattered with the burned-out remains of Tutsi homes, and now only Hutu were seen walking along the road. Gone for the time being were the familiar congregations of astonishingly tall men in flowing white robes, and gone forever were the tipoys bearing Tutsi women upon the shoulders of Hutu servants.

Prior to the rebellion, more than eighty percent of the students in the schools were Tutsi; now they were mostly Hutu. The classrooms were filled with sturdy young boys and girls with friendly, eager faces. Here and there you might see a slender Tutsi child with delicate features and frightened, doelike eyes, but they were the exception.

Several hundred thousand Tutsi fled to Uganda, where they were detained in a refugee camp near the town of Mbarara. I made the mistake of agreeing to accompany a Belgian priest to the camp to help him locate one of his parishioners, a young woman named Dafrosa. The priest was a peculiar-looking man to begin with, but on this particular occasion he was dressed in a pair of black dungarees with a matching Western-style jacket, black leather cowboy boots, and a black cowboy hat. The camp was enormous, situated in hot, barren desert land. Two hundred thousand Tutsi refugees were encamped in small thatched huts, and more than a million emaciated cows wandered aimlessly in search of grass in the dry scrubland.

We drove through the dusty camp for hours in a Volkswagen bug searching for Dafrosa and her family, but we were unable to locate them. It became late and we got lost, and suddenly two Ugandan military trucks approached us in an unmistakably hostile manner. Armed soldiers demanded to see our passports and permission papers to enter the camp. We had none. We were taken to the military barracks and arrested on the spot. Our captors refused to believe that my sidekick (Gene Autry) was actually a priest, and they did not seem at all inclined toward leniency. The prospect of being incarcerated in a Ugandan prison was more than I could bear, and the tears started to flow. My uncontrollable sobbing (which was completely genuine) seemed to have a softening affect, and after several hours we were finally told, "You are free to leave, but don't ever come back!" I never spoke to the priest again, and he was eventually deported from Ruanda for killing a roan antelope in the Akagera Park.

The rebellion of 1959 was a resounding (if somewhat Pyrrhic) victory for the Hutu. Although Kigeri was still nominally the king, the Hutu—by their sheer numbers—had brought an end to Tutsi domination and virtually dismantled the feudal monarchy in Ruanda. A people kept in servitude for centuries had at long last cast off its chains.

As the wild elation following their victory began to subside, the Hutu became painfully aware of their shortcomings and the challenges that lay ahead. They had at last discovered the power of their majority, but their country lay in shambles. The destruction was massive. Blackened hillsides still smoldered, and most of their crops had been destroyed. Moreover, they were faced with the prospect of creating a new government. They were lacking in the education, skills, and experience necessary to lead their country. Under the Belgian administration, many government posts had been held by educated Tutsi, and there were only a handful of Hutu capable of taking their places. Bankers, judges, accountants, doctors' assistants, veterinarians, and even the police had been predominantly Tutsi. Now these educated men with years of training and experience were being replaced by untrained and inexperienced Hutu workers.

There was a mad scramble for education. Every Hutu father urged his sons to go to school, and the Belgian universities were flooded with requests for scholarships. For those few fortunate Hutu young men who had attained an education, the future was limitless.

19

CONGO INDEPENDENCE

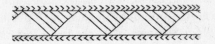

While the flames of rebellion swept through Ruanda, far greater troubles were brewing in the Congo with the emergence of militant nationalist leader Patrice Lumumba. Lumumba was a former postal clerk who had served time in prison for embezzlement and for inciting a riot which had resulted in the deaths of thirty people. He became active in regional politics in the mid-1950s and founded the Mouvement National Congolais (MNC) in 1958, advocating a centralized, independent Congo.

In 1959, Belgium adopted a five-year transitional plan to pave the way toward Congo independence. In January of 1960, Belgian officials met with Lumumba at the Round Table Conference in Brussels to contemplate the political future of the Congo. In a sudden and unexpected turnabout, the Belgians agreed to relinquish control of the Congo effective June 30, 1960—less than six months away—with national elections to be held in May of that year.

This startling announcement was followed by an outbreak of violence and a total breakdown of authority in the Belgian Congo. Lumumba's MNC party issued violent threats against the white population, spurred on by the popular belief that on Independence Day, all European-owned property would be confiscated by the Congolese. Many Europeans sent their wives and children out of the country. In the spring of that year, all commercial flights to Europe from Léopoldville and Stanleyville were completely sold out with families desperate to leave. Additional flights were added in the months that followed.

Lumumba's henchmen drove through the city streets and country roads in vehicles equipped with loudspeakers, spewing invectives and terrorist threats against the white population. Moreover, they strong-armed the Africans into joining the MNC by threatening that all men who did not join the party by Independence Day would be rounded up, roped together, and burned alive.

Belgium brought in large numbers of military troops to protect its nationals. The Belgian government announced the appointment of a minister-at-large to remain in the Congo for an indeterminate period of time following independence. Lumumba responded by demanding the immediate withdrawal of all Belgian troops. I listened to Lumumba's incendiary rhetoric on a local radio broadcast, where he said, "We must intimidate the whites! If the whites are frightened, they will do what we want!" I tried not to be frightened, but each day was filled with apprehension and uncertainty. I was thankful to be living in Ruanda, but I worried constantly about Kenneth and Per and all of my friends who were still in the Congo.

In May of 1960, Kenneth and I took a last sentimental safari to the Congo. This was my last visit to the Epulu River and the Beni and Mutwanga regions at the base of the Ruwenzori mountain range—known as the "Mountains of the Moon." In Beni, we learned that tea and coffee planters had armed themselves in anticipation of a revolt. Most of the women and children had already left the country, and those who remained were packing to leave. Everywhere we went, throughout the towns and villages, Africans angrily shouted *"Uhuru! Uhuru!"*—freedom. Only the Bambutti pygmies greeted us with friendly smiles and seemed completely unchanged and unaware of the impending crisis.

We caught a clear but fleeting glimpse of the icy peaks of the Ruwenzori and spent our last night on the Rwindi Plains. As I lay awake listening to the sounds of hippos foraging in the camp and the harsh cry of hyenas in the distance, I grieved for all of those belligerent Africans and despairing Europeans we had encountered. The entire colony seemed on the verge of havoc and violence—with independence only four weeks away.

The Congo held its first national elections in May of 1960. Lumumba's MNC party outpolled its principal opposition, Joseph Kasavubu's Abako alliance, although neither side was able to achieve a parliamentary coalition. As a result, an uneasy partnership was formed with Kasavubu as president and Lumumba as prime minister. Kasavubu favored a moderate coalition government with broad provincial autonomy, whereas Lumumba advocated a strong, centralized Congo.

On the eve of Congo independence, I listened to BBC radio commentator Edward Collins broadcasting from Léopoldville. He reported that the capital city was gloomy and quiet. King Baudouin had arrived that afternoon and met with the new president. Collins emphasized that President

Kasavubu and Prime Minister Lumumba espoused diametrically opposing policies, and it was difficult to envision how these two men could govern together effectively and manage to keep this enormous country from breaking apart.

On the morning of June 29, 1960, one of the headmen at Kania Plantation asked Per how they should celebrate Independence Day. "This is our biggest day, Bwana," he said, "but we don't know how to celebrate." When Per asked what the people at Kania would like to do, they said, "We want to celebrate with you." So Per organized an Independence Day party, which was held in the dining room of his house. He bought beer and a dozen chickens, which the men cooked themselves with rice and palm oil. There were impromptu speeches and innumerable toasts to the Congo, to the workers on the plantation, and to Bwana Moller. At midnight, they turned on the radio and listened together as the Belgian Congo was proclaimed the independent Republic of the Congo. The following morning, Per found a wooden board propped against the side of the house, and painted on it were the words: "Independence for All! Long Live Independence!" It was signed: "The Workers of Kania Plantation."

Many of the white settlers celebrated Congo independence. All over the Congo, Europeans rejoiced with their Congolese friends and neighbors. In Léopoldville, President Kasavubu spoke to the people of his hopes for the future. He thanked King Baudouin and the Belgian authorities for turning over the country in a state of prosperity and for granting independence in a timely fashion. His address was followed by an inflammatory speech by Prime Minister Lumumba, clearly intended as an insult to King Baudouin and the Belgian officials who were present. All in all, however, there was a great sigh of relief that the Independence Day ceremonies had taken place without incident and that a general spirit of peace and goodwill had prevailed.

The feeling of conciliation was short-lived. Within a week of independence, army and police officers mutinied, igniting an insurrection that swept across the country, plunging it into a state of anarchy. Congolese soldiers embarked on an orgy of rape and murder aimed at the European population from one end of the Congo to the other. It is not known how many women were violated, but two Belgian doctors reported administering injections of penicillin to more than three hundred white women who had been raped by soldiers and who feared they might have contracted syphilis. Among those women were nuns, missionaries, and the wives of Belgian officials and civilians.

On July 8, the Congolese army advanced toward the Kivu Province, and the European residents of Goma hastily prepared to flee. People loaded their cars with as many possessions as they would carry, snatched sleeping babies from their cribs, and joined the long line of overloaded vehicles heading into Kisenyi. At eight o'clock that night, the Congolese captured Goma and closed off all roads leading out of town—virtually imprisoning those who had not yet crossed the border into Ruanda. The soldiers rightly assumed that the Belgian troops in Kisenyi would not fire upon Goma while Europeans were being held hostage. Some families escaped by boat, crossing the lake in the middle of the night.

Unaware of what had taken place in Goma, the following morning Sembagare and I drove into Kisenyi for supplies. Approaching the outskirts of town, we knew immediately that something had happened. Kisenyi was unrecognizable. The streets were glutted with weary, frightened people. Bewildered children, many still in their pajamas, hugged cherished dolls or teddy bears. Cars were parked on the lawns and double-parked along the streets, loaded with what few possessions the owners had been able to salvage from the homes they had lived in for years—homes they had expected their children and grandchildren to inherit.

The residents of Kisenyi (myself included) were now cut off from banks, businesses, and shops, as Goma had been the commercial center for the region. I found myself with no money and very little food and had to rely for a time on the kindness and generosity of friends in order to get by. There were only a few small markets in Kisenyi, and their shelves emptied quickly. Within a few days there were shortages of food and gasoline. Hungry and desperate and overcome by despair, families began to leave Kisenyi, heading for the east coast of Africa by way of Uganda. For the next several weeks, a pathetic procession of overloaded vehicles crawled up the mountain road to Ruhengeri, and then on toward Kabale and Kampala, where they were received with kindness and offers of assistance by the Ugandan people.

Alone at Mugongo, I tried not to dwell on the fact that we were only six miles from the Congo border. I monitored my shortwave radio intently and learned that ten Europeans had been killed in Elizabethville. In Luluabourg, the Italian consul general and seven hundred white residents had been rounded up and held captive. Missionaries and planters in remote outposts broadcast horrifying tales and desperate appeals for help. Messages were sent to relatives abroad, and there were urgent pleas for rescue by helicopter and requests for food and milk and military assistance for isolated families threatened by Congolese soldiers.

On July 12, Lumumba appealed to the United States for three thousand troops to help restore order in the Congo. In response, the United Nations dispatched one of the first of the international peacekeeping forces from many countries, called *"Casques Bleus."* Their shiny blue sun helmets soon became a welcome and familiar sight.

Toward the end of July, the mineral-rich Katanga Province in the south, under the leadership of Moise Tshombe, announced its secession from the Congo. Before long, the Kivu and Kasai provinces signaled their intent to break away from Lumumba's centralized government as well. The United Nations refused to recognize Katanga as a separate state. At the same time, however, U.N. forces did nothing to help suppress the Katangese revolt. Consequently, Lumumba turned to the Soviet Union for assistance, which he received in the form of military advisers and personnel. The country was now occupied by Belgian, Congolese, and Soviet military forces in addition to U.N. peacekeeping troops from around the world. Katanga's radio station began each program with the following message: "Katanga— where President Tshombe is fighting against communism for the freedom of Katanga and Africa."

By the end of July, I had nearly four tons of pyrethrum stored at Mugongo. I had no way of knowing that those four tons, plus most of the pyrethrum Mugongo would produce that summer and fall, would go unsold for nearly a year. I was feeling terribly isolated and anxious. I had received no mail from the United States or Europe in months, and there had been little or no news of those friends who had fled the Congo—let alone of those who had not.

The presence of the U.N. peacekeepers brought a temporary respite from the violence, and by September, Sembagare and I began to venture into Goma once or twice a month to deliver small loads of pyrethrum to the extraction plant. It was a frightening and humiliating ordeal. Where a border patrol had never existed, we were now required to go through customs and formalities on both sides of the new Congo-Ruanda frontier. Our passports and laissez-passers were checked first by Ruanda customs officials, then by Belgian paratroopers, and finally by Congolese soldiers and police. We were required to have two sets of documents—one for Ruanda and one for the Congo, both of which had to be renewed every thirty days. The Irish U.N. peacekeepers stationed in Goma did what they could to maintain order, but they were powerless to prevent the insults and abuses administered by the Congolese soldiers upon those of us who dared to enter their country.

Tales of atrocities mounted. Thirteen Italian air force pilots were massacred in Kindu, and friends and acquaintances told of harrowing experiences of degradation and brutality. No European was safe from attack, particularly those living alone in remote areas. Kenneth and Per were finally forced to abandon their plantations and seek refuge in Ruanda. Kenneth still held an interest in two pyrethrum plantations in Mutura, so he moved into a cottage on one, called Nyaruteme, which was six miles from Mugongo, and Per moved into the other, called Rwamise, just two miles away.

It was a great comfort to have both Kenneth and Per so close by during this turbulent time. We were an odd trio, the three of us—me, my former husband, and the man I was hopelessly in love with. But these were unusual times. We were bound by the past and the present and the relentless onslaught of circumstances beyond our control. We saw each other almost every day and did our best to boost each other's spirits. Instead of the customary charm and wit of the old days, Europeans now measured one another in terms of bravery and perseverance. We lived in a state of constant tension and fear, with each day bringing news more dire than the day before.

In December of 1960, the Irish peacekeepers in Goma were replaced by Nigerians, most of whom were Moslems. In contrast to the boisterous, hard-drinking Irish, the Nigerians were an extremely disciplined and orderly group. Their battalion purchased a half ton of potatoes from Mugongo each week, which Sembagare and Per delivered to Goma. The Nigerian commanding officer ordered seventy-five Christmas trees from Mugongo to be distributed to the Christian U.N. peacekeepers throughout the Congo. The workers at Mugongo cut the cypress trees and bound them in dry banana leaves. Per and I addressed the tags, which we placed on every tree, and he added a message in Swedish for the Swedish troops stationed near Léopoldville.

Kenneth, Per, and I spent that Christmas together at Mugongo. Beneath the branches of our festive Christmas tree were presents for the workers and their children as well as for each other. It was a lovely warm day, and the garden was a blaze of color. In the valley below, Lake Kivu shimmered in the sunshine. Little did we know that as we sang Christmas carols and opened our gifts, more alarming events were taking place across the border.

On Christmas morning, thirty military trucks filled with MNC soldiers arrived in Goma and arrested the entire administration for its secessionist activities. The outnumbered Nigerian troops barricaded themselves in their camp and took no action. In Bukavu, at the southern end of the lake, Jean Miruho, the president of the Kivu Province, and his entire cabinet were captured and transported by truck to Stanleyville. Later that day, an announcement came from Lumumba's headquarters in Stanleyville proclaiming that the Kivu Province had been captured and was now part of the Congo's Eastern Province.

* * *

The new year brought no respite from the terror and violence that accompanied Congo independence. In January of 1961, there were reports of Congolese soldiers infiltrating Ruanda. On January 13, bands of Congolese insurgents crossed the border at Kibumba—just six miles from my home. That morning a carpenter had turned up to repaint the living room walls. The houseboys had completely dismantled the room and removed all the books from the bookcases, when suddenly we heard gunfire. Carrying a wobbly stack of books out to the terrace, I saw workers from Milindi running toward Mugongo, shouting, "The Congolese are coming! The Congolese are coming!" The workers at Mugongo threw down their hoes and ran from the fields.

Kenneth and Per arrived within minutes of one another, and we did our best to remain calm while we figured out what to do. It was agreed that the men would stay to look after the plantation while I drove to Kisenyi to report the shooting. A few miles down the road, I ran into Robert Ameye, the owner of a neighboring plantation, coming in the opposite direction. As I shouted frantically that Congolese soldiers were shooting their way into Mutura, he interrupted me with more stunning news.

"My dear," he said, "the Congolese soldiers are attacking Kisenyi. All the civilian population has been evacuated. I've come to take you to Ruhengeri—or to Uganda, if you prefer."

Only eighty Belgian paratroopers were on hand to defend Kisenyi against more than two thousand Congolese soldiers in Goma. Kisenyi had been under fire since the previous evening. Trembling with fear, I turned the truck around and headed back to Mugongo, my foot shaking on the accelerator. When we pulled into the driveway, Robert jumped out of his car and began flapping his arms about wildly.

"You all must leave at once!" he shouted furiously.

"I'm not leaving," I heard myself say, both surprising myself and confounding the men. Initially they didn't believe me, but after I repeated my declaration, Robert became so furious that he stalked off to the garden and sulked for a half hour before leaving for Ruhengeri, alone.

My refusal to leave was not so much bravery as it was the fear of *leaving*. I was terrified of leaving my home and everything I owned, not to mention my animals and all of the workers—all of whom depended upon me. What's more, all of my precious books were stacked in piles outside on the terrace. I couldn't possibly leave Mugongo now.

Per and Kenneth and I remained together at Mugongo, waiting for military help to arrive. The hours passed slowly, as we listened to the sound of sporadic gunfire echo through the hills. The next day came, and still no help arrived. Kenneth finally reached the breaking point and insisted that we all must leave immediately. Still, I refused to budge. "Rosy, you really are mad!" he shouted. Thoroughly exasperated, he got into his car and stormed off to Kisenyi to round up the militia. While Per and I waited, I took down a suitcase and filled it with pieces of silver flatware that had belonged to my family, negatives and precious photographs, money and my passport, a small jewel case, and a few articles of clothing. Per brought the pickup around to the front of the house, in the event that we had to make a quick getaway.

As the shooting continued, Per appointed sentinels and positioned them on hillocks throughout the pyrethrum fields. From where they stood, they could see in all directions and send warning signals to each other, and to us, if the Congolese came within shooting distance. By now, crowds of frightened people had gathered on the lawn, and it was only Per's calm presence that prevented an all-out panic. I turned on my radio and brought it outside so everyone could listen to the news broadcasts from Usumbura.

It was eventually reported that the eighty Belgian paratroopers had somehow managed to defend Kisenyi against the Congolese attack from Goma and that the shooting there had ceased. Miraculously, there had been no casualties, although nearly every building within shooting distance of the border had been damaged. The Belgians had acted under a "don't shoot to kill" policy, fearing retaliation in Goma, where a hundred and fifty Europeans remained sheltered at the U.N. barracks. Many of the women and children from Kisenyi had taken refuge at Bralirwa, the brewery, located several miles outside of Kisenyi.

At five o'clock that evening, Kenneth finally returned—followed by six truckloads of Belgian soldiers determined to drive the Congolese back across the border. During the first few hours, the paratroopers shot and killed dozens of Congolese inside Ruandan territory. The situation appeared to be more or less under control, so Kenneth and Per returned to their respective houses for the night.

Left alone at Mugongo, surrounded by darkness, the full magnitude of the peril we had encountered hit me full bore. My heart pounded and my body shook as I lay in bed listening to the volley of gunfire in the hills and fields nearby. Around midnight, I was startled half out of my wits by a loud, persistent knock at the door. With trembling hands, I struggled to light a small oil lamp and timidly opened the door a crack. I was stunned and relieved to find six Belgian paratroopers standing on my front stoop. They were hungry and asked if I had any food to spare.

I called to Edouard, who emerged from his hut wearing an old brown wool jersey dress I had tossed out many months before. I suppose it made a comfy nightgown, and under the circumstances, it didn't seem all that peculiar. In no time at all, Edouard had a fire going in the kitchen stove and was beating eggs and cooking sausages. I set the table—all the while tripping over machine guns which had been tossed about helter-skelter on the floor. After a supper of omelets, sausages, homemade bread, and coffee, the grateful soldiers thanked me and Edouard and bid us both a good night.

By the following morning the Congolese had retreated from Ruanda, and although we felt uneasy for many weeks afterward, they did not return. Additional paratroopers were brought in to Kisenyi, and the civilians eventually returned to their homes. Karin Bielska, who had spent three days and two nights holed up at the brewery, returned to her twin houses in Kisenyi and packed her bags and left for Europe. She wrote me a brief note to say she was leaving.

"After all, dear," she wrote, "this is a bit much."

I had to agree. It did seem a bit much.

20

TRANSITIONS

The political alliances underlying Lumumba's regime in the Congo had been extremely tenuous. He and his party leaders were ill-prepared for self-government, and there was stiff opposition within the highest ranks of his administration. Lumumba alienated and terrorized the white population, rather than including them as welcome and valuable assets to the country. He had no control over his army, and his civilian administration was untried and untested. The mutiny of his military forces escalated into a reign of terror which he was unable to contain. All of this, combined with Belgian military intervention and the threatened secession of the Katanga Province, resulted in chaos and brutality. Forces both inside and outside of his administration began to plot for his demise.

Patrice Lumumba was ousted as prime minister in the fall of 1960—just three months after taking office. His removal was orchestrated by President Kasavubu and led by twenty-nine-year-old Congolese army leader Joseph Mobutu. Lumumba was subsequently arrested and delivered to Katanga, where he was assassinated on January 17, 1961. The true circumstances of his death are known only to his captors.

The news of Lumumba's death was received in the Congo and Ruanda with no small measure of relief. The Soviets, on the other hand, depicted him as an international martyr, and Patrice Lumumba was mourned as a hero throughout Russia, Egypt, Ghana, Guinea, and Harlem. After Lumumba's death, Joseph Ileo was appointed new prime minister and General Mobutu was made commander in chief of all military forces.

Meanwhile, in Ruanda, a new government was being created under the tutelage of Belgium. It was headed by Grégoire Kayibanda, the leader of the Parmehutu party. Kayibanda was an eloquent and charismatic speaker who had studied for the priesthood. His energetic patriotism quickly aroused national pride among his countrymen, as preparations got underway for the first elections to be held in September of 1961. Peace and reconciliation were the first and foremost objectives of the new republic. Ruanda's ten districts became prefectures, each headed by a prefect appointed by the government as administrator. The *chefferies* of the old days (areas ruled by subchiefs) were replaced by communes. Kayibanda called for the abolition of the royal drum, the royal council, and all vestiges of feudalism. The feudal dynasty in Ruanda was coming to an end, and the hearts and hopes of the Hutu people were lifted by the promise of democracy.

In a move to distance the seat of government from the royal city of Nyanza, a small town in the center of the country was designated as its capital. Kigali, in 1961, was no more than a small outpost with dirt roads and one very modest hotel. A Quonset hut sitting alongside a small dirt airstrip served as its airport.

Elections were held under the auspices of a special U.N. mission and included a referendum on the fate of the Tutsi monarchy and the rule of Mwami Kigeri. All men and women over the age of eighteen were eligible to cast their ballots for one of the four political parties—Aprosoma, Parmehutu, Rader, and UNAR. This historic Election Day took on a carnivallike atmosphere. The Banyaruanda, dressed in their finest clothes, came out in droves to exercise their voting rights for the very first time. To accommodate the illiterate majority, ballots were printed with large blocks of color—red, black, white, and green—each color designating one of the four parties. Care was taken to avoid "favorite" colors. The voting took all day. At the voting grounds in Mutura, five babies were born—including one set of twins, which was considered to be a sign of God's blessing. Kayibanda's Parmehutu party received seventy-seven percent of the vote, and the Tutsi monarchy was rejected by an overwhelming majority.

Life at Mugongo gradually slipped back into a relatively normal routine. We were busy replanting and harvesting pyrethrum, which was piling up in enormous quantities in every shed and outbuilding on the plantation. Sacks of dried pyrethrum were stacked to the ceiling in every room of the house.

Sembagare and I resumed our weekly trips to Kisenyi, where we would invariably hear reports of continued atrocities in the Congo. One morning, while delivering flowers to the Hotel Regina, we happened upon a young coffee planter from the Congo who lay dying in the hotel lobby of head wounds inflicted by machetes. Workers on his plantation had found him lying unconscious in a ditch, and a neighbor had brought him to

Kisenyi. He died without regaining consciousness. Paul Stroumza, the manager of the Hôtel des Grands Lacs in Goma, who had bravely kept the hotel running through months of chaos and Congolese occupation, was forced to his knees at gunpoint and beaten on Goma's main boulevard. Many other Europeans were beaten and humiliated in a similar manner.

Per regretfully concluded that he would never be able to return to Kania and decided to go back to Kenya, where he had Swedish friends. Painful as this was, I had finally come to the realization that our love for one another could never be more than one of true friendship. The moon shone brightly during his last week in Mutura, and every evening after dinner we would pour our after-dinner coffee into a thermos and drive up the rocky path that led to Bihungwe at the edge of the forest. There, we would park the car and gaze out at Nyiragongo's flaming crater and watch for elephants.

The infinite glistening stars were diminished by the bright moonlight and crimson glow of molten lava, and the volcanoes stood out as stark silhouettes against the illuminated sky. The night air was crisp and cool, and we could hear the faint beating of the watchmen's drums and see their small fire in the distance. On only one of those nights did we actually see the large dark form of an elephant glide silently by—less than thirty yards from where we sat. A short time later, a second elephant followed, accompanied by her baby. I held Per's hand tightly in mine, grateful for this time we had spent together and thinking how very much I would miss him.

Per left Ruanda in March of 1961. Most of my friends were gone now, and the rest were preparing to leave. Oswald du Chasteleer had gone to South Africa, Jack Poelaert to Uganda, and Robert Ameye to Belgium. Karin Bielska and her three children had returned to Europe and had decided to stay, leaving Adam alone in Kisenyi. Zacharia, my plantation clerk, left Mugongo and moved to Rutshuru in the Congo.

Kenneth left abruptly for England, signing over his one-third portion of Mugongo to me. His affairs were in a tangle, which he left for me to straighten out. His old Plymouth was to be sold to pay his unpaid taxes, and his cottage at Nyaruteme was full of possessions for me to sort through and dispose of. What's more, he still had a two-year contract to manage Rwamise for its absentee owner. His parting words were, "You can run that plantation easily, Rosy!"—giving no thought to how I was supposed to sell pyrethrum from Rwamise when I already had tons of my own stockpiled all over Mugongo.

I was feeling pretty lonely and frightened. And to make matters worse, the situation on the political front was far from stable. There was still the threat of a Congolese attack from across the border a few miles away.

And now an even greater danger loomed. Tutsi exiles from the Congo, Uganda, and Urundi had banded together and were infiltrating Ruanda at night, killing, maiming, and pillaging, then fleeing back across the border before daybreak. The Hutu called them *"inyenzi"*—which means cockroach, because they only came out at night.

The raids were sporadic, but terrifying. Philippe Daublain, a pyrethrum planter at Kinigi, was gravely wounded when terrorists shot through the windows of his house with machine guns and then made off with his car. In the outskirts of Kigali, families were held at gunpoint and robbed. One of the newly elected Hutu officials was shot and killed, arousing anger and hostility among the Hutu populace. Infiltrators from Uganda attacked the Gabiro Guest House at Akagera Park, killing the Belgian director and seriously wounding four others. At Kiburara, near the Ugandan border, two hundred *inyenzi* torched thirty Hutu huts and massacred twenty-seven people in one nightly raid.

I hired two night watchmen—the stalwart Patani and the less stalwart Sebazungu. All the men in Mutura were now armed with spears, even during daylight hours. One afternoon the gardeners unveiled a demonstration of their strength and skill by hurling their six-foot-long spears over and over with all their might, using a tree as their target. It was an impressive display, but it did not provide me much comfort. I realized with disheartening awareness how pitiful those spears would be against terrorists armed with automatic weapons.

Roadblocks were set up throughout the country. Every vehicle was stopped and its occupants' papers examined by police. The people were united in their defiance of the terrorists and were determined to preserve their new government at any cost. Hutu civilians, who several months earlier would have fled from Congolese soldiers, steadfastly resolved to defend with their lives the emancipation they had so recently achieved.

During the spring and early summer of 1962, Belgian paratroopers maintained a steady presence in Mutura, and Mugongo took on the semblance of a small roadside inn. Every night they would patrol the Mutura road from Kisenyi to the Congo border, and every evening eight or ten fatigued and hungry paratroopers would use my house as a rest stop. They warmed themselves in front of the fire and filled up on the cookies, cake, and coffee I provided. They were extremely kind and friendly, and I felt very secure having them there. Their patrol schedules varied, so I never knew when to expect them. If they had not arrived by ten o'clock, I would throw some logs on the fire and leave a large thermos of coffee and a plate of cookies or cake on the table—leaving the front door unlatched before I went to bed.

Most nights, I would lie awake anxiously awaiting their arrival. But as soon as I heard the reassuring sounds of their heavy boots on the front stoop and their guns clattering to the floor outside my bedroom door, I would drift off to sleep. In the morning, the thermos would be empty and the cookies gone, but there was always a note or small token of appreciation on the table. This went on for the better part of a year.

Tons of dried pyrethrum continued to pile up unsold, as the border between Ruanda and the Congo remained closed and there was no access to the extraction plant in Goma. Many of the planters resolved to pack up and leave the day the Belgian troops left Ruanda. Everything seemed to be coming to an end for me—my physical safety, financial prospects, and friendships. The only true friend I had left in Ruanda was Adam Bielski. I would stop by to see him every week when I went into town, and occasionally he would drive up to Mugongo to visit and bring me the latest news. Once again the thought of leaving crossed my mind, but all I had to do was look around me and I knew it was impossible. A new life was beginning for the Ruandan people, provided they could establish a stable government and manage to preserve it. I wanted to be there to see it happen.

In May of 1962, to my utter surprise and delight, Per returned from Kenya—"To stay as long as you do," he said. Along the way, he had acquired an enormous black dog, which jumped out of his little Citroën as we were embracing and attacked Terry, one of my Irish terriers. Terry fought valiantly, but lost three of his front teeth and nearly lost an eye before Per was able to bring the dog under control. It was an inauspicious beginning, and it went downhill rapidly from there. Within days of his arrival, Per became quite ill and was diagnosed as having typhoid fever. We nursed him through it as best we could, but once he was sufficiently recovered, he left Ruanda and returned to Sweden permanently. Although I never saw him again after that, I have always kept a photograph of him in my bedroom.

Adam and I were now among the lone survivors of that world of privilege and entitlement we had all taken for granted, and the hostility and violence that had obliterated it forever. He and I together would stay to witness Ruanda's independence and follow the course of its difficult struggle toward peace and stability.

21

An Independent Republic

In all the years I have lived in Africa, I have never known anything to go exactly as planned, and Ruanda independence was no exception. The fledgling republic, under the patronage of Belgium and the United Nations, labored to implement its new government and overcome the shackles of its past. After centuries of oppression, the artless Hutu had been caught somewhat off guard by the stunning success of their grassroots rebellion. They were wholly unprepared for the challenges that lay ahead and were in no hurry to be liberated from their benefactors.

By 1962, however, the United Nations was fervently advocating independence for Ruanda. When U.N. observers visited the country in the spring of that year, they were greeted with large banners erected along the roadsides, painted with bold letters proclaiming: "No Immediate Independence!" and "Democracy First—Independence in Its Time!" Disregarding these impassioned sentiments, the U.N. representatives returned to New York and recommended that Ruanda be granted independence at the earliest possible date. It is conceivable that the United Nations was simply weary of its responsibility for Ruanda, which had been under its protection since the end of World War II (and before that the League of Nations since 1918). The announcement, however, came as an enormous shock to the barely established little republic.

The principal stumbling block was the U.N. insistence that the two small countries of Ruanda and Urundi be unified—a logical concept, since they were contiguous and similar in ethnic makeup. The problem was that neither country would even consider the idea. The people of Urundi were perfectly content to remain under the control of the Tutsi monarchy and were fervently loyal to their Mwami Mwambutsa. They rejected outright the concept of democratic rule and equality for the Hutu majority—the cornerstone of the new Ruandan republic. Ultimately, the proposal to merge the two countries was abandoned, and on June 27, 1962, the U.N. General Assembly Trusteeship Committee voted to grant independence to Ruanda-Urundi on July 1, 1962—just *four* days later—as two separate countries, to be known thereafter as Rwanda and Burundi.

The United Nations debated the question of maintaining Belgian troops in the two countries following independence. It was a foregone conclusion that without outside military intervention, Tutsi factions would attempt to overthrow the new Hutu government in Rwanda. Addressing the U.N. Security Council, the Belgian minister of foreign affairs reported that Belgium had no desire to maintain troops in Rwanda and Burundi indefinitely, but agreed to maintain a military presence until the two new countries had sufficiently organized and trained their own armies. To Rwanda's great alarm and distress, the United Nations arbitrarily ordered that all Belgian troops be withdrawn from Rwanda and Burundi by August 1—just one month after independence.

This was surely the most slapdash independence that ever took place. There was no time to organize ceremonies and festivities—or to prepare the people psychologically for this day they both longed for and feared. One old man asked, "What is independence? Is it a person?" Another answered, "Yes, it is a person who lived in Ruanda many years ago—the Mwami Ruganzu. He will return to us in July." Mwami Ruganzu had reigned in the early seventeenth century and was one of the most deeply revered of the Tutsi kings.

To enlighten the bewildered populace, army helicopters flew over the towns and countryside dropping leaflets hastily prepared by the government explaining the significance of independence. People scurried across fields to pick up the papers that tossed in the wind and gathered in solemn groups to listen, while those who could read recited the news they had been waiting to hear. The document was a disappointment to some of the more belligerent Banyaruanda. Rather than a declaration of unfettered freedom and militant nationalism, it emphasized hard work, a peaceful transition, and the absence of revenge. The major points, translated from Kinyaruanda, were as follows:

1. Some people think that when we are independent we will chase the Tutsi out of the country. Those who believe this are wrong. Independence is the time for all Banyaruanda to draw close together. It is the time when Tutsi, Hutu, and Batwa must unite.
2. There are those who think that on Independence Day we will expel Europeans and Asians from our country. This is not

true. To do so would be as foolish as throwing a stone and breaking your wooden milk container. We need these people to show us the way to prosperity.

3. Some people think that when independence comes they may rob people whom they dislike. Those who do so will be punished.
4. Some people believe that they will no longer have to obey those who are superior to themselves. This is not true.
5. There are those who believe that they will no longer have to work. We will all have to work harder than ever before.
6. Even if many Europeans leave our country, Banyaruanda will not be poor or unemployed. If we are good to the Europeans, it will encourage others to come and invest in our country.
7. Taxation will not end with independence. Taxes will still have to be paid.
8. Independence will not bring the termination of the bride price, although perhaps later the dowry may be reduced.
9. Do not think independence means the end of law and order. It does mean freedom and peace to people of all religious beliefs.

The proclamation ended with the words "Government officials, priests and pastors, Catholics, Protestants, Adventists, Moslems, and all people who can read must tell their brothers and sisters all that is written on this paper. Peace to you all." It was signed "Lazare Mpakaniye, Minister of the Interior."

Independence Day, July 1, 1962, was a Sunday. Spirits were dampened by a radio announcement saying that, due to the threat of terrorist activity by Tutsi exiles, Independence Day celebrations would be held at the capital city of Kigali for members of the government and foreign diplomats only. The rest of the people were ordered to "remain quietly in their homes and hug one another."

Independence Day was a quiet day indeed. Well-meaning acquaintances had warned me to leave the plantation for security reasons. It was feared that *inyenzi* would cross the border on foot and launch a raid on Mugongo in an attempt to steal my vehicles. I was the only white person living on the Mutura road at that time, and I had both a car and a pickup truck. The *inyenzi* had been known to kill for vehicles—and a great deal less. However, the Belgian paratroopers were very much in evidence, and I felt it was important to spend this day with the people of Mutura. So, I concealed my anxiety and remained at Mugongo.

In the morning, I listened to the radio broadcast from Kigali. Patriotic speeches accompanied the official announcement that Ruanda was now the independent "Republic of Rwanda." No one who had lived in Ruanda under the feudal regime of the Tutsi monarchy could fail to rejoice at this moment of independence and emancipation for the Hutu majority. Following the ceremonies, I sat in my garden, gazing out across the fields at the towering peaks of the volcanoes. The hot sun of the dry season had burnished each leaf and blade of grass. Thistledown floated in the air, and all around me there was the soft hum of bees and the brightly colored flash of wings. It was utterly peaceful, and I laughed as I recalled the harsh warnings I had received.

At noon, my friend Sergio Bottazzi, his mother, and his two small children stopped by for a visit and suggested that we take a picnic lunch to Lake Ngondo. I thought it was a marvelous idea. What better place to celebrate Rwanda's independence than at my favorite spot at the edge of the forest? I went into the kitchen to tell Biriko, my cook, to prepare some sandwiches for our outing. To my surprise, both he and Sembagare reacted with great alarm.

"No, No, Madame!" they insisted. "Do not go there today! If people see *wazungu* walking in the forest today, they will believe you are fleeing!" This seemed extraordinarily farfetched to me, but they were both so adamant, I finally gave in and agreed to have our picnic in the garden.

That evening, Sembagare stood with shining, excited eyes as I listened to the world news report on the radio.

"What is the world saying about our independence, Madame?" he asked.

In point of fact, there had been only the briefest mention of the independence of Rwanda and Burundi on BBC and Voice of America. How to explain to Sembagare that these events, which were so important to him and everyone in Rwanda, were insignificant to the rest of the world?

"The world is celebrating with us," I assured him. He was certain that this was so and seemed satisfied.

On July 3, a post–Independence Day celebration was held at our community center in Mutura. Children joyfully sang *"Indepandanzi! Indepandanzi!"* and a group of schoolboys ages ten to fourteen, called *"Les Soldats de Nyaruteme,"* marched across the field and performed a drill exhibition. The proudest moment of all was the flag-raising ceremony, complete with many impassioned speeches. Somehow, during the previous week, a national flag had been devised—a field of red, yellow, and green with a large

"R" in the center—which flew proudly above the enthusiastic crowd. The grand finale was a wild dance, in which almost everyone participated. Young men danced with pretty girls, married men danced with their wives (many with babies strapped to their backs), and gray-haired men danced with lively old women. Babies' heads wobbled about madly as their mothers danced with graceful, outstretched arms, and the entire crowd clapped their hands and stomped their feet to the rhythm of the drums. It was a truly joyous and unforgettable occasion.

Within a few days of independence, the threat of terrorist activities by Tutsi exiles became very real indeed. On July 5, the National Guard discovered a camp of more than eighty Tutsi infiltrators in the forest between the outermost fields of Mugongo and Lake Ngondo. Twenty men were killed and forty were taken prisoner. Four men were captured behind my pyrethrum drying house. The terrorists were heavily armed, and it was estimated that they had been camped in the area for at least five days, as their food supplies were low and those who were captured were very hungry.

Sembagare and Biriko must have known there were *inyenzi* in the forest on Independence Day. I don't know how they knew, but Rwandans have a peculiar way of knowing things. Perhaps a shepherd told them, or perhaps it was a message from Imana. In any event, it was terrifying to contemplate what might have happened to us if our party, with two small children, had wandered into the middle of the terrorists' camp on Independence Day.

The following day, pygmies alerted the authorities that a much larger group of *inyenzi* were encamped in the woods near Ruhengeri. In a surprise attack, almost all were captured, while the rest retreated across the border. Among the items confiscated was a notebook containing their military plans, including maps. Their plan had been to infiltrate into the center of the country where they were to be joined by groups of comrades from Uganda and Burundi. The notebook contained lists of people to be eliminated, including Hutu politicians and some Europeans. I was relieved to learn later that my name was not on the list. The notebook also contained the names of Tutsi sympathizers within the country who could be trusted to help them.

Other items confiscated were large stashes of hand grenades, submachine guns and revolvers, radios manufactured in Russia, and cases of ammunition and whiskey. They also had money—the equivalent of twelve thousand dollars in small denominations—a huge sum for Rwanda at that time. Spies reported that reinforcements were gathered at the base of Mikeno near the Congo-Rwanda border, waiting for the signal to join their comrades. The Congolese had been supplying them with food and provisions.

Rwanda independence had gotten off to a rocky start, but the Rwandan people remained united in their determination to preserve their new republic and defend their new freedoms at all costs. They would be called upon to test this resolve many times in the decades to follow.

It seems to be a modern-day African tradition to change the names of towns and countries at any given opportunity. At independence, Ruanda changed its name to Rwanda, and Urundi became Burundi. The small town of Kisenyi near my home was officially renamed Gisenyi. In 1964, Tanganyika merged with Zanzibar to become Tanzania. In 1971, under President Mobutu, the Congo changed its name to Zaire, and the Congolese capital city of Léopoldville became Kinshasa, Stanleyville became Kisangani, and Elizabethville became Lubambashi.

PART FOUR

22

ALYETTE

When I recall the many friends and acquaintances I have known in Africa, it is predominantly the women who stand out in my mind as having had the exceptional courage and fortitude necessary to survive in this sometimes harsh and intractable land. There is no doubt that within the Rwandan culture it is the women who are the backbone of the family structure and rural agrarian economy. Although it is traditionally Rwandan men who work for wages in factories, shops, and European houses, it is the women who work the fields, bear the greatest burdens, and carry the heaviest loads. Similarly, it has been my experience that among whites, it is too often the women who are destined to endure the hardships and cruel misfortunes that occur in Africa with painful regularity. Dian Fossey was certainly one of those women, and Alyette de Munck is another.

Whenever I think of Alyette, I am reminded of the song from *Annie Get Your Gun* called "Anything You Can Do I Can Do Better." In this case, anything I could do Alyette could do better. Alyette is a diminutive, energetic woman of numerous talents. She enters a room like a whirlwind and is unabashedly outspoken and self-assured. Moreover, she is compassionate and kindhearted and one of the most generous people I have ever known. Her ingenuity and dedication have brought her widespread recognition as an accomplished horticulturist, an outstanding photographer, a gracious hostess, and a superb plantation manager. Above all, Alyette is an extraordinary adventurer.

Alyette had spent most of her life in the Congo, having been brought there by her Belgian parents when she was five years old. As a young woman, she had climbed erupting volcanoes with French volcanologist Haroun Tazieff and spent many weeks exploring the Ituri Forest and camping with the Bambutti pygmies. On one photographic expedition in 1982, she ventured so close to the flaming crater of Nyiragongo that her hair was singed. Alyette is a dedicated naturalist with years of experience in the wild. She is also quite famous as a collector of snakes.

One of her most perilous snake adventures illustrates just how far Alyette was willing to go in pursuit of a specimen. Years ago, while driving through Queen Elizabeth Park in western Uganda in the company of a young guide, Alyette spotted a cobra on the path in front of them.

"Stop the car!" she shouted.

Startled, the young man slammed on the brakes. Alyette catapulted out of the open Land Rover and grabbed the snake with her bare hands. The snake slithered underneath the car in an attempt to escape, but she held firmly to its tail, dragging it out into the open. It was only at that moment that she identified the snake as a "spitting" cobra—a bit more than she had bargained for. In an instant, the snake whipped around and spat its venom in her eye.

The venom of a spitting cobra will blind its victims temporarily and can sometimes be fatal. Blinded in one eye and in agonizing pain, Alyette reached for her scarf to wipe the venom from her face. In so doing, she inadvertently smeared the venom into the other eye, so that now she was completely blind.

The young guide drove at breakneck speed to the park offices for the antivenom serum, which he administered himself. At least now, she told me later, she knew she was not going to die. She was taken to a small roadside inn at the nearby town of Gatwe, where she spent the night in agony. By the next morning some of her sight had returned, and not one to be deterred by a minor inconvenience such as blindness, Alyette got into her car and drove herself all the way back to Rwanda—negotiating the steep, winding mountain roads. When she pulled up to her house in Gisenyi, she was so weak she had to be carried from the car. She later told me that the pain in her eyes was more excruciating than anything she had ever experienced, including childbirth and the countless injuries she has suffered during the course of her adventurous life.

Alyette's husband, Adrian, was a devoted family man, and theirs was one of the happiest marriages I have ever known. For many years they lived in a large villa on Lake Kivu at Buheno in the Congo, fifteen miles south of Goma. Their household consisted of their own three children plus the four children of Alyette's widowed sister, Inez. Adrian had done well in tungsten mining and had retired at the age of fifty to enjoy his life and his family. He bought a small plane, a Piper Cub, and the two of them would take off and fly to exotic places at a moment's notice, with Alyette acting as navigator. Their house was a gathering place for their wide circle of friends and a variety of fascinating visitors from around the world. I so envied their happy and adventurous existence.

Although I had known Adrian and Alyette since I arrived in Africa in 1949, they were really more Kenneth's friends than mine. In fact, there was a period of time when they did not hold me in very high regard. I believe they felt that anyone who would leave a man as charming and fascinating as Kenneth must be very peculiar and foolish indeed. It wasn't until after Kenneth left Rwanda in 1961 that they became my friends as well.

At Congo independence, all seven children were sent to live in Belgium where they would be safe from the upheaval that had replaced their happy, carefree existence. In the tumultuous years that followed, Adrian and Alyette were robbed and harassed numerous times by Congolese soldiers. Soldiers would arrive at their house in the middle of the night and demand money—sometimes threatening to kill a female hostage they had picked up along the way if their demands were not met. They were finally forced to flee the Congo in 1966, and they ended up managing a plantation near Mugongo, called Mudende.

Adam Bielski had been farming Mudende and was experiencing some financial difficulties. At my suggestion, Adam agreed to take on Adrian and Alyette as partners, and for a time it was a very successful partnership for them all. Adrian and Alyette moved into Mudende, while Adam remained at his house in Gisenyi. Adrian took over the management of the household and supervised the renovations to the plantation house (which was practically falling down around them), while Alyette managed their half of the plantation—growing asparagus and raising merino sheep.

In June of 1967, Adrian de Munck died suddenly of a ruptured aorta while on a visit to Paris. Heartbroken and devastated, Alyette returned to Nairobi on August 12, where she was met at the airport by three young men—her son Yves, her nephew Philipe Bribosia, and their friend and college classmate Xavier de Failly. All three boys had recently graduated from the University of Louvain and had been on a photographic safari in Kenya, a graduation gift from Adrian to his son and nephew. Adrian's death had occurred while the boys were en route to Kenya, and—believing that this was what he would have wanted—Alyette insisted that they continue with their adventure. The boys had come to Kenya by boat and had brought with them an old Jeep painted in military-style camouflage, which they planned to drive to Rwanda via the Nairobi-Kampala road.

Alyette rode with the three boys as far as Uganda, where the Jeep broke down outside of Kampala. While in Kampala, Alyette met up with a friend who suggested that she ride back to Rwanda with him and that the boys follow when their mechanical problems were resolved. Alyette gratefully accepted—thinking she could prepare the house for the boys' arrival.

When the Jeep was fixed, the boys headed south to the border town of Kisoro where they were to spend their last night in Uganda at the Travelers'

Rest hotel and guest house, run by an Austrian named Walter Baumgartel, a longtime friend of Alyette's. Kisoro is situated at the juncture of the three countries of Rwanda, Uganda, and the Congo, and the Travelers' Rest is located just a short distance from both the Rwanda and Congo borders. From there, one road leads to the Congo and another to Rwanda. The Congo, at this time, was embroiled in a full-scale rebellion led by Moise Tshombe in a struggle to oust President Mobutu. The revolt was led by Belgian mercenaries aiding and supporting rebel soldiers from the southern province of Katanga. There was a bounty on Belgian mercenaries at this time and very strong anti-white sentiment among the Congolese government troops. The Congo was to be avoided at all costs.

The boys arrived at the Travelers' Rest and were warmly greeted by Walter. That evening at the bar, they spoke animatedly about their safari adventure and told a group of Rwandan men that they were eager to cross the border into Rwanda the following day. Early the next morning, they left. Walter, to his eternal regret, was still sleeping and did not see them off. Tragically, the boys took the wrong road—the road to the Congo— and were never heard from again.

One of the hotel workers said he saw them with the Rwandans that last morning and overheard them tell the boys, "We will show you the road to Rwanda." They were taken to the Congo border and handed over to Congolese soldiers as Belgian mercenaries. Despite the fact that the boys were dressed in civilian safari clothing and their passports were stamped with "student tourist" visas for Rwanda, they were immediately arrested.

No one knows for sure what happened to them. An Italian businessman crossing the border at about that time reported seeing three white boys being stoned by villagers. It is believed that they tried to escape by jumping out of the Jeep. I was later told that a missionary monitoring a short-wave radio overheard a Congolese officer request further instructions. "The Belgian boys are still alive," he is reported to have said. "What shall we do with them?" "Finish them off," was the response.

When the boys failed to arrive at Mudende as expected, Alyette became greatly alarmed and began making frantic inquiries. I spent much of the next several days by her side, waiting for news of their whereabouts. Finally, on the fourth day she received word that the boys had been taken captive in the Congo and that they were not "transportable," which she interpreted to mean that they had been severely wounded. Alyette went immediately to Goma to arrange for an ambulance to bring them back to Rwanda. It wasn't until the Belgian ambassador arrived in Gisenyi the following day that she learned that the three boys had been executed.

I went to see Alyette the moment I heard the devastating news. Never in my life have I wished I had more to offer a friend than I did at that moment, but Alyette was inconsolable and didn't want me to stay. To lose her beloved husband and then her young son and nephew less than three months later—in such a brutal and senseless way—was more than she could bear.

But somehow she did bear it. Alyette remained in Rwanda until 1994 and continued to play a significant role in my life and in the lives of many others over the years. She is truly one of the most remarkable women I have ever known, and I will forever admire her extraordinary courage and her uncommon spirit of adventure.

23

DIAN—THE EARLY YEARS

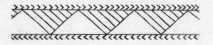

I first learned of Dian Fossey through Kitty Cyr, the wife of the U.S. ambassador to Rwanda. One afternoon while on a visit to Kigali, Kitty took me aside and said, "Roz, there's a young woman who has been studying the mountain gorillas in the Congo. She's going to ask if she can continue her work from your plantation. You be careful. She's a strange one."

This conversation took place in July of 1967, a time when the Congo was embroiled in a civil war—the same conflict that would claim the lives of Alyette de Munck's son and nephew and their companion several weeks later. Dian was just six months into her initial research project in the Congo at a campsite called Kabara on the northern slopes of Karisimbi, when Congolese soldiers raided her camp and forced her down the mountain at gunpoint. She was arrested and taken to a military camp at Rumangabo. Many versions have been told of Dian's ordeal in the Congo, including a rumor that she was gang-raped by Congolese soldiers. She always maintained, however, that this was not true. "I think they were saving me for their major," she would say enigmatically.

It was by no means an easy time for her, though. She managed to escape by convincing her captors that she had a large stash of money just over the Uganda border at the Travelers' Rest hotel in Kisoro run by Walter Baumgartel. If they would take her to the hotel, she assured them, she would give them the money in exchange for her freedom. The soldiers believed her, and a weary Dian arrived at the Travelers' Rest accompanied by a menacing gang of Congolese soldiers. She ran into the building and threw herself on Walter's mercy, pleading, "Hide me, Walter! I've told them I would give them money if they would let me go!"

Walter stood up to the soldiers unafraid. "You are in Ugandan territory," he told them firmly, "and you have no right to be here. Miss Fossey is now free to go, and there will be no payment for her captors." The soldiers were furious at having been duped by this feisty American female, but they eventually gave up and returned to the Congo empty-handed.

Before I met Dian, I received a letter from her, dated July 20, 1967. It came to me by way of the office of the American ambassador, Leo G. Cyr, and was typed entirely in uppercase letters.

DEAR MRS. CARR,

I WOULD VERY MUCH LIKE TO DISCUSS WITH YOU
TOMORROW THE POSSIBILITIES OF MY WORKING ON A
GORILLA SURVEY FROM THE RWANDAN SIDE OF
KARISIMBI.

I'VE RECENTLY BEEN ORDERED DOWN FROM THE
CAMPSITE BY THE CONGOLESE MILITARY. I'VE BEEN
WORKING UNDER THE AUSPICES OF DR. LEAKEY, THE
NATIONAL GEOGRAPHIC SOCIETY, THE AFRICAN
WILDLIFE FOUNDATION AND THE N.Y. ZOOLOGICAL
SOCIETY, AND THIS INTERRUPTION OF MY WORK IS
MOST UNFORTUNATE.

THE MILITARY IN THE CONGO HAVE TOLD ME IT
WILL BE ANOTHER FOUR MONTHS BEFORE I CAN RETURN
TO THE CONGOLESE AREA, BUT IN VIEW OF THE FACT
THAT I ESCAPED ACROSS THE BORDER SOMEWHAT
ILLEGALLY, I'M UNCERTAIN IF I CAN RETURN AT
THIS MOMENT. FOR THIS REASON, I WOULD VERY MUCH
LIKE TO CONTINUE MY WORK ON THE RWANDA SIDE OF
THE MOUNTAIN IN THE HOPES THAT I MIGHT FIND A
FEW GROUPS OF GORILLAS TO HABITUATE AND STUDY.
WHEN I LEFT THE CONGO SIDE I HAD ONE GROUP
HABITUATED TO THE POINT WHERE THEY WOULD
APPROACH ME TO WITHIN TWENTY FEET.

I'M GOING TO NAIROBI ON TUESDAY TO TALK TO
DR. LEAKEY ABOUT THE CONTINUATION OF MY WORK,
AND MENTION TO HIM THE POSSIBILITIES OF
CONTINUING MY STUDY FROM YOUR PLANTATION, IF I
CAN GET THE PERMISSION OF THE MINISTER OF
AGRICULTURE. THUS, THIS RUSHED NOTE TO EXPLAIN
THINGS TO YOU BRIEFLY, BUT I KEENLY HOPE TO
TALK TO YOU FURTHER TOMORROW.

YOURS SINCERELY,
Dian Fossey

The following day I was to attend a luncheon in my honor hosted by the American military attaché in Kigali. The moment I arrived, I was accosted by an exceptionally tall young woman dressed in a lovely lilac linen dress (which I later learned had come from I. Magnin) and filthy dirty tennis shoes. Her dark hair was worn in a thick braid over one shoulder, and her brown eyes were startling in their scrutiny. She conveyed in her demeanor no sense of friendliness or charm whatsoever, but rather a steely, defiant determination.

In all fairness, I was not aware at the time of what she had been through in the Congo, or that her escape had taken place just three days earlier. Her tennis shoes were what she had been wearing when she was arrested and forced down the mountain, and she had no others. I never did learn how she managed to salvage the pretty dress.

Dian was not the least bit interested in polite conversation. The moment we sat down to lunch, she brought out a small, well-worn notebook and got right to the point. "Now, Mrs. Carr," she said quite abruptly— taking everyone by surprise— "I have some questions to ask you." We all thought she was quite peculiar.

The interrogation began as follows: "Question one—," "Question two—," "Question three—," and so forth. Her first question was to ask if she could establish a temporary campsite on my plantation at the base of Karisimbi. I saw no harm in it, so I agreed. Then I was bombarded with questions about the volcanoes and the gorillas.

"There are no gorillas on my side of the mountain," I stated with absolute confidence. "For years, people have been parking their cars on my plantation to climb Karisimbi, and no one has ever reported seeing a gorilla."

"I know they are there," she said flatly.

Dian was not the sort of person to be put off lightly, and I began to wonder what I had gotten myself into. Several days later, Dian arrived at Mugongo with a carload of equipment and supplies and pitched a small tent at the base of Karisimbi. I came to know her better during the weeks that followed, as she shuttled back and forth between my house and her temporary headquarters at the base of the mountain. Although she kept her distance and I kept mine, we maintained a cordial relationship, and there were moments when I detected in her a certain warmth and humor which I found difficult to resist, in spite of myself. She finally had to concede that there were no gorillas on the Rwanda side of Karisimbi, but it was common knowledge that gorillas did exist in Rwanda on Visoke, Sabinyo, Muhavura, and the northern slopes of Karisimbi. I saw in Dian a spirit of boldness and dedication to her work that was reminiscent of my friend Alyette de Munck. Perhaps these two headstrong and adventurous women—each of whom had recently suffered a traumatic loss—could discover in one another a mutual interest and common bond.

In August, Dian left for Nairobi to meet with Dr. Louis Leakey to discuss the possibility of continuing her research project in Rwanda. I knew that Alyette would be returning from Paris at about the same time, so I wrote a letter of introduction and suggested that Dian try to contact her. Having just lost her husband, I thought it might be therapeutic for Alyette to become involved with this eccentric young woman who was determined to study the mountain gorillas in Rwanda.

Dian was waiting for Alyette at the airport in Nairobi when her plane touched the ground. She told me later that she knew it was Alyette when she saw a small European woman being escorted by three handsome young men. Dian rushed up to meet her and said, "Mrs. de Munck, Mrs. Carr has told me a great deal about you and suggested that I look you up. I do so want to talk to you!" Alyette did talk to her and, in fact, invited her to join their party for dinner that evening. Alyette felt an instant spirit of kinship toward Dian and was intrigued by her passion for the mountain gorillas. That was the beginning of a great friendship that lasted for many years.

When Dian returned from Nairobi, she came to my house and I broke the news to her about the murder of Alyette's son and traveling companions in the Congo. She was devastated to learn that the three bright young men with whom she had so recently had dinner in Nairobi were dead, and she rushed immediately to Mudende to be with Alyette.

The next morning, Dian marched angrily into my backyard, gesturing wildly and shouting at the top of her voice. "We've got to find out who did it!" she screamed. "I'm going to offer your houseboys money to go into the Congo to find out who did it!"

I looked at her aghast. "Oh, no you're not," I said. "No employee of mine is going into the Congo right now. It's far too dangerous. And besides," I added, "they won't go."

"Oh, yes they will," she insisted. "Africans will do anything for money. You just watch. For a thousand francs, they'll do it."

"Go ahead and try," I said, thinking how very little I liked this woman.

Dian pulled a thousand-franc note from her purse and began to wave it around madly. "Who will go into the Congo for this money?" she shrieked. "Who will go and find out who murdered the son of Mrs. de Munck?" She didn't speak Swahili, so I had to translate this tirade. The houseboys and gardeners just looked at her, then at me, then back at her. Nobody moved.

Dian went absolutely wild. She pulled handfulls of bills from her pockets and threw them into the air. "Who will go into the Congo for this money? Who will go?" Everyone just stared in silent shock at this crazy woman shrieking and throwing money around.

"Dian," I said, by now thoroughly offended and my patience wearing thin, "you're welcome to stay the night, but tomorrow morning you're going to have to leave."

"Fine," she said. "That will be just fine."

The next morning she did leave, and I was very relieved to see her go. For years, Alyette was Dian's closest friend in Rwanda. She accompanied her on excursions into the volcanoes to locate gorillas and was instrumental in getting her research project established. Dian spoke almost no Swahili at the time, and it was Alyette who translated for her and taught her the language. It was also Alyette who helped establish Dian's camp in the Virunga volcanoes, called Karisoke—so named because it lies in the saddle between Karisimbi and Visoke.

In time I got over my initial dislike of Dian and we eventually became good friends. I cannot say exactly when this happened, but I soon forgave her behavior during those initial months. I came to realize that when she first came to Rwanda, she was terribly scarred by her experiences in the Congo and had formed an unfavorable opinion of Africans in general. The brutal murder of the three boys in the Congo pushed her over the edge, and her natural instinct had been to try to avenge the terrible injustices that had been done. Dian's life experiences had been very different from my own. Despite the fact that she was twenty years younger than I, my feelings toward her were never in any way maternal in nature. Dian was far too self-assured for that, far too prepared to take on the world.

Ultimately, I came to love her and admire her very much, but it was never an easy friendship. Dian was absolute in many things. She violently objected to my fur rugs and coverlets and anything I owned that was made of ivory. And when she discovered that I had been married to the famous hunter Kenneth Carr—the man responsible for killing fourteen mountain gorillas on Prince William's expedition in 1921—she stated flat out that any friendship between us was out of the question. She had to concede, however, that divorcing Kenneth was probably the smartest thing I had ever done, and reluctantly allowed as how we could remain friends— provided that Kenneth's name never be mentioned in her presence. I was careful to see that it never was.

I visited Dian at Karisoke for the first time in January of 1968. Today, a rocky road leads to the foot of Visoke, but in those days it was a two-hour hike through the *shambas* of the Hutu farmers just to reach the base of the mountain. As I trekked through the fields with my porter, children appeared from all directions and trailed behind us in a happy procession. The first five-hundred-meter stretch on the Visoke mountain path is very steep and difficult, but from that point on it was an easy climb for me in those days, and I reached the camp in a little over three hours.

Karisoke is situated on a high plateau amid towering hagenia trees and dense bamboo rain forest. Beside it, a stony creek cuts through a deep ravine. At that time the camp consisted of three tents—one large tent, which served as Dian's office and living quarters; a smaller tent for storage; and a pup tent with a folding cot and small table for guests. The privy was nothing more than a hole in the ground, with the remnants of a privacy curtain made of burlap sacking strewn about pell-mell—the result of an elephant raid a few nights earlier.

I was immensely grateful to Biriko, my cook, for packing a roasted chicken and a basket full of fresh vegetables and fruit, as Dian had nothing of the sort on hand. I learned to my chagrin that her diet consisted primarily of junk food. She disliked vegetables and pretended to be allergic to fruit. Meals were taken at a wooden table perched at the edge of the ravine, and in the evenings a fire was built just close enough to envelop us with smoke but too far away to provide any warmth. Our supper that first night was tinned mushroom soup, cold chicken, and rice. We laughed and talked in the flickering firelight with tears from the smoke rolling down our cheeks. Through the smoke and the tears we kept a watchful eye on the opposite bank of the stream, where Dian assured me that elephants would come to drink after dark. The evening air was bitterly cold, and I asked her if she got undressed at night.

"You must be joking!" she laughed. "Of course not! I have to go outside three or four times every night to chase away buffalo and elephants!"

That night, an elephant came so close to my little pup tent that I could hear his stomach rumbling. I was terrified he would stumble over the tent ropes, causing the tent to collapse on top of me, or possibly step on *me*, crushing me like a bug. I have never been more frightened—or cold—in my life. I didn't dare move or make a sound, but I could hear Dian typing away in her tent—completely oblivious to my peril.

That first visit to Karisoke lasted four days, but we saw no gorillas. Each day, we hiked through dense jungle of bamboo and stinging nettles from nine in the morning until three in the afternoon, aimlessly following a sad excuse for a tracker. The trackers in those days were not particularly adept at locating the gorilla groups. We could hear them in the distance, and occasionally Dian would catch a glimpse of one or two with her binoculars. But that was the closest we came. She did find some consolation in the fact that we were able to locate and examine gorilla nests from the night before, which were rampant with dung.

During our daily marches, we kept body and soul together with a thermos of tea and Oreo cookies. Back at the camp, we retired to our tents with another thermos of tea and a cooking pot full of popcorn saturated with margarine. At night, when the chicken was gone, we ate Spam and potato chips. I had a stomachache for four days.

It was several years before I returned to Karisoke, but I saw Dian frequently when she came to Gisenyi to stock up on provisions. And whenever she was ill—which was often—she would come to Mugongo to recuperate and indulge in some much-needed pampering.

Later in 1968, Alyette directed and financed the building of the first cabin at Karisoke. It was made of corrugated iron sheeting and painted a dull green to blend with the vegetation. Dian gratefully moved out of her tent and into the large, sturdy cabin. Her gorilla studies were producing astonishing results. She had soon identified fifty-one gorillas in family groups which she numbered "Four," "Five," and "Eight." The gorillas' instinctive fear of Dian soon gave way to curiosity and acceptance, and they gradually began to welcome her into their secluded world.

I visited Karisoke many times in the following years and experienced the unique joy of observing the mountain gorillas in their natural habitat. On one visit in 1977, we hiked for four grueling hours before we located the research group. I was on the verge of collapse when there suddenly appeared before us twenty or more gorillas in a small clearing in the dense bamboo jungle. Some were resting comfortably or tending to their young, while others groomed one another with serious intent. The juveniles climbed trees and swung from branches, cavorting and performing acrobatic stunts—not unlike human children. As I crouched very quietly on the damp forest floor, I was astounded to see a huge blackback walk right up to Dian and sit down beside her. He looked around (to make sure I was paying attention), then leaned against her, as if to say, "Good to see you, old friend." Quite unexpectedly, one of the juveniles, a young male named Pablo, swung down from a tree and jumped into my arms. My initial fright was immediately overcome by wonder and delight at his gentleness and playfulness. He demonstrated a childlike curiosity about me and meticulously examined my hair, face, and clothing and pawed through my knapsack. After he had inspected me thoroughly, an adult female took him by the hand and led him away, as though scolding him for his cheekiness. It was truly one of the most memorable experiences of my life, and I will always be grateful to Dian for giving me that gift.

In the spring of 1969, Bob Campbell, a *National Geographic* photographer from Kenya, came to Karisoke to make a documentary film on Dian's work. Bob remained at Karisoke for almost three years. A romance developed between them, and I believe that those were the happiest years of Dian's life. Her work was receiving international recognition, and she was no longer alone on the mountain. It was during this time that a huge blackback named Peanuts reached out and touched her hand. Bob's photographs of that poignant moment and Dian's tears of joy drew the world's attention to Dian and her efforts to protect the endangered mountain gorillas.

Years later, Dian and Alyette had a falling-out. I never knew exactly what had caused it, but I believe it was because Alyette continued to visit Bob Campbell whenever she passed through Nairobi—long after the romance between Dian and Bob had ended. Perhaps she felt that if Alyette was her friend, she could not be Bob's friend as well. Dian was difficult in that sense and often became her own worst enemy. She and Alyette never reconciled.

24

THE PALM BEACH HOTEL

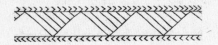

In the fall of 1967, President Mobutu of the Congo closed the Rwanda-Congo border in a dispute with President Kayibanda of Rwanda. The dispute erupted over the fate of European mercenaries who had taken part in a failed attempt to topple the Mobutu regime. The mercenaries surrendered at Bukavu, along with Congolese rebel soldiers from the southern province of Katanga. With them were the wives and family members of the Katanga soldiers who had accompanied them into combat.

Under the auspices of the International Committee of the Red Cross, an agreement was reached between Mobutu and Kayibanda. The agreement contained two provisions—one being that Mobutu would allow the mercenaries safe passage into Rwanda, from where they would be transported back to Europe; and the other being that the Katanga soldiers and their families would be granted amnesty and be allowed to return to their homes in Katanga. Mobutu reneged on both of those promises. I can only speculate as to the fate of the Katanga soldiers and their families.

As for the mercenaries, they were initially allowed to enter Rwanda. Mobutu immediately changed his mind, however, and demanded that they be extradited back to the Congo. Kayibanda stood up to Mobutu and refused to turn the mercenaries over. He had given his word that they would be granted safe passage to Europe through Rwanda, and he intended to honor that commitment. The situation developed into a full-scale confrontation. Kayibanda found that his neighboring countries had turned against him, and the Belgian planes that were to transport the mercenaries out of Africa were denied permission to fly over any of the surrounding African countries or refuel at their airports. The mercenaries remained in hiding for several weeks, until one African country finally agreed to "look the other way" and allow the planes to fly over its territory and refuel within its borders. To everyone's great relief, the mercenaries safely departed Rwanda.

In the meantime, several of the mercenaries had been wounded and were recuperating at the French Hospital in Ruhengeri. One was a handsome young man from a prominent Belgian family who had come to the Congo in search of adventure after graduating from university. He had received a bullet in the base of the neck and was paralyzed from the neck down. Dian and Alyette took a keen interest in this young man and visited him frequently at the hospital. For all her brashness, there was a side to Dian that was very tender and caring. Prior to coming to Africa, she had worked for many years as an occupational therapist for handicapped children in Louisville, Kentucky, and she spent hours working with this young man, helping him to move his fingers and hands. Sadly, his condition was very serious and her treatments were only mildly successful.

The closing of the Rwanda-Congo border, which lasted from the fall of 1967 until March of 1970, was a catastrophe for me financially. Its effect was to cut off access to the extraction plant in Goma, making it virtually impossible to market Rwandan pyrethrum. I had no idea how I would survive or manage to keep the plantation running. Pyrethrum must be picked and culled and carefully tended year-round. If I dismissed my workers, I risked losing my valuable plants. Yet, without the extraction plant, there would be no sales and no income to support the farm. I was desperate. Finally, in 1969, I accepted a position as manager of a small hotel in Gisenyi, called the Palm Beach Hotel.

The Palm Beach was situated on the lakefront and consisted of eleven guest rooms, a dining room, and bar. It was not nearly as glamorous as the name suggests, but it did have a certain amount of charm. The Palm Beach was owned by a Belgian named Van Der Steen, who had leased it to a Swiss named Martin Sollaire. It was Mr. Sollaire who hired me and to whom I reported.

I knew next to nothing about running a hotel, but I embarked upon this new venture with as much enthusiasm as I could muster and came up with innovative ideas for attracting new customers, as well as the local clientele. With only eleven guest rooms, my focus was to liven up the dining room and bar in an effort to generate new business. I organized bridge parties and afternoon teas with scones and cookies, which turned out to be quite popular. I bought the most extraordinary birdcage imaginable from a European family that was leaving Gisenyi. The birdcage was eight feet long and had tiny trees and birdhouses inside it and came with eleven little budgies in a rainbow of colors. I set it up between the bar and the lounge as an attraction and amusement for the patrons—adults and children alike.

Mr. Sollaire was wildly opposed to the birdcage. He protested that the birds would die from the cigarette smoke and that they wouldn't be able to sleep at night with all the noise and loud dance music. As it turned out, they were the happiest budgies I have ever seen. They produced seven baby budgies, and they danced to the music and seemed to tolerate the cigarette smoke far better than I.

The dining room was quite large and demanded a significant portion of my time. The chef was a disagreeable man named Bernard, who had been sacked for drunkenness prior to my arrival. I knew Bernard and knew that he was a very good cook, so I immediately hired him back. For a month or so, Bernard was a perfect angel. He arrived in the morning to prepare lunch and worked until two in the afternoon. He then had time off from two until five, at which time he was supposed to return to begin preparing for dinner. For the first few weeks, Bernard showed up promptly at five—then he began to slide.

To act as Bernard's assistant, I hired Biriko, my cook from Mugongo. Biriko was a friendly, unassuming sort who got along well with everyone and learned very quickly from Bernard. Bernard soon realized that it made no difference what time he showed up, since Biriko could quite capably get the dinner preparations underway without him. Periodically, I would give Bernard a dressing-down about punctuality, but the simple fact was that I truly believed he was indispensable in the kitchen. Biriko did have a few specialties, but Bernard was an accomplished French cook.

As room boy and all-around handyman, I hired a friendly, cheerful fellow who had once worked for Kenneth. We used to call him Kenneth's "Good Man Friday," although his name was Micheli. Micheli cleaned the rooms, walked babies in strollers, and did odd jobs around the hotel. He was also in charge of wake-up calls, for which I provided him with a large windup alarm clock with a very loud clangor. It reminded me of the sort you see depicted in animated cartoons. Micheli believed wholeheartedly that the ultimate success or failure of the hotel rested entirely upon that alarm clock. Many of our hotel guests were airline pilots who were required to get up very early in the morning and be served breakfast prior to their departure times, and Micheli faithfully made sure that no one ever overslept. He had accepted the job on the condition that he be allowed to sleep at the hotel, so I fixed up a small room for him in the back.

One morning, Micheli called me into the men's lavatory and asked me to reach up on top of the water tank above the toilet. When I did, I was startled to discover four frozen chickens sitting there. Micheli confided to me that Bernard frequently used this hiding place to stash food from the freezer before taking it home with him. We returned the chickens to the freezer, and later that day when Bernard showed up for work, I said, "Bernard, I found four frozen chickens in the men's lavatory. To my knowledge, you're the only employee with access to the freezer." The freezer was kept locked, and he and I had the only keys. "I am far too busy to discuss this with you right now, but I want you to know that I am extremely upset!" Bernard said nothing, but he did look a bit chagrined.

It did not take long for Bernard to figure out who had spilled the beans. A few nights later—while the dinner hour was in full swing and every table occupied—the door to the kitchen burst open and Micheli flew through the middle of the dining room with Bernard hot on his heels, brandishing a machete and screaming in Swahili at the top of his lungs, "I don't care if I go to prison for life! I'm going to kill him!"

What followed was a masterpiece in precision choreography, as all heads turned at once and the patrons froze, forks poised in midair. Micheli vanished into the night and didn't reappear for three days, by which time I had sacked Bernard. From that point on, Biriko took over the kitchen and things ran somewhat more smoothly. Biriko ultimately became a very fine cook and went on to work as chef for the Hôtel Meridien in Gisenyi and the American ambassador's residence in Kigali.

It was during this time that my Aunt Margaret came to Rwanda for a six-month stay. She was the first member of my family to visit me in Africa, and I was thrilled to have her—although somewhat disheartened by the fact that her long-awaited visit came at a time when I was plagued with so many difficulties. Aunt Margaret and I shared a room at the Palm Beach, and she adapted to the routine of running a hotel in Africa as though it was the most natural thing in the world. She tended to the budgies, dispensed Phillips' Milk of Magnesia tablets by the hundreds, and charmed all the tourists. Everyone called her "Madame Tante." On Sundays we served a large continental buffet with an enormous fruit compote, which Madame Tante generously laced with peach brandy. It was extremely popular.

Dian was a frequent guest at the Palm Beach and became a great friend and admirer of Aunt Margaret. They maintained a lively correspondence for many years, until Dian's death. One afternoon, Dian came into the hotel carrying a large cardboard carton. Before I could ask what was in it, the carton burst open and out jumped a two-year-old long-haired golden monkey. She had seen it being offered for sale on the roadside and felt compelled to rescue it from some dreadful fate.

"Oh, no, Dian," I said. "I'm sorry, but you cannot keep that monkey in your hotel room!"

"Just pretend you didn't see her," she whispered impishly, as she hustled off to her room with the monkey struggling to free itself from her grasp. Against my better judgment, I went along with Dian and pretended that I hadn't seen her, but I dreaded what I would find when I went up to her room after she checked out.

She had kept "Kima" shut up in the bathroom, and the destruction exceeded even my wildest imaginings. Banana peels were stuck to the ceiling, and shredded sweet potatoes covered the floor. Broken glass was everywhere. She had made a bed for Kima out of bath towels, and gooey messes of droppings covered every surface. Dian had made no attempt whatsoever to clean up after the monkey. I was furious—at the monkey, at Dian, and at myself for allowing it to happen in the first place. Kima remained one of Dian's cherished pets at Karisoke for many years, although it was generally acknowledged that she was cherished by precious few.

Dian often treated people rather poorly, but she would never tolerate the mistreatment of animals. She would go to extraordinary lengths to rescue an animal from what she perceived as cruel or inhumane treatment. One morning as she was driving down Gisenyi's Avenue of Palms in her Volkswagen combi, she spotted a Rwandan man walking an alarmingly thin dog on a leash. Dian stopped the car and announced to the man that she wanted to buy the dog. The man told her the dog was not for sale.

"Oh, yes it is," she said. "I'll give you five hundred francs for him."

"No, no," the man insisted. "He is not for sale."

Dian would not take "no" for an answer. She picked up the dog and put it in the combi. Then, after stuffing five hundred francs into the bewildered man's shirt pocket, she got in the car and drove off. The man turned around and ran back to the house where he was employed and reported that a tall woman in a Volkswagen combi had stolen their dog. It turned out that the dog had worms, and the man was taking it to the veterinary clinic for its second in a series of treatments.

Managing the Palm Beach was exhausting work. I got up at five-thirty in the morning and didn't go to bed until long past midnight. I was constantly on my feet—running up and down the stairs, attending to guests, and checking on the guest rooms. The building was in terrible disrepair, and nothing worked as it should. The roof over the dining room leaked, and every single toilet in the building had its own peculiar idiosyncrasy. Each time I showed a guest to his room, I would point to the toilet and say, "Now, there's a slight problem *here* . . ." I would then go on to explain that with this one you had to jiggle the chain; with another the lid was off because you had to reach inside and lift the metal bar; with another you had to fiddle with something else. It went on and on, and I lost fourteen pounds during the five months I worked there. I was getting no sleep at all, and I eventually became quite ill.

I finally went to see my doctor, who prescribed a three-month vacation. Mr. Sollaire refused to let me out of my contract. But fate stepped in when the owner, Mr. Van Der Steen, arrived suddenly and announced that he was taking over. I was gone within the week.

My salary from the Palm Beach just barely covered my expenses and allowed me to keep the plantation running. A few months later, the border reopened and I was able to deliver more than forty tons of stored pyrethrum to the extraction plant in Goma. I also began to sell cut flowers again to clients in Goma and Gisenyi.

By this time, I had paid off my debt to Gino Imeri, and Mugongo belonged solely to me. This piece of land that I have struggled so hard to hold on to represents a great deal more to me than simply a home and a symbol of my independence. As any farmer or factory owner knows, ownership bears a heavy responsibility. Hundreds of people over the years have relied upon me to support their families, and it is this obligation and interdependency that has kept me bound to Mugongo as much as my love of the land.

So we struggle through droughts and mudslides and hailstorms. We replant when disease strikes or when elephants trample the fields. We persevere through political upheavals and border closings and when the price of pyrethrum hits rock bottom. I have been close to bankruptcy many times in my life, but somehow I have always managed to hang on.

25

DIAN—THE LATER YEARS

Dian Fossey was one of my dearest friends in all the world, but she was surely one of the most complex and enigmatic people I have ever known. Although I loved and admired her deeply, there is no denying that she was at times a bit of a handful. She could be loving and lighthearted one moment, and thoughtless and hurtful the next. She was loyal and generous to her friends, affectionate and tender with children, and fiercely protective of animals—unless they happened to be cows. She had no patience with people who disappointed her, and many people did—sometimes myself included.

Life on the mountain was a hard existence. It took a person of exceptional physical stamina and impassioned dedication to withstand its relentless onslaughts and deprivations. For all its haunting beauty, it was cold and wet and lonely. It was also dangerous. Karisoke was terribly isolated, and the forest was inhabited by wild and terrifying animals, not to mention poachers, all of whom considered Dian to be their enemy. Dian suffered countless injuries and routinely ignored the warning signs of illness, to the endless frustration of those who loved her. She suffered from chronic asthma and emphysema, which were aggravated by the high altitude and heavy smoking. Over the years she broke numerous bones, fractured ribs, punctured a lung, and was bitten by sundry animals.

On one occasion, Dian tumbled into a deep drainage ditch while trying to outrun a charging buffalo and fractured her fibula. She set the leg herself—binding it with tape and a splint—and continued to walk on it for weeks afterward, supporting herself with a crude walking stick. She said she was far too busy to have it taken care of properly. The leg was later rebroken and reset in Germany.

One afternoon in November 1969, Dian and Bob Campbell stopped by for a visit on their way back to Karisoke from a trip to Gisenyi. Dian was limping badly and had a large bandage wrapped around her leg. When I

Tutsi boys performing Intore dance.

Mwami Kigeri V with Belgian administration officials, 1959.

At Mugongo, 1965.

Hutu man on first election day.

Independence Day celebration in Mutura, July 1962.

Grégoire Kayibanda, first president of the Republic of Rwanda.

Per Moller, 1958.

Per Moller, 1961.

Gahereri, Tutsi shepherd, 1958.

Dian Fossey's original research camp at Karisoke, 1968.

Dian Fossey at Karisoke, 1970.

Dian in her cabin at Karisoke.

Dian with Coco and Pucker, 1969.

With young
gorilla Pablo,
1977.

Pickup loaded with
cut flowers.

Young boys
dressed as
soldiers,1960.

Mugongo plantation house and gardens.

Picking flowers, 1991.

With Sembagare,
1987.

Mikeno.

Lake Kivu.

Sunday dances, 1989.

Drying house prior to renovations, October 1994.

Orphanage during renovations, 1994.

Imbabazi Orphanage, December 1994.

With a little friend, 1997.

Sembagare taking inventory.

Fina and Clemence.

Sembagare and me with chil-dren, 1998.

asked her what had happened, she casually replied that she had been bitten by a wild dog, which was more than likely rabid.

"My God, Dian," I cried, "when did this happen?"

"Two weeks ago," she said, demonstrating a total lack of concern.

When I insisted that she go immediately to the hospital in Ruhengeri for vaccine, she said, "I haven't got time for all that."

To my annoyance, Bob seemed to agree that it was nothing to be all that alarmed about. When I asked him if he believed the dog actually was rabid, he said, "Well, I had a hard time loosening its jaws from Dian's leg." This being one of the first indications that an animal may be rabid, I was extremely upset that they weren't taking it more seriously.

Later that day, I told Alyette about the dog bite, and she immediately dashed off to Karisoke to insist that Dian go to the hospital for treatment. "Do you have any idea what it's like to die of rabies?" she asked Dian. "It's the most painful death in the world! You foam at the mouth and bite people. You go insane and break your back in agony!" Dian refused to listen even to Alyette.

The next day she developed a high fever and had to be carried down the mountain on a tipoy and taken to the hospital in Ruhengeri. I found her there four days later, flushed with fever and lying on the bed dressed in blue jeans and a denim shirt. She sat up and said, "Thank God you've come. You're taking me home with you." The doctor was appalled at the idea and refused to release her. She had received antibiotics and a tetanus shot, but she had just begun the painful rabies vaccine treatment—a series of fourteen daily injections administered in a circle around the navel.

"Of course I can leave," she announced firmly. "This isn't a prison!"

We argued about this, but Dian could be infuriatingly stubborn and usually managed to get her way. I knew that she would make herself miserable and everyone in the hospital miserable if I didn't agree to take her, so I relented. The doctor was furious at us both and threatened to contact the U.S. Embassy to have Dian deported. He finally allowed that if I was crazy enough to take her home, I could, but I had to promise that she would receive her daily injections of vaccine every day for the next eleven days. These injections, he emphasized, had to be administered by a doctor—not a hospital nurse. To cheer us on our way, he added that there was still a fifty percent chance that Dian would develop rabies, since she had waited so long to begin the vaccine treatment.

Every day for the next eleven days, Sembagare drove Dian all the way to Gisenyi for her daily injections of the rabies vaccine. She was by no means a cheerful patient, and the strain of the twenty-three-mile trip each way over rough roads did little to improve her disposition. She was cantankerous and disagreeable toward everyone who tried to make her more comfortable.

One morning, I entered the guest room and found her sitting up in bed reading my *Merck Manual*, the medical bible used by Europeans in Africa for the diagnosis and treatment of illnesses. Dian looked up and said, "Now I know I have rabies. I have all the symptoms—depression, great thirst, and irritability. I am very *irritable!*" I had to agree. Dian eventually recovered from the dog bite, but she never completely got over her irritability.

My house servants used to say to me, "Madame, Mademoiselle does not love you! She only comes to you when she is sick."

There was some truth to this. I did nurse her though many illnesses. One incident that stands out in my mind occurred in 1971. Dian arrived at my house in a very weakened state and told me she was hemorrhaging. I assumed that she meant she was menstruating, so I put her to bed with her feet up. Four days later, she announced that she was feeling better and was ready to return to Karisoke. On the climb up the mountain, she started hemorrhaging again and had to be carried back down. She was taken by taxi to the hospital in Ruhengeri, where a very competent French surgeon, Dr. Weiss, operated on her and saved her life.

I later learned that Dian was suffering from a botched abortion. She had been pregnant with Bob Campbell's child and had undergone a back-room abortion in Goma. She later confided to Alyette that if Bob had asked his wife for a divorce on his most recent trip to Nairobi, she would have told him about the pregnancy. He did not; and, as a result, she aborted the baby and almost died.

One of the unforeseen outcomes of this near tragedy was that Dr. Weiss fell head over heels in love with Dian. He was in his early sixties at the time and had a houseful of children by a variety of women, among them his former French wife and his African mistress. Nevertheless, Dian became quite smitten with him. They spent occasional discreet, romantic weekends together in Kigali, which Dr. Weiss evidently interpreted to mean that they were engaged to be married.

One afternoon, I arrived in Kigali to hear the astonishing announcement that Dr. Weiss had published the banns at the French Embassy. I was surprised and shocked, as I had no idea they were considering marriage and I was not at all convinced that he was the right man for Dian.

Dian was out of the country on a lecture tour at the time, raising money for her gorilla research. I wrote her a letter of congratulations on her upcoming nuptials, but added that I thought this decision was perhaps a bit premature. When Dian returned to Rwanda she was furious.

"He had no right to publish banns," she stormed. "We talked about an engagement, but it never went as far as all this!"

"Well, dear," I told her, "frankly, I'm relieved. Where would he live? Up on the mountain? Or would you live in Ruhengeri?"

"Yes," she admitted. "That is a problem."

That was one problem that Dian and I shared in common. Even if one of us were to find true love, and even if the man happened to be available, the likelihood of any man giving up his life and career to live in the seclusion of Mugongo or the rugged isolation of Karisoke was extremely remote.

Their relationship continued, and Dian went on believing that she had the upper hand, until she learned that she was not the only woman in Dr. Weiss's life. She came storming into my living room acting for all the world as though her heart was broken. I tried to sound sympathetic, but told her I thought it was probably all for the best. She was having none of my opinion, however. There was a great scene, but she eventually got over it.

Dian frequently turned on her friends for no apparent reason. The rift with Alyette was particularly distressing, since Alyette never knew what had caused it. They had been inseparable—never even had an argument. Alyette had done so much to help Dian and considered her to be a devoted friend and soul mate. Several attempts were made to effect a reconciliation, but all were rejected outright by Dian. There were times when she simply stopped speaking to me as well. These events were usually preceded by an offhand or hurtful remark. For weeks afterward, there would be no visits and no letters. Then we would bump into each other in Gisenyi, or she would stop by the house, and she would greet me with a big smile and a hug, as though nothing had happened.

As Dian's work became more widely known, she was urged to accept zoology and anthropology student interns at the camp. This she eagerly agreed to do. Unfortunately, many of the young students who came to Karisoke either could not tolerate the rugged conditions and isolation or they failed to live up to Dian's exceptionally high and, in some cases, capricious standards. She got along well with only a handful of the students and had no tolerance for anything less than total dedication to her work. She discouraged distractions of any kind, such as excursions down the mountain or close relationships among the students. She resented the fact that her research center, and heretofore her own private domain, was overrun with hippies, adventure seekers, and elitist would-be scientists. What little patience Dian had to begin with evaporated entirely. Sometimes she would sign her letters to me "Old Cranky Puss."

Difficulties with interpersonal relationships were probably unavoidable at Karisoke. The living conditions were extremely primitive. Foul weather, stinging nettles, poisonous spiders, and dysentery were routine aggravations. The temperature in the mornings was just above freezing. Bathing facilities were never more than buckets of water heated over an open fire, and the privy was always outdoors. In a gesture of friendship and goodwill, U.S. Ambassador Frank Crigler gave Dian a gift of a porcelain bathtub, but she never bothered to install it. Instead, it was used only by the guides for brewing large quantities of banana beer. There was never enough firewood for heat, and the students were required to buy their own food and prepare it themselves. They were miles by foot, plus an hour by car, away from anything even remotely resembling a town.

After Dian's death, one of the first changes to be made at Karisoke was the establishment of a communal dining room. I never understood why Dian insisted upon eating alone (except on rare occasions) and leaving the students to fend for themselves, or why she discouraged any sort of camaraderie or gaiety in the camp. By contrast, Dian enjoyed a relatively active social life. She traveled periodically to the United States and Europe and made frequent jaunts to Kigali, where she was entertained in grand style by the American ambassador and his family and the Embassy staff.

Beneath her brash exterior, there was a soft, feminine side to Dian which many people never knew. She loved to shop and she loved beautiful clothes. Most of her clothes came from Saks Fifth Avenue in New York or I. Magnin in San Francisco. I thought her beautiful, particularly when she was dressed up. At the parties she attended in Kigali, she was always the most glamorous woman in the room. She spent a small fortune on face creams, body lotions, and Giorgio perfume. Whenever she came to my house, she would spend hours in the bathtub, washing her beautiful hair and soaking in bubble bath. She used to say that we three—Dian, Alyette, and I—were the three women in Africa with the dirtiest fingernails—she with her gorillas, me with my flowers, and Alyette with her sheep and asparagus beds.

Although the early 1970s were perhaps the happiest years of Dian's life, they were surely among the saddest as well. She had fallen deeply in love with Bob Campbell, and when he returned to his wife in Nairobi in 1972—after nearly three years together—she was heartbroken. This, followed by the brutal slaying by poachers of her beloved silverback Digit, brought Dian close to the breaking point. The successful habituation of the gorillas was her only consolation.

In 1970, Dian was accepted for Ph.D. work at Cambridge University. Between 1970 and 1974, she left Karisoke three times for periods of four months at a time to study at Cambridge. She received her doctorate degree in 1976.

By the mid-1970s, Dian's relationship with the Rwandan authorities had become extremely contentious, due largely to her unwillingness to accept any human habitation of the Volcano National Park. In 1968, the park area was radically diminished by a European Economic Community project (ILACO) which allocated more than thirty-eight square miles (forty percent) of the parkland to peasant farmers in a program to grow pyrethrum. Trees were cut down and large portions of the forest were destroyed. The animals' natural habitat was replaced by countless acres of cultivated fields that encroached deeper and deeper into the park. Large numbers of elephants, gorillas, and buffalo were forced higher into the mountains, and many eventually disappeared into Zaire. Scores of elephants and buffalo were killed. Dian protested violently, but to no avail. She subsequently railed against the Rwandan government for allowing Tutsi shepherds to pasture their cattle in the park. Still her protests were ignored.

Although hunting had been forbidden in the park since its creation in 1925, the authorities had traditionally allowed shepherds to pasture their cattle on the volcanoes during the dry season. Moreover, the government turned a blind eye toward the hunting and trapping activities of the Batwa pygmies, and the penalties for setting traps were rarely enforced. The traps were intended primarily for antelope, but very often gorillas became caught in the snares. In most cases, the gorillas were able to break free, but the deep wounds often festered and became gangrenous. Sometimes they were fatal.

As one gorilla after another fell victim to poachers, Dian became the lone voice in the wilderness battling for their survival. She embarked upon a policy of "active conservation," whereby she pursued poachers, burned their camps, and herded illegal cattle out of the park. She hired guards to destroy the traps and haul the poachers to the police station in Ruhengeri. If the authorities would not enforce the laws, Dian would. And she would make up her own laws as she went along.

One day she turned up at my house with a collection of the most frightening Halloween masks I have ever seen. She had bought them on a recent trip to California. One in particular was grotesque. It was a witch's mask with long protruding teeth and eyes that bugged out of their sockets when you squeezed a little rubber ball. She donned the mask and appeared suddenly before Biriko in my kitchen. He let out a shriek and ran like an antelope. Dian was thrilled. Her idea was to use the masks to scare away the poachers. If they would frighten my cook, she reasoned, they would surely intimidate her antagonists on the mountain.

She ran from the kitchen and burst out the front door, just as Sembagare was coming up the walk. Sembagare was far too dignified to run, but he stopped dead in his tracks and uttered not a word. He was so furious he could barely bring himself to address the matter. When he did, he told me privately, "Madame, if she wears that mask on the mountain, they will surely kill her. The first man who sees her will throw a spear right through her heart."

I had conflicting feelings about Dian's anti-poaching activities. I was at the same time awed by her bravery, appalled by her tactics, and genuinely frightened for her safety and welfare. This was a country where such interference and high-handedness by a foreign visitor was looked upon with considerable resentment, and I felt there should have been some flexibility on her part. Dian and I argued frequently about people versus animals, and I believe there were many things about Rwanda that she didn't understand. There is no doubt, however, that it was Dian's dogged determination and sometimes controversial methods that rescued the mountain gorillas of Rwanda from almost certain extinction.

In 1976, Ambassador Crigler made an attempt to ease the dissension between Dian and the Rwandan authorities. National Geographic had produced a film called *Gorilla*, which contained some of Bob Campbell's footage of Dian at Karisoke. Frank Crigler organized a showing of the film at his residence and invited all the Rwandan cabinet ministers to attend. I was invited as well.

Dian looked lovely that evening in a stunning black lace skirt and white silk blouse and was on her best behavior for the introductions and the showing of the film. Then the lights came on and the questions began.

"Why will you not share the park with the shepherds?" the ministers asked.

"A park is for *wild* animals," she insisted.

On the matter of her anti-poaching activities, one of the ministers ventured to remark, "With all due respect, Mademoiselle, the poachers are being punished."

"Not severely enough!" Dian responded vehemently.

The minister looked skeptical.

"They should be hung!" she declared. She then lunged forward and made a neck-breaking gesture with her hands around her own neck and shouted, *"Hung!"*

Ambassador Crigler cringed, and the room became deathly silent. When the discussion got off the ground again, the ministers were unanimous in their praise of cows and their right to seek pasturage during the dry seasons.

Dian was maddeningly exasperating, but she could be deliciously funny as well. She ran roughshod over people who disagreed with her, but at the same time she desperately craved love and affection. We both adored Christmas, and after coming to one of my Christmas parties at Mugongo, Dian began to throw even bigger parties at Karisoke. Her Christmas trees were of giant heather decorated with garlands of everlasting flowers, strings of popcorn, and candles. All the workers and their families were invited. Sometimes as many as a hundred people showed up, including children and babies. One Christmas Day, a pygmy baby was born at Karisoke. I believe that these were some of Dian's happiest moments on the mountain, surrounded by her loyal workers in a spirit of friendship and camaraderie. Dian had gifts for everyone, and the festivities went on long into the evening, with singing and dancing and lots of *pombi*.

In January 1984 I received a letter from Dian. She wrote, "Just think, long after you and I are gone, our Africans will remember us just as happy, giving, caring people. I rather doubt they will grieve or, if so, only for a short while. I, for one, have a great deal to learn from the Africans, although this involves crossing into another culture."

Some may take issue with the term "our" Africans, but I like to believe that Dian was finally acknowledging a respect for and a humility toward the Rwandan culture—sentiments she seldom exhibited in her day-to-day existence.

Less than a year later, Dian was dead—savagely murdered in her cabin by multiple machete blows to the head. In her typewriter, I learned later, was a letter written to me explaining that her Christmas party had been postponed until after Christmas in order to include the film people who were coming from New York to shoot a nature film based on her book *Gorillas in the Mist*. I still grieve when I think of her brutal murder on that night after Christmas in 1985. Her Christmas tree was beautifully decorated, and piles of carefully wrapped gifts were placed all around it. Hanging on her front door was a Santa Claus wearing a red ribbon and a sign that said "Howdy!"

In the last years of her life, Dian's relationship with the Rwandan authorities continued to disintegrate and became a great hardship for her. Dian's dogged opposition toward the use of the park and the gorillas as a tourist attraction put her at loggerheads with certain factions both inside and outside of Rwanda. The minister of tourism, Laurent Habiyaremye, withheld the issuance of her visa as a means of harassing her. Toward the end, she was granted two-month visas only, each one requiring an official letter of approval from the minister himself.

Renewing her visa every two months became an agonizing ordeal for Dian. Her physical condition had deteriorated to the point where she required an oxygen bottle to withstand the arduous climb up and down the mountain. By this time, she had no car and had to hire a taxi to take her to Ruhengeri. From there, she would haggle for a seat (two seats, actually, to accommodate her long legs and all her belongings) on one of the overcrowded taxi-buses that traveled between Ruhengeri and Kigali. Once in Kigali, she would go directly to the minister's office, where she would be forced to wait until the minister's secretary would announce that, much to his sorrow, the minister was unable to see her that day. Often, Dian had to wait three or four days before the minister would agree to see her and grant her the necessary documents to renew her visa.

Several weeks before her death, Dian received what appeared to be an extraordinary stroke of good fortune. Over dinner at the Hôtel des Mille Collines in Kigali, she was greeted by a high-ranking government official. He asked her how she was getting on, and she told him of her troubles.

"Mademoiselle," he said, "come and see me tomorrow."

By the next day, Dian had a *two-year* visa stamped on her blue American passport. She was jubilant and told everyone she met. It is my belief that the visa was her death warrant. Whoever it was that wanted her out of Rwanda now knew that she would be there for at least two more years. The identity of Dian's killer remains a mystery to this day.

I made my last climb up the mountain path to Karisoke on the morning of her funeral. I was seventy-three years old, and I was numb with shock and grief. My hands grabbed at the dense vegetation as I slipped and stumbled on the muddy slopes. In the days since her death, the American Embassy had managed to obtain permission from her family to bury her at Karisoke, where she would have wanted to be.

Many people attended the service, but I believe I was the only person there who had loved Dian. The Rwandans present were all police officers or soldiers, and the foreigners were principally Embassy functionaries or journalists lugging around heavy photographic equipment and dressed inappropriately. All of the Rwandans who had been close to Dian were in the Ruhengeri jail, being held for questioning; and most of the officials at the American Embassy were out of the country for the Christmas holidays. The minister who presided over the service was a dear friend of mine, Dr. Elton Wallace, but he was not a Catholic, as was Dian, and he had never even met her. His eulogy was beautiful and very moving, but it was in English, and very few of those present understood it.

I was heartbroken to be among this assemblage of strangers, most of whom had come either out of duty or curiosity. I could not stop weeping. When the earth fell upon the plain wooden coffin, I moved away from the gathering and walked unsteadily toward the meadow near Dian's house. Standing in the meadow, closer than I had ever seen him before, was a great old bushbuck that Dian had often watched from her window. He had always been wary of people and noise, but now—despite the crowd of strangers and commotion nearby—he was standing on the lawn gazing toward Dian's house, as if to say good-bye.

26

VISITORS TO THE FARM

Following Rwanda's independence in 1962, European and American diplomats established embassies in Kigali, and the dusty little town was gradually transformed into a modern city filled with imposing government buildings and visitors from around the world. The United States purchased and renovated an old butcher shop on Kigali's main boulevard and converted it into a handsome Embassy building. At the time, I thought of it as my own private Embassy, for although there were eleven American missionaries in Rwanda in 1963, I was the only American landowner and full-time resident.

The very idea of an American Embassy in Rwanda was so thrilling to me that I planned a special trip to Kigali to call upon the chargé d'affaires, whose arrival in Rwanda had preceded the ambassador's by some months. So pleased and proud was I at this remarkable new development that I invited Adam Bielski to accompany me, and together we made the six-hour journey to Kigali, bouncing along the rutted dirt roads and marveling at the changes that had taken place in Rwanda over the past decade. I wanted so much to make a good impression that I chose my outfit with meticulous care, down to a pair of never-worn white gloves I had discovered tucked away in the back of my bureau drawer. Adam looked quite distinguished as well—it was the first time I had ever seen him wear a necktie.

We arrived at the Embassy in the late afternoon—teatime for me, but cocktail hour for most Europeans. The chargé d'affaires himself appeared at the front door, dressed in blue jeans and a T-shirt.

"I'm Rosamond Carr," I said, "and I've lived in Rwanda for ten years." With my indelible Yankee accent, I didn't feel it necessary to explain that I was an American citizen. When no welcoming response was forthcoming, I motioned toward Adam and said, "And *this* is my friend Count Bielski of Gisenyi."

The young man simply stared at us with a stunned expression on his face. Perhaps it was the white gloves and necktie that rendered him speechless, but to our surprise, he did not invite us in. Nor did he demonstrate any curiosity about us at all—or exhibit even a modicum of friendliness or common politeness. Instead, what he said was, "Is there something in particular that you want?"

"Not a thing," I said. And Adam and I turned around and left.

I was utterly deflated. This was hardly the reception I had anticipated. Clearly, the white gloves had been too much. My faith was restored, however, when the first U.S. ambassador, Dudley Withers, arrived in early 1964 with a very professional and efficient staff of young officers, and from that moment on I have always been shown the utmost courtesy and consideration by the Embassy personnel. Many of the officers and their families have become dear friends, and I have spent many happy weekends entertaining them at Mugongo. The embassies and their bright young diplomats brought to Rwanda a certain cachet and sophistication it had never seen before, and I was frequently invited to parties and luncheons and reciprocated with invitations of my own.

I have had the pleasure of entertaining a host of ambassadors and diplomats from numerous countries over the years, but one that stands out in my mind was a visit from then-U.S. ambassador to the Congo, MacMurtrie Godley, in 1965. He arrived at Mugongo with his sister and brother-in-law and a staff of seventeen. They were making a tour of the Kivu Province in a U.S. military plane decorated with stars and stripes painted on its wings. As I recall, the luncheon was a success, with Adam Bielski and Alyette de Munck adding an international flavor to the group.

After lunch, Ambassador Godley surprised me by saying, "Did you know that you are a 'pin' on the U.S. State Department map?" He then added, "I was told you must be queer as a three-dollar bill." He must not have found me all that queer, however, for he invited me to accompany his entourage to Rwindi Park the following day. It was my first visit to this marvelous wildlife reserve since my last safari with Kenneth just prior to Congo independence. I recall the ambassador scoffing long and loud about the "timid Belgians" and their penchant for undue alarm. I didn't say a word, but I knew that military planes had flown low over the Rwindi Plains all day that day and the day before to ensure that the ambassador and his party would be safe from insurgents in the area. It was thrilling to return to this glorious place that held so many fond memories for me. Elephants and hippos frolicked in the Rutshuru River. Enormous herds of zebra, buffalo, and impala thundered across the plains in great clouds of dust. We even saw lions. It was a wonderful excursion, and I was so grateful that I had been asked to go along.

* * *

My social and political contacts have by no means been limited to Europeans and Americans. Prior to independence, Rwanda was governed by Belgian administrators, and it was to them that the white settlers turned for leadership and assistance. Following independence, these positions were filled by Rwandans. As the years have gone by, children whom I have watched grow up in Mutura have risen to positions of power and influence in both the local prefectures and in the central administration in Kigali. I have been honored and proud to have entertained Rwandan president Juvénal Habyarimana and his wife at my home on several occasions, and I am privileged to have been a guest at the Presidential Palace for numerous receptions and gala events.

It has never seemed necessary for me to leave Mugongo to see the world—the world has always come to me. Over the years, most of the European and American community in Rwanda has, at one time or another, come to visit at Mugongo. Moreover, as the mountain gorillas lured tourists into Rwanda, many of those tourists would travel up the rocky road to see my gardens and stay for tea. I still feel a tingle of anticipation each time I hear the sound of a car pull into the driveway. The dogs and I race outside to see what new faces will appear at my door and what fascinating tales and adventures they will have to tell me.

Many of the visitors have come to see the Sunday dances, which have been a permanent feature at Mugongo since 1960. This was during the time of the troubles in Rwanda, when every little boy in Mutura yearned to be a soldier. One afternoon, a group of boys—ages eight to twelve—marched onto the lawn beside my house, dressed in khaki shorts and shirts and wearing little caps of folded green banana leaves. They carried wooden guns and homemade flags on tall staffs. The captain was a small boy named Jean Biramahire, who barked out commands: "*Un, deux, trois! Un, deux, trois!*" They separated into two groups and attacked one another—the "dead" collapsing on the ground. Apart from myself, the audience was made up primarily of their younger brothers and sisters. Some were very tiny children who tumbled around on the soft grass looking like animated bundles of rags in their fathers' cast-off clothing. Small boys wore ragged shirts that came to their knees to cover their small naked bodies, and little girls wore sarongs of faded cotton cloth tied under their armpits.

After watching and applauding the troops for three or four Sundays in a row, I became a bit weary of the soldiers and asked the little girls if they would dance for me. They did, and eventually the boys joined in. Before long, the marching was forgotten and the Sunday afternoon dances became a regular event.

They soon became so popular that we started drawing crowds. It seemed only fitting that we elevate the entertainment to a more professional level. I had six large African drums specially made, and Sembagare and I held auditions for the dancers and drummers. The selection process took weeks. Every little boy and girl in Mutura wanted to perform for Madame Carr, so the competition was extremely intense. After great deliberation, we finally selected our dance troupe. There were three age groups—the little ones under the age of ten, the teenagers, and the adults. In addition, we had a band consisting of six female drummers. Regular practice sessions were held, and special costumes were assembled. The boys wore white skirts with matching T-shirts and bells around their ankles, and the girls wore full skirts of colorful fabric with blue-and-white knit blouses and long, filmy white sashes.

Each group consisted of four girls and four boys, and they danced a traditional courtship dance called *"ikinimba,"* in which the boys perform a series of movements and contortions designed to attract the girls. When Rwandan girls marry, they are no longer permitted to perform this dance. As a result, every year we had to replace one or two of the older girls. The men, on the other hand, are allowed to perform this dance all their lives. Consequently, many of our older male dancers have been performing and perfecting their artistry since they were children.

The dances became a local attraction of some renown. There was rarely a Sunday when fewer than two hundred people converged on the lawn around my garden to watch the dancers perform to the singing and clapping and beating of the drums. The spectators have been predominantly local people from Mutura, but over the years countless friends, visitors, and tourists have come to Mugongo to spend a Sunday afternoon in my garden enjoying the spectacle. One visitor wrote in my guest book: "I visited a place in Rwanda where time doesn't exist, apart from teatime, where children and adults from all places in the world come together and are at home, where Sunday is celebrated by dancing, and your belief in the Creator is restored."

The dancers have performed for many distinguished guests over the years, among them Supreme Court Justice Sandra Day O'Connor, who was visiting Rwanda in the summer of 1990. Dian Fossey spent many Sundays at Mugongo and particularly enjoyed the dances. She would often step out onto the lawn and join the dancers with a surprising animation and grace. Among the guests one Sunday was a lovely British girl who had been a member of the London Royal Ballet. With bare feet and long dark hair streaming about her face, she spun and pirouetted across the lawn to the beat of the drums. Although my drummers had never seen a ballet, they accompanied her with perfect rhythm as she performed on the grassy stage in the foothills of the Virunga volcanoes.

Perhaps my most glamorous visitor of all was Madame Giscard d'Estaing, who was visiting Rwanda with her husband, French president Valéry Giscard d'Estaing, in 1979. Following a visit to the new maternity wing at the French Hospital in Ruhengeri, Madame Giscard was brought to Mugongo for a prearranged luncheon. She wore a lovely pale green linen suit and was without a doubt the most elegantly dressed woman I have ever met. I particularly recall that as we strolled together through the gardens, she was able to identify every flower by name. The dancers put on a special exhibition in her honor and truly outdid themselves—performing for *"le grand monde!"*

Biriko had prepared a marvelous luncheon of chicken flambéed in cognac, fresh asparagus, and artichoke hearts. Dessert was a bit more complicated, however. The French Embassy had notified me in advance that for dessert, only cake would do. Biriko had many elegant desserts in his repertoire, but cake was not among them, as it is virtually impossible to bake a cake in the uneven heat of my wood-burning stove. Nonetheless, if Madame Giscard demanded cake, then cake it would be. When the cake was brought to the table, it was a masterpiece of mocha icing arranged in artfully decorated garlands, and I thought for a moment that it just might be a success. Biriko's face fell as the first slice revealed a very soggy middle and his beautiful creation collapsed in a heap. Madame Giscard was most kind and sympathetic toward his obvious embarrassment. Before she left, she presented Biriko with a gift of a cigarette lighter inscribed with the date of her visit, which he cherished for many years.

Madame Giscard's visit to my house was reciprocated with an invitation to attend a state luncheon in Gisenyi the following day. The luncheon was in honor of Madame Giscard and the seven first ladies from seven African countries—Rwanda, Zaire, Burundi, Senegal, Ivory Coast, Mali, and the Central African Republic—whose husbands were attending a summit meeting in Kigali. The first lady of Senegal was a blond Frenchwoman dressed in a shocking pink suit with matching spiked high heels. I was seated beside the first lady of Mali, who looked absolutely stunning in an exquisite white robe with dozens of silver necklaces and bracelets encircling her neck and wrists.

In the interest of national pride, it was decided that a traditional Rwandan lunch would be served. The first ladies dined somewhat dubiously on tough, stringy chicken and dried fish, served with beans, potatoes, and rice. The after-lunch entertainment was a uniquely Rwandan experience as well. The ladies were escorted onto a newly plowed, muddy field near

Ruhengeri, where neat, straight rows had been staked out in preparation for the planting of pyrethrum plants by the eight honored guests. Dressed in their beautiful clothes and wearing dainty sandals (and, in one case, pink high heels), the first ladies picked their way uncertainly across the muddy field and performed their diplomatic duty with as much dignity as the exercise would allow. When they finished, young Rwandan girls came to the rescue with bowls of water and cakes of soap. It was said that Madame Giscard was later seen surreptitiously cleaning her beautifully manicured fingernails. I feel certain that her afternoon at Mugongo was a bit more to her liking.

The dances were held in my garden every Sunday afternoon until April of 1994, when everything in Rwanda stopped. There came a time when Sembagare began to find the dances tiresome and continued to participate only to humor me. One Sunday many years ago, bemused to find me looking forward to the upcoming dance with as much enthusiasm as I had the very first one, he turned to me with a weary expression and said, "Don't you ever get tired of these silly dances, Madame?"

"Not at all!" I replied. "I could watch them every day and never tire of them."

Sembagare shook his head in mild exasperation. "Madame," he said, "you're just like an Italian with her macaroni!"

27

THE POTATO PROJECT

While the early 1970s were an exciting time for me socially, I was once again plagued by financial worries. The Rwandan government had lowered the price it paid to farmers for dried pyrethrum to rock-bottom levels, and pyrethrum became increasingly less profitable to produce. Ironically, the international demand for pyrethrum had never been greater, but it was becoming more and more difficult to earn a living as a pyrethrum planter in Rwanda. As financial ruin loomed, I gradually increased the acreage of commercial flowers at Mugongo, but this was a faltering business at best, and I was certain the end was near.

In a last-ditch effort to keep the wolf from the door, I embarked upon a venture which very nearly proved to be my undoing. The director of the pyrethrum cooperative in Ruhengeri, a Dutchman named Wouter Yonker, suggested that I might earn a decent profit by drying pyrethrum for other planters. Not far from my property was an abandoned drying house, and I proposed to the owner that I renovate it and pay her a monthly fee for the use of it. She happily agreed.

I invested nearly one thousand dollars in the renovations—a great deal of money for me at that time (or any time, for that matter). When the renovations were completed and the dryer was filled to overflowing with pyrethrum flowers, Wouter came to see it. As he was leaving, he asked if the building was insured.

"I'm going to do it on Monday," I replied.

Sunday night the pyrethrum dryer burned to the ground. The masons had built the trays too close to the indirect heat used to dry the flowers, and they ignited. I must confess it was a spectacular blaze, as the ceiling was made of ancient bamboo which was filled with oil. The bamboo logs exploded like firecrackers. People came from miles around to watch my high-stakes investment go up in smoke.

This time I knew my options had run out. Facing utter ruin, I gave in to the inevitable and conceded that I had no choice other than to sell Mugongo and leave Africa for good. I announced my decision one day at lunch to a Belgian visitor, who immediately asked how much I wanted for the property. I named a sum in haste, knowing it was far too low. He left, assuring me that he could readily find a buyer at that price. I should have been pleased, but I was not.

Sure enough, the man arrived the next day with a firm cash offer at my asking price. With a severe case of cold feet setting in—or just delaying the inevitable—I stalled and told him I would need a week to think it over. Somewhat disgruntled, he left.

News travels fast in Rwanda, and several days later a complete stranger showed up at my door. He was a young Swiss named Henri Peyer. To my astonishment, he presented me with an offer from a consortium of four businessmen to lease forty hectares of my land to grow potatoes. He said they had been experimenting with plots that had produced three to four times the normal yield per hectare, and they were certain they could achieve similar results on my land. They offered to pay me forty thousand francs a month for a period of three years. I was ecstatic. Forty thousand francs would just barely cover my expenses, but it would allow me to keep Mugongo. It seemed that potatoes were to be my salvation.

I immediately agreed to the proposal, but I felt it only fair to warn him that I did not believe they would obtain the amount of potatoes from my land that they anticipated. Unlike the land they had been experimenting on in the forest, Mugongo was not virgin soil. It had been producing pyrethrum for many years. Henri remained stubbornly optimistic, however, and said they would send a contract around in a few days.

The potato project was a disaster from the start. Henri and his partners hired as foreman an out-of-work Russian from Kigali, who knew nothing about potatoes. Nor, as they later learned, did he even know how to drive. They rented a tiny house for him in nearby Tamira and built him a small office in the fields. Sembagare had to teach him how to drive the brand-new pickup truck they bought for him, which he wrecked within two months. The partners spared no expense and cleared out one of the large caves on my property to store the potatoes once they were harvested. Metal gates were installed at the entrances for security. The cave was two hundred and fifty meters long, and oil lamps were hung throughout for lighting. It was quite beautiful inside when they were finished. Unfortunately, it never was filled with potatoes as they had envisioned.

The Russian, who had a wife and children in Kigali, immediately took as his mistress a young Tutsi girl. This offended Sembagare mightily, and the two never got along. As I feared, the potato yield did not measure up to their expectations. It was slightly above average, but nowhere near the original estimates—and evidently not enough to meet their expenses.

After eighteen months, one of the partners came by to tell me they had lost so much money they were giving up. He said he was sure I would understand that they would be unable to make the monthly payments for the remainder of the contract. He said he felt certain that the newly fertilized fields would more than compensate me for my losses. And to sweeten the deal, he offered to throw in the "fully furnished office," which was nothing more than a shack in the middle of a field with a table and chair.

I was not quite as understanding as he had hoped. I needed the money desperately, but finally agreed to forego the third year of the contract if they would pay me through the end of the second year. The matter was settled—or so I thought. Henri and one of the other partners insisted upon paying me the full amount through the end of the third year out of their own pockets. They said they had signed the contract in good faith and I was entitled to the money. I was too desperate to refuse. Once again, Mugongo was saved.

And that was the beginning of one of the dearest friendships of my life. Henri Peyer and his wife Suzanne lived on a beautiful property on the lake in Gisenyi where I have spent many happy days. On overnight visits, I always slept in their lovely guest house, which had a balcony extending out over the lake. I would wake up in the mornings to the sounds of waves lapping against the shore and the faint singing of fishermen returning from a night on the water.

Henri had very definite views about my welfare, and—whether he was right or wrong—we generally did things his way. He redesigned my kitchen, rebuilt my front entrance, and built a lovely flagstone terrace in front of my house. He loaned me a truck or combi whenever mine broke down (which was often), and during the long droughts he arranged for truckloads of water to be delivered to Mugongo. I used to say that Sembagare was one of my adopted sons, and Henri was the other.

Nineteen seventy-seven, the year the potato project failed, began with a bang. On January 10, Nyiragongo erupted. The lava level in the crater had been rising steadily during the previous years, but the eruption was completely unexpected. There was a terrifying BOOM! followed by mushrooming black clouds (which appeared ominously similar to photographs of the atom bomb) accompanied by a deep roaring sound. Within minutes, in clear view from my house, a river of molten lava flowed down the mountain slopes toward Goma at the rate of a hundred and fifty miles an hour. It slowed to three miles an hour on level ground and stopped just before it reached the Goma airport. As I watched from my terrace, the enormous crater emptied itself in less than three hours.

Nyiragongo had been a landmark and an important feature of life in the Kivu area for many hundreds of years, and our view of it was one of the great delights at Mugongo. White smoke rose from its giant crater during the day, turning pink at sunset and intensifying to a flaming crimson against the night sky. The intensity of the glow varied. Sometimes only the rim of the crater glowed, and at other times an effusion of fiery red ashes spewed into the sky. I never went to bed without first going outside to stand on my front porch in my bathrobe and slippers and gaze at it for several minutes or more. When Mikeno and Karisimbi were snowcapped, it was quite extraordinary to turn from their snowy, towering peaks to the fiery eruption of Nyiragongo less than twenty miles away. For weeks, tiny particles of gray ash fell from the sky, filling the air and covering everything in sight.

The eruption caused a temporary evacuation of Goma, but there was mercifully little loss of human life, as the foothills of Nyiragongo were mostly uninhabited. A campsite for mountain guides was buried in the river of lava, a tourist's minibus disappeared forever, and several people living in the foothills suffocated from gaseous fumes.

When the Goma-Rutshuru road finally reopened with a hastily built bridge over the solidified lava, I accompanied U.S. ambassador Frank Crigler and Belgian ambassador Jean-François de Liederkerche and their wives on an excursion up the volcano. It took us one hour to drive across a half kilometer of lava plain, stopping from time to time to gaze into open fissures where red-hot coals glowed deep beneath the surface. We got out of the car and picked our way slowly across the charred ruins of giant trees. Everything was coated with black lava, still brittle. It crunched under our feet, and as a light drizzle of rain began to fall, steam rose all around us. There was not a bird or a leaf or a sign of life anywhere. As we left the foothills and climbed higher, we found the blackened hulk of a half-buried elephant, one of the thousands of animals that had perished in the devastation.

Scientists predicted that it would take thirty years or more for Nyiragongo's huge crater to fill up again with lava. To everyone's surprise, it became active again in 1994, and in the haunting gloom of Rwanda's darkest hour, its fiery red ashes lit up the night sky once more.

28

THE 1980s

By the early 1980s, it was no longer possible for me to earn a living growing pyrethrum, so I converted Mugongo into a flower farm. It was with mixed emotions that I gave the order to dig up acres and acres of pyrethrum plants and replace them with lilies, gladiolas, carnations, agapanthus, iris, and alstroemeria. And it was with deep sadness that I let most of my longtime field hands go, keeping only a dozen or so of the best workers to tend to the flowers. The fields of white daisies gradually gave way to a vibrant landscape of pinks and blues and yellows, and every Friday, Sembagare and I would drive into Gisenyi and Goma to deliver fresh-cut bouquets wrapped carefully in cellophane to my growing number of clients.

During this period, both my business life and social life flourished, due largely to the paving of the main road between Gisenyi and Kigali. The project was financed by Germany, but the work was performed almost entirely by Chinese laborers, some of whom died during the massive construction project. A Chinese cemetery with white vertical markers and black symbols denoting the names of those who died sits beside the road as a memorial and a curiosity to those traveling to or from Kigali. Now, instead of a six-hour journey over bumpy roads, the trip to Kigali could be made in less than three hours. It revolutionized transportation in Rwanda and helped preserve many tires and shock absorbers—not to mention our backsides.

Political and economic stability brought to the country a lively group of Europeans and Americans, and a whole new world opened up to me, both socially and professionally. These were some of the most enjoyable years of my life, filled with good friends and happy times. My sense of isolation evaporated entirely with the advent of new friendships and a whirl of social activities that extended from Gisenyi all the way to Kigali.

Just down the road from Mugongo at Mudende—where Alyette de

Munck once farmed—the Seventh-Day Adventist Church built a modern university called L'Université Adventiste de l'Afrique Centrale. Dr. Elton Wallace from California became its director, and he and his wife Evelyn and many others came to stay and run the university. What a joy it was for me to have American neighbors and dear friends just two kilometers away.

Rwanda's two main export products are coffee and tea, and it was around these two industries and the people who ran them that much of my business and social life began to revolve. Fabulous luncheon parties were held at Cyohoha, the tea factory and estates belonging to Joe Wertheim of Westport, Connecticut, and managed by Michael Boyd-Moss, one of the world's great tea makers. His wife Shelagh had created magnificent gardens that were the rival of my own, and weekend tennis parties became a regular social event.

Rwandex, the company that bought and marketed all of Rwanda's coffee, began to play an increasing role in my life during this time. Rwandex was originally owned by three men—Anthony Wood, George Drew, and Robert Hasson. Tony Wood managed the company in Kigali and at the same time served as British honorary consul to Rwanda. He was, and still is, one of my dearest friends in all the world. Tony has a lovely house on one of Kigali's main thoroughfares, and his compound of house and gardens has always been a favorite gathering place for all Anglophones in Rwanda. One of the most eagerly anticipated social events of the year was Tony's annual bash to celebrate the queen's birthday. Tony is perhaps best revered for his charming wit and irreverent sense of humor. He once incurred the wrath of a visiting British ambassador named Snodgrass by teaching his three African gray parrots to repeat the words "Snodgrass, Snodgrass, silly old arse." On another occasion, he attracted the ire of a Belgian government official (and owner of the only horse in Rwanda) by refusing to attend an equine barbecue the night old Dobbin was put down.

In 1982, Tony suggested that Rwandex trucks be used to transport and deliver flowers from Mugongo to customers in Kigali, opening up a whole new market to me. As the twelve-ton lorries shuttled back and forth between the factory in Gisenyi and Kigali, baskets of fresh-cut flowers rode along on top of the dried coffee beans. The flowers were carefully packed in large, openwork bamboo baskets, four feet long and two feet wide, and each bouquet was wrapped in fresh green banana leaves for coolness and covered with well-thumbed issues of the *Daily Telegraph*.

Suddenly, fresh-cut flowers from Mugongo were in great demand, and my business began to prosper as it never had before. Among my clients were the hotels and embassies in Kigali, as well as the wives of the diplomatic corps and a flower shop called Iris. In time, I began to ship flowers to Kinshasa and Lubumbashi by air from Goma.

Tony's assistance with the transportation of the flowers turned my faltering business into a thriving one, and for that I will always be grateful. In recognition of his service as honorary consul, Tony was awarded an Order of the British Empire by Queen Elizabeth in 1985. He invited four of his friends from Rwanda (myself included) to fly first-class to London to be his guests at the investiture. How very impressive Tony looked as he arrived at Buckingham Palace in a Rolls-Royce, dressed in tails and an elegant gray top hat. After a celebratory luncheon and dinner party for a hundred and fifty people, Tony escorted our merry group through the elegant trappings of London society. We attended a performance of *Romeo and Juliet* at Covent Garden Opera House and dined at some of London's finest restaurants. For a small farmer from Rwanda, it was a heady experience. Back home at Mugongo, it took me a full week to come down from my cloud.

Throughout the 1980s, Rwanda experienced an unprecedented period of peace, prosperity, and growth. The country was transformed by improved transportation and communications systems and the construction of a modern international airport in Kigali. Even so, the greatest obstacle toward the advancement of the Rwandan people remained access to higher education. The government provided free primary school education for every child up through the sixth grade. The secondary schools were boarding schools, and although they were subsidized by the government, some tuition was required. Few families were inclined to encourage higher education for their children, and even fewer could afford the tuition for secondary schooling. There were a limited number of secondary schools in Rwanda, and, as a result, competition for acceptance was extremely rigorous. Only the brightest students qualified. Upon the successful completion of three years of secondary school, students received a teacher's certificate; but if they went on to complete four more years of secondary schooling (the equivalent of high school and junior college in the United States), they received a diploma and were automatically eligible for acceptance at the university in Butare, which was free. Any student who completed the full seven years of secondary schooling could easily find work in Rwanda, but a university degree guaranteed a student his or her choice of almost any job he or she desired. The secondary-school step was the big stumbling block.

In 1982, I started a student scholarship program with the help of a wide network of family members and friends from all over the world. I matched students with sponsors and sent a photograph and description of each child to his or her sponsor. Often, a lasting correspondence would develop between the students and their sponsors. The tuition costs averaged about two hundred dollars a year per student. I kept meticulous records—keeping track of each student's rank, financial status, progress, and grades. If they did not measure up, they were out of the program. As a result, I have been able to help hundreds of young Rwandan boys and girls attend secondary school over the years and go on to have successful and rewarding careers in teaching, commerce, agriculture, and government. In 1994, I had seventy-two students active in the program and enrolled in secondary schools throughout Rwanda.

Under the terms of the original plantation grants established by the Belgian administration many years ago, the thirty-five-year lease on one half of Mugongo was due to expire in 1984. This meant that half my land would no longer belong to me. Land was scarce in this densely populated country, and good farmland was at a premium. During the early 1970s, I had allowed some of the local people to settle on a portion of my land, allocating approximately one hectare per family—the minimum acreage required to feed an average family. By 1974, forty families were living at Mugongo, and I was very happy to have them there. When I gave them the land, I had cautioned them not to plant trees or build permanent houses, because I knew that in 1984, when the lease expired, they might be forced to vacate. Believing I had acted in everyone's best interest, I confided to an acquaintance at the local commune office what I had done.

"Oh, no, Madame," he whispered conspiratorially, "you gave them very bad advice indeed. If they plant trees and build substantial houses, they will *not* be forced to leave."

I immediately called the men from the forty families to my house and told them what had to be done. Within days, the grass-roofed mud huts were dismantled, and sturdy houses made of wooden poles and roofs of corrugated iron began to emerge. These roofs would become an important factor in the final outcome. When the lease expired in 1984, the *préfet* of Gisenyi came to pay me a visit. He was extremely upset that I had invited all of these people onto my land. I suspect he may have had plans of his own for this prime real estate.

"Madame," he said, in a voice quaking with rage, "the land was not yours to give away!"

"I didn't give it away," I said, as innocently as I could. "I told the people they could farm the land for ten years, but that the final decision when the lease ran out would be entirely up to the *préfet*."

"But, Madame," he protested, "you didn't have the right to do that!"

"Well, actually, I did." I said. "At the time, the land was still mine to do with as I pleased." He had to admit that this was true. "And one thing more," I added. "These families have built houses on the land."

The *préfet* was not impressed. "That is not important," he said. "Those are just mud huts with grass roofs."

"No," I replied. "They are sturdy houses with corrugated iron roofs."

The *préfet* was furious, but he had to concede that a house with an iron roof was a serious matter and that it would be difficult indeed to remove families from substantial houses such as those. To my delight and enormous relief, the families were allowed to remain on the land.

I certainly don't need all of my land to grow flowers, so in recent years I have allowed my workers to plant crops or graze their cattle on the remainder of the property. They understand that this is just a loan and that if the property is ever sold, they will have to discontinue farming it.

In 1983, Dian Fossey published her book called *Gorillas in the Mist*, a fascinating and highly regarded account of her reminiscences and activities with the mountain gorillas. She worked on it over a period of several years with a talented editor at Houghton Mifflin, who pared it down and rearranged numerous passages. Dian was delighted with the results. She told me that the publishers had objected to the title she had chosen and insisted that it be changed. Dian was equally insistent, and *Gorillas in the Mist* it remained. Universal Studios bought the screen rights to the book in 1984.

The film project began as a nature movie while Dian was still alive. The film's producer, Arne Glimcher, arrived in Kigali with his son Paul on December 27, 1985, to meet with Dian at Karisoke the following day. Dian had postponed her Christmas party in order to include them in the festivities. When Arne and Paul checked into the Hôtel des Mille Collines in Kigali, they were stunned to learn that Dian had been murdered the night before. Plans were immediately altered to turn the nature film into the story of Dian's life.

Ironically, it was Dian's death more than anything else that focused the world's attention on her work. Journalists descended upon Rwanda, and many articles—some filled with inaccuracies and falsehoods—were written about her. One such article was bought by Warner Bros. as the basis for a movie about Dian. Immediately, a bidding war erupted in Hollywood over the rights to Dian's life. After much wrangling and legal maneuvering, an agreement was reached and the project became a joint venture between Warner Bros. and Universal Studios.

In the summer of 1987, the film people converged on Mugongo, and this became a very exciting time for all of us. Only Sembagare seemed completely unfazed at the prospect of having Hollywood stars and celebrities in our midst. Sembagare believes that Rwanda is the center of the world and that, sooner or later, everyone will eventually come to Mugongo. Sigourney Weaver was the perfect choice to play Dian, and I was portrayed by the exceptional actress Julie Harris. Both women have remained dear and valued friends. Julie told me that I was the only living person she had ever portrayed, and for that reason we would always have a very special bond. It is one that I treasure.

My dancers played a role in the filming, although those scenes were later cut from the final version. The costume designer was not at all happy with the outfits the dancers wore and went to elaborate lengths to dress them according to her satisfaction. She was delighted to find some colorful patterned fabric at the market in Ruhengeri, which she artfully wrapped around their bodies. The premise was that the dancers had simply wandered in off the road and started dancing, although why this might have happened I cannot imagine. Sigourney, as Dian, danced in my garden with the dancers, just as Dian had done so many times, wearing a lovely peach-colored dress and adding some much-needed color and lightness to the film. Unfortunately, the entire sequence ended up on the cutting room floor.

Sembagare had a prominent role in the film as well—although not quite as prominent as he had hoped. The screenwriter was a brilliant woman named Anna Hamilton Phelan, and when she came to Mugongo to work on the script, she found that she particularly liked the name "Sembagare"—and, more important, she liked the *idea* of him. Although Dian had many loyal workers at Karisoke, she never had one longtime tracker and companion, so Anna borrowed Sembagare's name and character for the film. Sembagare was a bit put out that he wasn't chosen to play himself in the movie, and even more disgruntled by the fact that a Kenyan actor was selected for the part—one who, as he put it, "didn't speak Kinyarwanda and had never even met Dian." But once he had seen the film, he had to concede that John Omirah Miluwi did a very fine job and that he probably could not have mastered the English required for the part. Sembagare did, however, enjoy a certain amount of celebrity status throughout Rwanda for quite some time.

He told me that people would often ask him, "Is that you in the film, Sembagare?"

"And what do you say?" I asked.

"I must say 'no,' " he responded somewhat sadly, a victim of his own honesty. "I explain that I am not Mademoiselle *Fossey's* Sembagare. I am Madame *Carr's* Sembagare."

"That's right," I said. "You are."

Then came the painful admission. "Sometimes I get tired of saying 'no,' Madame." He added with a guilty look, "And then I say 'yes.' "

The 1980s were not without problems, for these were the years that brought the AIDS epidemic to Rwanda. Scientists believe that the AIDS virus originated in Central Africa, perhaps mutating from a harmless virus carried by monkeys. Whatever its origin, by the mid-'80s we were hearing more and more of people dying from this terrible new disease. The virus spread along the truck route from Mombasa, which winds its way up through Uganda and down into Kigali and on to Bujumbura. Sadly, the greater the development of the region in terms of urbanization and transportation, the faster the virus spread. Gradually it spread from the cities to the countryside, and eventually found its way to the lush, green hills surrounding Mugongo.

Homosexuality in Rwanda is extremely rare. The exceptionally high rate of AIDS infection throughout Central Africa has been spread predominantly through heterosexual contact and unsterile medical practices. Until recent years, hygiene in clinics and dispensaries has been very poor, and hypodermic needles were reused over and over until they no longer functioned. Disposable needles were not commonly used in Rwanda until the late 1980s. By 1990, it was estimated that as much as thirty percent of the population of Kigali was HIV positive, and men, women, and children were dying at an alarming rate in both the towns and rural areas.

When it first surfaced, the Rwandan people adopted a very fatalistic attitude toward the disease, or denied the seriousness of the epidemic. Their feeling was that they all must die of something—whether it be cholera, dysentery, or AIDS. In the early 1990s, the government initiated aggressive educational programs to both acknowledge the epidemic and confront it head on with centers for the treatment and prevention of the disease. Sadly, when war broke out and people were dying by the thousands of machete and gunshot wounds, the AIDS epidemic was largely forgotten.

One case that stands out in my mind was that of a friend named Naftali Mutabazi, a highly educated and well-respected employee at Rwandex in Gisenyi. There came a time when Naftali began looking extremely gaunt. He was tested and found to be infected with the AIDS virus, as were his wife Madeline and their young daughter Gloria. It was believed that he had contracted the virus from unclean needles at a dispensary, and everyone who knew him was shocked and saddened by the news.

Naftali's father had been a schoolmaster and pastor of a Protestant church, and he had instilled in his children a deep religious faith. From the moment his illness was diagnosed, Naftali went to church every day and spent hours in prayer. In the early spring of 1993, he returned to work and appeared to be well again. One day in April, I stopped by the Rwandex office to see him and he said to me, "Madame, have you heard of my miracle?"

"No," I said, wondering what he was going to say. As I listened to him speak, I had to struggle to fight back the tears.

Naftali's face was radiant with joy as he told me that one night he had seen a vision of God. God had appeared before him, and the Holy Spirit had told him that he, Madeline, and Gloria were completely cured of AIDS, and that he, Naftali, must now tell the whole world that God had cured him as a testament to his deep and abiding faith. Others must know what true belief in God can do, he said, and everyone should be told of this miracle and follow his example. He made me promise to tell others of his miracle and to invite my friends and all my employees to a church service in Gisenyi on May 4 to listen to the story of the vision, to learn of God's promise, and to see for themselves how healthy and strong he and his wife and child were.

Two thousand people, including many Protestant ministers, came to the small church and gathered outside to hear Naftali's story. Naftali and his family stood before the crowd and spoke convincingly of their miracle. In August, Naftali became ill again. He assured me that it was only malaria and that he would be back to work in three days. He died in early September. Thousands attended his funeral and burial, and all of Gisenyi grieved. His wife died several years later, but his daughter is still alive and living in Kigali with relatives.

As the years went by, Rwanda prospered, and so did I. I'm not quite sure how or when it happened, but suddenly I got older. I began to rely more and more on Sembagare for the day-to-day management of the plantation, and eventually I made him my business partner. The flower business brought me enough money to live on, the rains came and went, and the workers and their families came to my back door to tell me of their troubles and their joys. Sundays were filled with visitors and dancing, and I thanked God every day for the blessings of Mugongo and my happy and fulfilling life.

PART FIVE

29

THE WAR

Excerpts from a speech given by President Habyarimana on the occasion of the fiftieth anniversary of Akagera National Park—November 25, 1984:

> In a world which is dominated more and more by techniques which exploit nature, we must participate intensely in the battle for the protection of the environment, not only for our own national and regional interests, but for the preservation of a heritage which belongs to all mankind. . . .
>
> We strive to maintain the balances which we consider vital— the balance between population and food supply, the socio-ecological balance, and the cultural balance. We are handicapped by our population growth, the exhaustion of our arable land, and the modest dimensions of our territory. In the face of these challenges to development, we risk being tempted to turn to easy solutions which do not take into account ecological problems. . . .
>
> In the face of the decreasing availability of agricultural land, the opening of Akagera National Park (to human settlement) could make it possible to reduce the pressure for agricultural space. In my opinion, if the government showed itself to be irresponsible and said "yes" to such suggestions, Rwanda would soon have to give account for having traded off an essential and vital asset for advantages of a risky and specious nature. Because of their fragility, the natural balances in this region would be quickly disturbed by a massive human influx. The consequences would be incalculable, but most certainly disastrous.

—Major-General Juvénal Habyarimana
President of the Republic of Rwanda

President Habyarimana, a charismatic and highly educated Hutu from Rwanda's northwestern province, came into power in 1973 in a bloodless military coup d'état. He received his military training in Europe and became minister of defense under the Kayibanda administration. As president, he founded the Mouvement Révolutionnaire National pour le Développement (MRND) and established the Second Republic— pledging stability, national unity, and an end to ethnic hostility in Rwanda. Under his administration, a national quota system was established whereby positions in government, business, and education were allocated according to the ethnic distribution of the population—eighty-five percent Hutu and fifteen percent Tutsi. Throughout his twenty-one year presidency, Habyarimana was enthusiastically supported by the vast majority of the population, Hutu and Tutsi alike.

Under his leadership, Rwanda enjoyed many years of relative peace and prosperity, due largely to the steady flow of economic aid into the country. Dispensaries, maternity clinics, and family planning centers were established in every commune. Progressive agricultural and veterinary projects were successfully implemented nationwide. Free and compulsory education was made available to all children through the sixth grade, and secondary schools and universities were filled to capacity with students eager to learn. Infrastructure improvements included transportation projects, telecommunications systems, hydroelectric power plants, and the construction of a modern international airport in Kigali. Reforestation projects were initiated, and the preservation of national parks and wildlife became a top priority. In 1990, the tiny country of Rwanda contained more preservation land per square mile than any country in the world. Akagera National Park alone encompassed more than ten percent of Rwanda's land surface. Its fertile soil and large agricultural labor force produced an abundant food supply to feed its burgeoning population of almost eight million people. Workers were paid good salaries, and pensions and disability benefits were guaranteed. Although Rwanda relied heavily upon foreign aid for development, it was one of the few countries in Africa that made a genuine effort to repay its debts.

I was fortunate to know President Habyarimana and his family personally, and I believed him to be a man of great integrity and vision. By the late 1980s, however, rumors were rampant of corruption and nepotism within his administration. Citizens were forced to carry ethnic identity cards, and it was alleged that the quota system was being used to restrict Tutsi participation in business and education. Decreasing world prices for coffee— Rwanda's main export product—created a sharp economic decline. By 1990, the government had devalued the Rwandan franc by more than sixty percent, increased import duties, regulated prices, and imposed a ten percent sales tax on goods and services. Crime was on the rise in the cities, and the AIDS epidemic was spreading at an alarming rate. There were reports that Habyarimana had been the target of assassination attempts by enemies within his own administration.

By 1990, the Rwandan government was under mounting pressure from the United States and Europe to establish a multiparty democracy. When the World Bank and other financial institutions threatened to withhold foreign aid, Habyarimana was forced to allow the establishment of opposing political parties. Within a year, there were sixteen organized political parties in Rwanda—not based on any particular ideology, but rather on ethnic and regional associations. Many of these political parties resembled social clubs more than political organizations, and the result was that they fractured the country at a time when national unity was essential. Differentiating one party member from another became so confusing that hats of different colors were devised to identify party affiliation. Everywhere, people wore brightly colored hats. Little caps of green and blue identified one party while caps of pink and yellow identified another. Party squabbling became so contentious that I finally had to ban all party hats at Mugongo. My cook, Mikingo, said, "This democracy will kill us all, Madame."

During the last week of September 1990, President Habyarimana attended a World Summit for Children at the United Nations in New York. On October 1, he was scheduled to fly to Denver, Colorado, where he was to be honored for his administration's vigilant protection of the endangered mountain gorillas and exemplary record in wildlife conservation.

On the morning of October 1, soldiers from the Ugandan Army, under the leadership of Major-General Fred Rwigema, invaded Rwanda from the north, killing Rwandan officials at the Uganda-Rwanda border post of Kagitumba. They advanced to the nearby town of Gabiro and easily captured the Rwandan military camp located there. Rwigema was a legendary military figure in Uganda, having formerly served as deputy commander of the Ugandan Army and deputy minister of defense. He was killed on the first day of the invasion.

Habyarimana immediately left the United States and returned to Rwanda, after brief stops in Paris and Brussels to request military assistance to suppress the unprovoked attack. Belgium sent six hundred paratroopers to protect its sixteen hundred Belgian citizens living in Rwanda, and France sent one hundred and fifty French Foreign Legionnaires to evacuate its nationals and secure the international airport in Kigali.

Rwandan officials anticipated international condemnation of this act of aggression against the Rwandan people and assumed that the world would leap to their defense in the conflict—as it had when Iraq invaded tiny Kuwait. To the shock and bewilderment of the Rwandan people, the world press and public opinion came down overwhelmingly on the side of the Ugandan rebels. The invading army consisted primarily of Ugandan army deserters and Tutsi exiles—many the sons and grandsons of Tutsi who had fled to Uganda during and after the rebellion of 1959. These men were born in Uganda and were trained by the Ugandan Army. They spoke English, not French, and many did not even speak Kinyarwanda. The entire world seemed captivated by these tall, handsome, English-speaking officers being interviewed from Kampala, while poor besieged Rwanda was criticized for not handing over its country to them on a silver platter.

Rwanda had invested its resources in agriculture, infrastructure, education, and the preservation of its natural resources—not militarization. As a consequence, Rwanda's army was a poorly trained outfit of barely five thousand men. They were no match for the highly trained and heavily armed Ugandan forces, whose initial numbers exceeded ten thousand troops. The rebel army called itself the Rwandan Patriotic Front (RPF), or *inkotanyi*, which means "invincible ones," and its mission was to overthrow the existing government and restore Tutsi supremacy in Rwanda.

From the moment of the first attack, ethnic hatred was aroused and Hutu fear of Tutsi domination was reignited. The Rwandan military began immediately to enlist army recruits. Most of those who volunteered were unemployed men who were half giddy at the prospect of a uniform, a pair of boots, a salary, and the promise of two bottles of beer at the end of each day. In the beginning, they were a ragtag, undisciplined group.

Rwandan authorities conducted house-to-house searches looking for arms and ammunition. Every Tutsi house was searched, and thousands of suspected Tutsi sympathizers were arrested and held without charges. When the home of one prominent official was searched, he was reported to have said, "You should be searching the houses of the president's friends!" On October 4, another official was quoted as saying, "Eighteen years of extraordinary reconciliation have been undone in three days."

In mid-January of 1991, Ruhengeri was captured. The commanding officer of the Rwandan regiment, a Tutsi, surrendered without firing a shot and handed over the keys to the prison, releasing hundreds of political prisoners. Fierce fighting took place in the volcanoes near Karisoke, where an IMAX film crew was making a movie on the mountain gorillas. Among those involved in the film project were primatologist George Schaller and his wife and a photographic crew from National Geographic sent to film the IMAX team at work. The entire outfit was ordered to cease operations and vacate the Karisoke camp without delay. The IMAX crew, the Schallers, and the Karisoke research team were eventually evacuated to Kigali by French paratroopers. The National Geographic photographers found themselves hiding under their beds at the Hotel Muhavura in Ruhengeri, as bullets shattered the windows and ricocheted off the walls. They were subsequently taken captive by the rebels and held hostage, before finally being released.

Dr. Liz McFie, the veterinarian at the Volcano Veterinary Center, bravely fled from her compound at Kinigi, bringing with her more than a dozen frightened civilians and a black mangabey monkey named Kiki. They arrived at Mugongo with tales of terrified residents fleeing Ruhengeri with only spears and bows and arrows for protection. Kiki's favorite food was flowers, so he had come to monkey heaven. Liz hoped to return to Kinigi to rescue two chimpanzees she had left behind, but it was learned several days later that her house and the veterinary center had been destroyed and the chimps were presumed dead.

The rebels closed the Rwanda-Uganda border, blocking off transport lines for oil and other imports. The RPF was extremely well armed with sophisticated weapons and equipment from Uganda—armored vehicles, automatic machine guns, and cannons. As they marched toward Kigali, civilian peasants were used as human shields. Atrocities and human rights abuses proliferated on both sides, and a dusk-to-dawn curfew was imposed nationwide.

The rebels remained hidden in the obscurity of the volcanoes, from where they would launch their nightly raids. One cloudy day in February, a Rwandan military helicopter flew low over Mugongo, spraying gunfire and mortar shells into the fields and forests along the lower slopes of Karisimbi. I watched from the garden wall, fearful that *inkotanyi* would emerge from the forest at any moment. Many nights, I would go outside and stand near the asparagus beds with my night watchman and the shepherds—each of whom stood valiantly clutching long, wooden spears. In the moonlight and cold night air, we would listen to the sound of gunfire from a military camp six miles away and the thundering of cannons coming from the direction of the volcanoes.

The Rwandan military forces eventually recaptured Ruhengeri, and on March 31, 1991, a cease-fire agreement was signed in the Zairian capitol of Kinshasa. Tutsi prisoners were released, and military observers from three African countries were appointed to monitor the truce. The cease-fire was broken just two weeks later, and sporadic fighting continued throughout 1991 and 1992.

One of the principal issues at stake was the RPF demand that more than a half million Tutsi exiles living outside of Rwanda be allowed to return to their homeland. Rwanda was at that time the most densely populated country in Africa, with a population of almost eight million people living in an area half the size of Switzerland. Being staunchly Roman Catholic, its fertility rate was the highest in the world. Its demographic pressures, the scarcity of land, and an overburdened economy made the mass influx of large numbers of people virtually impossible without causing dire economic and environmental consequences.

In early February 1993, the RPF launched its biggest and most successful offenses of the war, and Ruhengeri was captured for the second time. As massacres and artillery battles raged throughout the towns and countryside, the death toll mounted. Fearing an attack on Gisenyi, all French nationals were urged to evacuate, and the American Embassy strongly advised me to go with them. Once again, I stubbornly refused to leave Mugongo. How could I leave my home and abandon my animals and all the people who depended upon me and looked to me for courage and reassurance?

In one of the most tragic episodes of the war, rebels infiltrated the northern region of Akagera National Park and slaughtered much of its wildlife, including elephants, hippopotamus, rhinoceros, chimpanzees, and lions. More than half of the forty-two elephants in the park were killed. In a desperate measure to clear the land for human settlement, one fourth of the park area was burned and destroyed.

The war also encroached upon the Volcano National Park, home to half the world's population of mountain gorillas. The rebels established campsites in the park, destroying the gorillas' habitats and threatening their existence. Game wardens, veterinarians, and researchers were driven out, and the Karisoke Research Center was ransacked and vandalized. The Volcano Veterinary Center was bombed and rebuilt four times during 1992, and three of its guards were shot and killed.

Flower sales plummeted as chaos and disruptions of every kind plagued the region. Many of my customers had left Rwanda for security reasons, and military roadblocks and open gunfire in the streets often made the delivery of flowers to Gisenyi and Kigali difficult, if not impossible.

As fear and helplessness gripped the nation, President Habyarimana urged the people to remain "vigilant." Simple farmers stood watch along the roadsides with spears or bows and arrows clenched in their fists, being as vigilant as they knew how to be. Ragged civilians set up makeshift roadblocks of rocks strewn across the road and checked the papers of everyone who passed by. In most cases, they had no idea what they were looking at, and often they would meticulously scrutinize the documents upside down. At one checkpoint, a group of Canadians was asked to produce their baptismal certificates.

* * *

In April 1992, peace talks began in Arusha, Tanzania. All of Rwanda was hopeful that negotiations would bring an end to the war, but the RPF's demands were so intransigent that the negotiations dragged on for almost eighteen months. Under pressure from world leaders, and with mounting casualties within both the military and civilian ranks, Habyarimana made many concessions to the RPF which were received with fear and condemnation by the Hutu majority back home. The peace settlement mandated the formation of an interim government with shared control between the RPF and the existing administration. In addition, it provided for the integration of the Rwandan and RPF military forces and guaranteed the repatriation of all Tutsi exiles. Although Habyarimana would remain president, his power would be diminished drastically.

The peace-accord ceremonies were attended by the presidents of Rwanda, Burundi, Tanzania, Uganda, and the Organization of African Unity, as well as the prime ministers from Egypt, Kenya, Zaire, and Senegal. Although the treaty was signed on August 4, 1993, it was never implemented.

After nearly three years of war, sixty-five hundred lives had been lost and more than a million people had been displaced. Farmers from Rwanda's most fertile region had been forced to abandon their fields and flee, threatening a severe food shortage and mass starvation. Squalid displacement camps sprang up along the route between Ruhengeri and Kigali, where ragged refugees whose homes and fields had been in combat areas were living off emergency relief supplies and stripping the forests for shelter and firewood.

The hearts of the displaced, the wounded, and the families of those killed in battle were consumed with bitterness toward the Tutsi rebels from Uganda who had devastated their peaceful country. I shared their heartache, but I never could have imagined—nor would I have believed—that what was to follow would become the standard by which the world would measure human tragedy forevermore.

30

Genocide

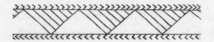

On the evening of April 6, 1994, a plane carrying President Juvénal Habyarimana was shot out of the sky as it made its descent into Kigali and plummeted into the gardens of the Presidential Palace. Also on board were President Cyprien Ntaryamira of Burundi, five cabinet ministers, and a crew of three. The plane was returning from a peace conference in Tanzania. There were no survivors.

The identity of the assassins has never been determined. Many blamed the RPF, who were openly dissatisfied with the nonimplementation of the peace accord. Others blamed hard-liners within the Presidential Guard opposed to reconciliation of any kind. It was even rumored that the Belgians were responsible, as the plane was shot down by a surface-to-air missile—believed to be beyond the capabilities of the Rwandan or RPF militaries.

I received the news the following morning in stunned disbelief. When I told my cook, Mikingo, that the president was dead, he said with eyes wide with shock, "This is the end of the world, Madame." No one came to work that day, and our community of Mutura was gripped in an eerie silence. I felt sick with sorrow and apprehension. Within days, shock and grief turned to violence and revenge, as gangs of militant Hutu extremists spread across the countryside, rounding up tens of thousands of young men and inciting them into a frenzy of hatred toward the Tutsi.

On the afternoon of April 8, a gang of hostile young men armed with heavy clubs was discovered searching the outbuildings on my property. When I demanded to know what they wanted, they shouted angrily that they were looking for Tutsi. One called out, "We know you have Tutsi hidden here!" I ordered them to leave, and eventually they retreated. The fact was that Tutsi families *were* hiding on my property. My shepherd Gafeza, his wife, mother, and children were hiding inside my house, and more than

a dozen others had sought refuge in the drying house and other outbuildings on the plantation.

The following morning, I awoke to find the house surrounded by
twenty or more teenaged fanatics wielding clubs and shouting wildly.
Some of these boys I had known since they were babies. They stormed
through the house and searched the grounds, looking into cupboards and
under beds for people who had been their neighbors and friends all their
lives. I could do nothing but watch in silent fury and pray that those poor,
frightened people had somehow been able to escape.

By late afternoon, the men had returned and were sitting on the garden
wall brandishing their weapons. I approached them and demanded to
know what they wanted.

"There is still one we haven't found yet," they shouted. "We think he is
in the attic of your house."

"You don't mind killing old women," I said. "If you want to kill someone, here I am. Kill me!"

They looked at me in horror and said, "Oh, no, Madame!"

At least eight people were killed at Mugongo that Saturday, including
Gafeza and his wife and baby. They were clubbed to death in the fields as
they tried to flee from the murderous young thugs. That evening, I found
pieces of torn clothing, photos, and indentity cards on the garden paths.
Never before in all my years at Mugongo had such violence occurred on
my own land. I was overcome with sorrow at the senseless slaughter of
these innocent victims and consumed with rage at the people who had
done this. I was also gripped by a paralyzing fear. At the time, I believed
that this was an isolated incident. I had no way of knowing that the same
thing was happening all over Rwanda. And it wasn't until some weeks later,
as reports of atrocities mounted, that I began to comprehend the full extent of the carnage.

The day after the president's assassination, Kigali dissolved into a state of
anarchy and terror, as soldiers and guards loyal to Habyarimana went on a
rampage, rounding up opposition leaders and their families. Cabinet ministers were abducted and the acting prime minister was executed. Amid the
violence, ten U.N. Belgian peacekeepers and seventeen Jesuit priests were
tortured and killed. Fighting broke out between the Rwandan military and
the Tutsi-backed RPF, and disparate army factions and civilian gangs took
to the streets, attacking Tutsi and Tutsi sympathizers and any members of
the political opposition they could find.

I was awakened at six o'clock on Sunday morning to the sound of

Belgian soldiers banging on my front door, ordering me to leave immediately. "You have exactly five minutes to pack!" they shouted. This time I did not hesitate. Dazed and still in my nightgown, I hastily stuffed precious papers and photographs, my jewel case, and a few articles of clothing into a small suitcase. I considered taking the dogs, but decided against it, as I believed I was only going as far as Gisenyi until things calmed down. I left Mikingo with some money and told him I would be back in a few days. I never had a chance to say good-bye to Sembagare.

The American Embassy had arranged for my evacuation, along with dozens of foreign nationals, mostly Americans, from the Seventh-Day Adventist University at Mudende. Our convoy of thirteen cars and military vehicles left the shattered campus of Mudende and slowly made its way down the Mutura road. Men and boys armed with clubs and spears lined the road, shaking their fists and shouting angrily. These were people I had known for years and whose hearts I thought I knew. Some had been children I had loved. What had happened in just a few days to turn them from peaceful farmers into cold-blooded killers? They stood three deep all along the roadside with hatred in their eyes. I rolled down the window and shouted, "You are devils!" The Belgian officer sharply warned me not to provoke them.

In Gisenyi, I parted company with the Adventists and was taken to the house of Henri and Suzanne Peyer on Lake Kivu, where we assured one another we would never leave Rwanda. But on Monday, April 11, all foreign nationals were forcibly evacuated to Goma. As we entered Zaire, friends were waiting to welcome us with warmth and kindness. In the ensuing days, reports of atrocities filtered across the border, and most of the evacuees made arrangements to leave for Europe. When I received word that hundreds of Tutsi had been killed in Mutura and it was believed that Sembagare was dead, I fell to pieces and reserved the last space on a private plane bound for Bujumbura.

Numb with grief and sorrow, I left my beloved Rwanda. From Bujumbura, I was flown to Brussels, where I spent several heart-wrenching days with the dear Boreel family. From there, I flew to San Francisco, where I was met at the airport by loving friends, Elton and Evelyn Wallace and Scott and Diane Heldfond. Scott and Diane kindly lent me their guest house at St. Helena in the Napa Valley, where I stayed for several weeks recovering my strength. Eventually I flew to the East Coast to be with my family.

During April and May, the genocide escalated to horrific proportions. I spent hours glued to the television watching images that will haunt me for the rest of my life. The violence was carried out by Hutu extremists with an unsparing ethnic hatred toward the Tutsi. They devised hit lists and marched through Kigali conducting house-to-house searches, rounding up opposition leaders and their families. Government officials, nuns, priests, relief workers, and human rights activists were killed. Radio stations spewed daily hate-filled broadcasts calling for the elimination of all ethnic Tutsi and members of the opposition. Extremist Hutu militia groups, called *interahamwe*, meaning "those who attack together," formed death squads and took to the streets. No Tutsi was safe. People were dragged from houses, offices, and churches and were executed by gangs of drunken young men using guns, grenades, machetes, and axes to carry out their deadly mission. Patients were slaughtered in hospital beds. Mutilated bodies littered the streets of Kigali and piled up in every building. As many as twenty thousand men, women, and children—most of them Tutsi—died in the first four days.

Soon there were food shortages, and drinking water became scarce. Power supplies were cut, phone lines were down, and sanitary facilities were nonexistent. Chaos reigned, and the air was thick with smoke from burned-out villages and the stench of thousands of rotting corpses. Amid the carnage, there were also moments of extraordinary bravery and sacrifice, as many Hutu risked their lives to protect Tutsi friends and neighbors.

Two wars raged simultaneously in Rwanda. One was the battle between the two armies—the Rwandan military and the RPF—for control of the country, and the other was the systematic slaughter of all ethnic Tutsi by the *interahamwe*. Although twenty-five hundred U.N. peacekeeping troops were stationed in Rwanda at the time, they did little or nothing to intervene in either conflict. At the height of the carnage, the United Nations pulled out all but two hundred and seventy "observers," leaving Rwanda to the fate of the butchers.

The streets were ruled by hostile young thugs urged on by government radio and fueled by cane liquor or banana beer, greed, and tribal hatred. There were no sanctuaries. Thousands of Tutsi were killed in churches, schools, convents, and orphanages. Tens of thousands of Rwandan women were raped. Civilians were ordered at gunpoint to round up their friends and neighbors for execution. They were shot, clubbed, and hacked to death. Many were dismembered, the body parts stacked neatly in piles. The dead were buried in mass graves in the lush valleys of Rwanda's rolling countryside. Bloated, mutilated bodies clogged the Akagera River all the way to Lake Victoria.

By the end of April, two million Rwandans had left their homes for refugee camps both inside and outside of Rwanda. Tutsi fled in fear for their lives, and Hutu fled in fear of retaliation. Two hundred and fifty thousand refugees, mostly Hutu, fled to neighboring Tanzania, creating what was then the largest refugee camp in the world. By the end of May, it was estimated that up to five hundred thousand Tutsi—almost half the entire Tutsi population of Rwanda—had been killed, and the rest were either in hiding or in flight. One missionary is reported to have said, "There are no devils left in hell—they are all in Rwanda."

Through friends in Goma, I occasionally received news from Mugongo. Mikingo and Sebashitzi, my houseboy, had remained at Mugongo to watch over my house and animals, which at the time included a yellow lab and a Jack Russell terrier, a Siamese cat, and two African gray parrots. In the first bit of good news I had received in months, I learned that Sembagare was still alive, but in hiding.

Kigali fell to the RPF on July 4, 1994, and Ruhengeri was captured less than two weeks later. During the last weeks of the campaign, Tutsi rebels chased the remaining Rwandan military forces westward, pushing more than a million civilians ahead of them. Hutu leaders issued radio broadcasts inciting their countrymen to flee. "If you stay in Rwanda," they threatened, "the RPF will kill you in revenge—or we will kill you as traitors." Thus began the greatest mass flight of people in modern times. Fearing retaliation, more than two million Rwandans, mostly Hutu, fled across the borders into Zaire, Tanzania, and Burundi in a period of just a few days. They were driven out of Rwanda—not by the Tutsi victors—but by their own leaders.

The vast majority of those who fled were innocent of any wrongdoing. Terror-stricken men, women, and children fled to Zaire at the rate of ten thousand per hour, overwhelming a tiny border crossing staffed by just one guard. Hundreds of refugees—many of them children—were trampled to death in the stampede. The Mutura road was thronged with desperate, frightened people heading toward Zaire. Among them were all of my neighbors and workers and their families, including Sembagare. By the final days of the mass exodus, Mikingo and Sebashitzi were no longer able to hold out at Mugongo, and they fled to Zaire as well, leaving my house and animals to their own fates.

The refugee camps in Zaire were situated at the base of Nyiragongo on hard, barren volcanic rock, making drilling for water or digging latrines all but impossible without heavy machinery. Lake Kivu was polluted by dead bodies and human waste. The refugees were desperate from hunger and thirst. While their crops lay rotting in the fields back home, many died of starvation waiting for relief supplies to come. Cholera hit the camps like a medieval plague. People lay dying at a staggering rate. Eight thousand bodies were counted in two days. In the first few weeks, as many as thirty thousand people died from cholera, typhoid, and other diseases. Their bodies were rolled up in straw mats and left in piles. Children wandered aimlessly, crying for their mothers. Rwanda's three-month reign of terror had left up to a quarter of a million children lost or orphaned.

At long last, the world took notice and international relief agencies and military assistance slowly began to arrive. In mid-August, the United Nations deployed fifty-five hundred peacekeeping troops to Rwanda in a mission called UNAMIR (United Nations Assistance Mission in Rwanda). Dozens, and then hundreds, of NGOs (Non-Governmental Organizations) brought relief supplies, medical assistance, and humanitarian aid to Rwanda and the refugee camps outside its borders.

The RPF had won the war, but they had acquired a country without people. It was a country with empty towns, empty fields, and empty hearts. As many as eight hundred thousand people were dead, two million had fled the country for squalid refugee camps in neighboring countries, and an additional two million had sought refuge in camps inside Rwanda. Well over half the population was gone.

I have asked myself a thousand times, how could such a thing happen in this time in our history? How could such a thing happen in a country that had known two decades of relative peace and prosperity? The Hutu and Tutsi populations in Rwanda shared a common language and a common culture. Hutu farmers and Tutsi cattle herders had coexisted in unity and cooperation. They lived side by side and intermarried. They were neighbors and friends.

The question still lingers, why was the world so slow to react? Why did it take so long for the international community to label the slaughter of hundreds of thousands of people *genocide*? There is no doubt that what took place in Rwanda was more than a spontaneous outpouring of tribal rage. What took place was a systematic campaign of extermination orchestrated by political leaders and backed by the military.

Why did the world close its eyes for so long to the suffering of so many helpless people? Perhaps the answer lies in the fact that what happened in Rwanda defies comprehension, defies explanation, and defies all conventional remedies. Perhaps it is because there is no frame of reference for such a cataclysmic event. It is too complex, too remote, too unthinkable.

Words are insufficient to describe my feelings of helplessness and despair, as newspapers and television reports depicted the horrors unfolding in this country that I love and call my home. I was tormented night and day by the images of so many dead bodies, so many orphaned children, so many hopeless faces. I was sick with worry for the people I loved and wracked with guilt for abandoning them in such haste. I was consumed by unbearable heartache and an irrepressible desire to go back. I had to go back. I knew that the Rwanda I had known was gone forever, but I could not forsake my country and its people in its most desolate hour.

Somewhere in the back of my mind, I had the crazy idea of converting the old pyrethrum drying house into a shelter for lost and orphaned children. I didn't know how I was going to do it. I didn't even know if any of my workers were still alive or if my house was still standing. I only knew that I had to go home.

31

RETURN TO RWANDA

It was suggested to me in none too delicate a fashion that I was a bit old to be attempting such a perilous journey with such an uncertain outcome. I was at that time just a few weeks shy of my eighty-second birthday. Without putting too fine a point on it, the consensus was that I had lost my mind entirely. A friend from California, Scott Heldfond, had offered to accompany me back to Rwanda, if and when I wanted to go. By the end of July, my desire to go back had become overpowering, and nothing or no one could stand in my way. On very short notice, Scott canceled all his personal and business commitments and began making travel arrangements for our excursion into the unknown. Against the advice of friends and family, and against the advice of the U.S. State Department, Scott and I left New York's JFK International Airport on August 10, 1994, to journey to the most dangerous place on earth.

Traveling to Rwanda is a long and arduous enterprise under the best of circumstances. This particular trip was made more difficult by the fact that all commercial flights into Kigali had been suspended and we had no idea how we would get into Rwanda or what we would find once we got there. We were traveling with an enormous amount of baggage—me with an accumulation of donated clothing, personal articles, and household supplies, and Scott with an arsenal of survival equipment, including food and provisions, sleeping bags, a water purifier, and camp stove. We were also carrying a significant amount of cash, carefully folded and concealed in money belts.

We landed in Nairobi on the morning of August 12 and checked into the famed Norfolk Hotel, an elegant relic of earlier times and happier memories. Weary from two long, all-night flights, we were now faced with our first big challenge—how to get into Rwanda. The only way in was to hitch a ride on a U.N. military or relief cargo plane. That being the case, luck was with us when we ran into Willard Munger, a Seventh-Day Adventist missionary from Mudende. I had known Willard for a number of years, and he and I had been evacuated together in April. As it happened, Willard was returning to Rwanda as well, to assess the damage at the university just down the road from Mugongo. Willard is a quiet, unassuming sort with a knack for achieving the impossible with little or no fanfare. We told him of our predicament, and two days later we were miraculously escorted onto a Russian-built cargo plane bringing relief supplies and personnel into Rwanda. To our astonishment, Scott and I were listed on the manifest as Adventist missionaries under the auspices of ADRA (Adventist Development and Relief Agency). To my further amazement, we were harnessed into bench seats (used for parachute jumpers) along the side of the fuselage in the cargo section of the plane, where we sat among huge, rattling crates of relief supplies. It was cold and noisy and extremely uncomfortable, but the atmosphere was charged with a palpable air of excitement and anticipation as the huge jet, with its small group of passengers and crew, hurtled toward war-ravaged Rwanda.

As we made our descent into Kigali, any thoughts of madcap adventure were quickly forgotten. There was no doubt that we were entering a war zone. The tarmac was lined with military and cargo planes bearing the insignias of the United Nations, CARE, and the Red Cross, and the airport was teeming with armed military personnel. When we stepped off the plane, my good friend Dave Rawson, U.S. ambassador to Rwanda, was there to greet us. His light blue seersucker suit and tie stood out among the sea of khaki military uniforms. Kigali's beautiful airport—once the pride of Rwanda—had been ravaged by mortar shells and riddled with bullet holes. The windows had been blown out, and broken glass littered the floors. I was stunned by my first glimpse of the destruction, but it would be several days before I fully understood the extent of the devastation that had taken place here. Ambassador Rawson guided us through what can only be described as extremely tense and chaotic formalities at the airport, and we said good-bye to Willard, agreeing to meet the following day to plan our excursion to Mudende and Mugongo.

Kigali was unrecognizable. The city was in shambles, with rubble everywhere. Every house, hotel, and business had been damaged and looted. Every building bore the scars of shelling, and some were simply heaps of stones. Street lamps had been wrenched from the ground and were lying helter-skelter on the sidewalks. There was no running water and no electricity. Nothing remained of the beautiful city I remembered.

Apart from the soldiers, the streets were deserted. The victorious RPF had renamed itself the Rwandan People's Army, and RPA soldiers were positioned in bunkers on every street corner, armed with machine guns and rocket launchers. We were put up at a "safe house," which we shared with

U.S. Embassy and military personnel. Army officers slept on the floors and couches with loaded guns at their sides or under their pillows. With each passing moment, my expectations dwindled and my concept of reality redefined itself.

Two days after our arrival, we determinedly set out for Mugongo and Mudende. Scott and I, accompanied by Laura Lane of the State Department and a driver, rode in a U.S. Embassy car with a paper American flag taped to the windshield. Willard Munger followed behind in a rented taxi filled with all of our luggage—as we optimistically hoped to be able to stay. I had previously been told that a relief worker for the International Organization for Migration, Jan de Wilde, had paid a visit to Mugongo two weeks earlier and had found my house occupied by RPA soldiers. They were "guarding it," they told him. He thanked them and looked around and saw that most of my furniture and belongings were still there. Only the beds appeared to be missing, which the soldiers said had been stolen before they arrived. As he was leaving, Jan told the soldiers, "Mrs. Carr is returning in ten days."

We rode along in an uneasy silence, struck by the absence of cars on the road. The only other vehicles in evidence were military Jeeps and huge relief trucks, many of them traveling in tandem, passing one another and barreling along the steep, winding road. Here and there were small groups of ragged refugees carrying all of their pitiful possessions on their heads or in rickety wooden wheelbarrows. Some were headed toward the refugee camps in Zaire, and a few brave souls were returning to their homeland. Littered along the side of the road were dozens of overturned trucks and the charred remains of cars in which people had been shot and set on fire. Progress was impeded by countless roadblocks manned by surly RPA soldiers, where we were forced to stop and wait for permission to proceed. Various relief agencies had set up field hospitals and food distribution centers along the way, and huge crowds of dazed and weary people stood in line waiting for food and medical treatment. The fields and houses were empty, the towns and villages war-ravaged and deserted. By the time we finally turned onto the Mutura road, I was trembling with a mixture of anticipation and dread. I looked around for friendly, familiar faces, but all I saw were tall strangers.

Mudende was a Seventh-Day Adventist university built in the early 1980s at a cost of eleven million dollars. The large campus consisted of lovely houses, classrooms, a church building, administration buildings, dormitories, and expansive open areas for agricultural projects. Nothing could have prepared us for what we encountered as we approached the complex from the long entrance drive. The beautiful campus was in ruins. Every building had been looted and vandalized. Toilets were overflowing; debris and human waste covered the floors. Dead dogs were left rotting in the sun. Although the bodies had been removed and hastily buried in mass graves, there was evidence that many people had died there. Cows had been sheltered in Willard's spacious house, and the few pieces of furniture that remained had been deliberately damaged. I thought to myself, "My house can't possibly be as bad as this." But it was.

Stunned and shaken, we left Mudende and continued on toward Mugongo. My heart lifted as we turned in at the stone pillars that mark the entrance to the drive, but fell immediately when my house came into view. The windows had been smashed, revealing large, gaping holes, and those that were not broken had been spray-painted with bright orange paint. A grotesque figure was painted on the front door. Trash and debris were strewn everywhere, and the carcass of one of my African gray parrots lay rotting on the stone terrace.

Inside, the devastation was complete. Everything was gone—family silver, crystal and china, antique Flemish mirrors, almost every piece of furniture, all cooking utensils, every stitch of clothing, all of the curtains, rugs, blankets, towels, and table linens, and all of my precious books, photographs, and diaries. Even the gardening tools and flower supplies were gone. The Volkswagen minibus had been stolen, and there was a large empty space where the kerosene refrigerator used to be. A lifetime of hard work and memories was all gone.

The safe in a corner cabinet in the dining room had been blown apart by a grenade. The floors were ankle-deep in torn, dirty papers, letters, documents, photos, negatives, and refuse, combined with millions of feathers from down pillows that had been slit open and emptied onto the floors. Most of the plumbing fixtures had been either broken or stolen. Even the water pipes had been ripped from the walls. The toilet was overflowing, and the vile stench coming from the lavatory was overwhelming. I looked around at what used to be my lovely home and wept with hopelessness and despair. I wept with shame for the people who had done this, and I wept with anger at the utter violation of my life and the senseless destruction of the country I loved. It was the greatest heartbreak I have ever known.

My moment of grief was interrupted by the faint sound of a familiar bark. My emotions turned to wild elation as I stumbled outside to embrace my two beloved dogs, Freddie and Tiffany, so weak they could barely walk—but still *alive*. They had not been fed in more than four weeks. Just moments later, a pitiful yowl announced the return of Kim, my fourteen-year-old Siamese cat, scolding me for leaving him and letting me know how much he had suffered. I am certain that it was Kim who had kept the dogs alive by killing small animals for them to eat. Discovering my pets alive and in desperate need of love and care was truly my salvation. That was perhaps the defining moment, when my thoughts turned from leaving in defeat to believing that I had a reason to stay. Amid the throes of our joyful reunion, I looked up and saw the dear face of Biriko, my old cook. He was thin and dressed in ragged clothes, and his face bore the haunted look of a man who had returned from the bowels of hell. With what little strength I had left, I threw my arms around him and wept with sorrow and untold anguish.

When Rwanda fell to the RPA, all of my Hutu workers and their families fled to an enormous refugee camp in Zaire called Kibumba, located across the border just six miles from Mugongo. Biriko told me he had left Kibumba after only five days at the outbreak of the cholera epidemic. If he was going to die, he said, he would rather die at home in Rwanda than in a refugee camp in Zaire. To my enormous relief, he had news that Sembagare, Mikingo, Sebashitzi, and several of the gardeners were still alive, but living in exile at Kibumba with their families.

With assurances to Biriko that we would return in two days, we put both flea-ridden dogs in the car and started back to Kigali around midafternoon. We had no choice but to leave poor Kim behind. As promised, we returned two days later with gallons of white paint, cleaning supplies, pails, brooms, nails, and a hammer. When we pulled up to the house, Biriko was waiting for us with seven children and a man named Joeli, ready to go to work. While the men scrubbed, swept, and painted, the children and I sorted through the papers on the floor, separating photos from letters and bank statements. To my great surprise, Scott found the deed to the plantation tossed in the bushes outside the dining room window. It had been in the safe along with jewelry, money, and some precious pieces of family silver. The thieves had taken all the valuables and thrown the deed out the window.

Again, we returned to Kigali that evening, as the house was far from livable and it was now time for Scott to return to San Francisco. The option was open for me to go back with him—to leave the shattered remnants of my life behind and live out my remaining years in America. But I have come to realize that I am just a visitor in the United States. My life is spiritually and emotionally embedded in Rwanda and in the lives of the Rwandan people. Only here does my life have true meaning and purpose, and it is only here that I feel I am at home. My ship had set its course a long time ago, and it was far too late to turn back now. I will be forever grateful to Scott for bringing me back to Rwanda and getting me started repairing my home and rebuilding my life. The rest was now up to me.

On August 24, 1994, I returned to Mugongo to stay—alone. The most joyful moment of all came when I arrived at the house and a weary Sembagare emerged from the doorway to greet me. He was very weak and haggard, but *alive*! I was overjoyed to see him and felt for the first time a sense of well-being and optimism. Days later, I learned of his heroic deeds during the genocide and his three narrow escapes with death. Most of his family, although scattered, were alive, but his wife's sister and brother-in-law had been killed, leaving eight orphaned children for him to raise. My dream of building an orphanage had by this time become firmly embedded in my mind, and now with Sembagare there beside me, I knew that together we could somehow make it a reality.

Looking around at the empty rooms of my house, I felt as though I was reliving my life of forty years ago. The floors had been scrubbed and the walls had been whitewashed, but none of my possessions accumulated over a lifetime remained. I was starting all over again with plastic cups and dishes, cardboard packing crates for chairs, and no kitchen utensils. I had purchased a used mattress in Kigali, which was torn and soiled, and I had two warm woolen blankets and a pillow stuffed with lumpy cotton given to me by a colonel in the U.S. Army. From America, I had brought six silver teaspoons and a small linen tablecloth. I had no car and no indoor plumbing. I had never owned so little, yet I have never felt quite so blessed. I was home again, and my beloved pets were with me and most of the people I loved had survived.

That first night on my own was very frightening. Many of the windows were still broken, and there were no curtains to shut out the terrors of the night. It was extremely cold in the dark, empty house. The chimneys were still choked with debris from the army occupation, so there were no fires in the fireplaces. I had one oil lantern, a flashlight, and some candles (but no candlesticks). When darkness fell, I was surprised to see Nyiragongo's crater flaming against the night sky for the first time since the eruption in 1977. I took this as a propitious and welcoming sign. I lay down on my unfamiliar mattress on the bare cement floor and stayed awake shivering most of the night—while armed soldiers walked around the house and peered in through the open bedroom windows.

The bright morning sunshine banished most of my immediate fears. A carpenter turned up later that day to repair the broken windows with glass panes Scott had managed to find in Kigali. The U.S. Embassy had given me a set of dark blue curtains which I hung at the bedroom windows, using plastic bracelets I had picked up at the market in Kigali as curtain rings. The curtain rods had been stolen, so we improvised using bamboo poles. Over the next few weeks, I would become a master at the art of improvisation. The simplest tasks became a challenge, and the smallest achievements a triumph.

In the following weeks, Mikingo and Sebashitzi returned from Kibumba and life gradually began to take on a new brand of normalcy. With the generous help of UNAMIR personnel and many relief organizations, my house was slowly put back in working order. Canadian soldiers replaced the water pipes and plumbing fixtures, fixed the toilet, repaired the water pump and water tanks, repaired some of the damaged furniture, and donated blankets, flashlights, batteries, cleaning supplies, boxes of army rations, and much, much more. I lived off the army rations for months.

Although the war had ended, Rwanda's problems were far from over. In the months that followed, there was little or no movement of the refugees back into Rwanda. Instead of existing as temporary safe havens, the refugee camps quickly became permanent settlements, with houses, roads, shops, restaurants, and schools. The United Nations and hundreds of relief agencies poured money and technical assistance into the camps, with state-of-the-art medical facilities and water purification and distribution systems that were the envy of every Third World country. Cargo planes laden with food and relief supplies arrived in Goma daily, paid for by taxpayers around the world at a cost of a million dollars a day. Members of the *interahamwe* and former Hutu militia groups took control of the camps, threatening to kill any refugee who attempted to cross the border and return to Rwanda. They confiscated relief supplies, which they sold on the black market or traded for arms, while those in need—pregnant women, children, the sick and elderly—were forced to buy what they needed or go without. They threatened the lives of relief workers and held more than a million refugees hostage in a campaign of terror, while they openly trained recruits, rearmed, and prepared to mount an attack against the RPA-controlled government in Rwanda. It was common knowledge that this was taking place, yet no one stepped in to stop it. The Zairian government did nothing, the RPA did nothing, and the United Nations did nothing.

At the same time, tens of thousands of Tutsi poured into Rwanda from Uganda, Zaire, and Burundi. Many were the descendants of Tutsi exiles who had fled Rwanda during and after the rebellion of 1959. The UNHCR (United Nations High Commissioner for Refugees) drew no distinction between Tutsi exiles who had left Rwanda thirty-five years earlier and

Hutu refugees who fled in terror in July of 1994. Instead of dismantling the camps and bringing the Rwandan refugees home, their efforts and resources were directed at repatriating new Tutsi arrivals from surrounding countries, welcoming them at the borders with bundles of relief supplies, and allocating land to them that was not theirs to give away. They resettled them in Hutu homes in Hutu villages where their cows would graze over fertile farmland, and when there were no more houses to give away, they settled them in thousands of blue plastic tents, which were scattered across the landscape as far as the eye could see.

The genocide and its aftermath brought about a dramatic redistribution of the population in Rwanda, and the consequences to the region were catastrophic—both economically and ecologically. In my commune of Mutura, where the population was once ninety percent Hutu and ten percent Tutsi, it is now the reverse. The Tutsi refugees flooding into Rwanda were born in Uganda, Zaire, and Burundi. It is from these countries that they bring their language and cultural heritage. Their children greet me in Swahili, not Kinyarwanda. The once fertile potato fields of the Hutu are now pastures for the long-horned cattle of the Tutsi. Without the Hutu farmers to farm the land, an economic imbalance has developed and severe food shortages are occurring. A large segment of the population has become dependent upon foreign aid for subsistence.

More than two million refugees remained in refugee camps outside of Rwanda for almost two and a half years. More than half of those were in eastern Zaire. The refugee camps encroached upon Zaire's Virunga National Park, one of the world's richest national parks in terms of diversity and the number of species of birds and mammals. Refugees foraged in the park, setting traps for meat and stripping the forests for firewood. The park became a dumping ground for refuse and human waste, further endangering its wildlife through the spread of disease.

With no functioning judicial system in Rwanda, there has been no due process and no retribution for crimes committed on both sides. Tens of thousands of Hutu suspected of taking part in the genocide were arrested and crammed into overcrowded prisons where thousands of men, women, and children have remained. None of the guilty have been tried or convicted, and none of the innocent have been released. At last count, more than one hundred and thirty thousand prisoners were being held in squalid prisons throughout Rwanda, waiting for an absolution that never will come.

At the same time, the perpetrators of the genocide, operating from the camps in Zaire, continue to conduct military offenses across the Rwanda-Zaire border, massacring Tutsi civilians and posing a security threat to the Rwandan government. In addition, thousands of Hutu civilians have been the victims of reprisal killings by RPA soldiers and Tutsi civilians, further intensifying the fear and distrust of the new government and heightening the instability of the region.

I had returned to a country where nothing worked. There were no banks, no schools, and no factories. There was no money, no postal service, no electricity or telephones. Almost every house and business had been looted, and almost everyone had lost everything. It was a country with a large portion of its population either dead or living outside its borders. Few foreigners had returned to Rwanda after the war, and those who did came back to empty, damaged, or confiscated houses and defunct factories or businesses, with most of their friends and workers either dead or detained in prisons or refugee camps. All business records had been destroyed, every safe had been looted, every factory had been dismantled, every vehicle had been confiscated, and everything of value had mysteriously left the country. It was not clear exactly who had been responsible for the systematic dismantling of Rwanda, but it was undoubtedly carried out in stages by a combination of the Tutsi-led RPA, Hutu militia groups, and unruly civilian mobs on a rampage of looting and destruction.

This was the reality of the Rwanda I had come home to. The idyllic, tranquil country I had known was gone forever. Its innocence and simplicity had been replaced by hatred and brutality, and it would never be fully restored in my lifetime. Was it possible to start over again in a country whose soul had been extinguished? Could I find it in my heart to forgive the desecration of an entire country and its people? My answers would be found in the enduring beauty of Rwanda's thousand hills, in the quiet courage and effortless faith of Sembagare, and in the faces of the children whose innocence had been so savagely taken away and lost forever.

32

IMBABAZI

The old pyrethrum drying house was a large, rambling affair made of brick and timbers. Abandoned since the late 1970s, its walls were crumbling in spots and the roof leaked, but the structure was basically sound. In the fall of 1994, Sembagare and I turned our attention toward the task of converting this old relic into a facility suitable for housing children. It was a huge undertaking, and one which would involve the work of many laborers, exhaustive searches for building materials in a country decimated by war, and endless amounts of determination and faith.

We began by hiring two masons, two carpenters, and eight assistants. With no electricity or power tools of any kind, work was slow but steady. Crude handsaws and machetes were used to fashion new support beams and floorboards. Large open windows were created to provide light and ventilation, and new tiles replaced the broken tiles on the roof. An outdoor kitchen was built with a large brick oven, and bathing and latrine facilities were added. The first floor was renovated into a large open area for eating and playing, with a small dispensary and office. A potbellied stove was miraculously found and installed in a corner to provide warmth in the cool evenings. The second floor was converted into sleeping quarters with two large dormitories—one for the girls and one for the boys. A new stairway was built, complete with a low railing—just the right height for small hands to hold on to.

In October and November of that year, my niece, Ann Halsey, came to visit and assist with the building of the orphanage. Ann's arrival did wonders to boost the morale of everyone involved in the project, and her cheerful enthusiasm brought to Mugongo a spirit of renewal and vitality that had been missing for some time. Since my return, it had become painfully clear to me that no one in Rwanda had been spared the unspeakable horrors that had occurred here. I was haunted by the fear in the people's faces and the sadness in their eyes. As work on the orphans' shelter progressed, a noticeable change began to take place. The workers eagerly showed up for work each day and went about their tasks with a renewed sense of pride and excitement. Soon there was laughter and chatter throughout the house and gardens, and singing and whistling among the carpenters and masons as each brick and plank fell into place. Mugongo had become a haven of safety and a symbol of hope for us all.

Our project was benefited greatly by the assistance of many of the UNAMIR corps and numerous relief organizations. My niece Ann was utterly shameless about asking for donations of materials and supplies, which we received in great quantities and with immense gratitude. Creative begging, she called it. Relief agencies donated mattresses, blankets, clothing, cooking utensils, and a generator. From UNAMIR personnel we received untold technical assistance, dozens of bags of cement mix and lime, and enough corrugated iron sheeting to cover the roof over the new kitchen. The Canadians built a shower with an outdoor water tank, and the Australians built a jungle gym, installed glass panes in the second-story windows, and leveled a large outdoor area for a soccer field. Once the orphanage opened, the Nigerian Medical Corps sent doctors and nurses every week to examine and treat the children. Médecins Sans Frontiers and other organizations provided medical services and inoculation programs as well. The World Food Program delivered food staples in large quantities, and UNICEF and UNHCR provided potable water. We received assistance from so many kind and generous individuals and organizations that it would be impossible to mention them all.

During this time, Rwanda was overrun with U.N. military personnel and humanitarian aid workers from around the world. Equipped with two-way radios, cellular phones, and laptop computers, they descended upon the tiny, war-ravaged country and took over hotels, villas, schools, convents, and office buildings. Restaurants and nightclubs sprang up overnight, and the towns were bustling with their energy and enthusiasm. Inevitably, they would hear about this elderly American woman who lived on a flower farm and was building an orphanage in the foothills of the Virunga volcanoes near Gisenyi. Many made the long trip up the rocky Mutura road to see this anomaly for themselves, and this turned out to be a very busy time for me socially. Rarely did a day go by when I didn't have at least several visitors—sometimes ten or twenty or more. Mugongo offered these remarkable, dedicated people a brief respite from the horrors they faced daily, and their visits brought me an enormous amount of comfort and enjoyment. Many became good friends. Enjoying tea and cookies in the garden, surrounded by the tranquil beauty of Mugongo, it was sometimes possible to forget for a brief moment what had brought us all together.

The orphanage needed a name, so we decided to hold a contest. We all felt the name should be in Kinyarwanda—a very complex language to decipher. Everyone participated—the houseboys, the gardeners, and all the workers at the children's shelter. They each wrote their suggestions on a piece of paper, and after a convoluted translation process, we had a vote. The winner, by an overwhelming majority, was "*Imbabazi z'i* Mugongo," which means "Mugongo is a place where you will receive all the love and care a mother would give." That afternoon, the men carved a wooden sign with the name "Imbabazi" on it and hung it over the front door.

On December 17, 1994, four and a half months after my return to Rwanda, the Imbabazi officially opened. It was built to accommodate up to fifty children, although we exceeded that number a long time ago. Most of the children are brought to us by CARE, the International Committee of the Red Cross (ICRC), and Save the Children (UK), although a few have simply arrived all on their own. Our original intent was to provide a safe and loving environment for the children while efforts were underway to locate family members or suitable permanent homes. Unfortunately, foster care is not a viable solution in present-day Rwanda. Tutsi families will not accept a Hutu child, and vice versa. And most of those who do accept foster children take them only to herd goats or work in the fields. The sad reality is that there are very few families in Rwanda still intact—families that have not been shattered by the war, either through the genocide or the suffering in the refugee camps. That being the case, the Imbabazi will remain a permanent shelter for as long as there are children who need a home and as long as Sembagare and I are able to keep it going.

I can only surmise that God didn't feel I was ready to have children until I was eighty-two years old. Then he sent me forty all at once. Our first group of children was brought to us by Save the Children and ICRC. Many were unaccompanied children who had left Zaire on their own, hoping to find relatives still alive in Rwanda. Most of the younger ones had no memory of who their parents were.

Our very first child (brought to me before the orphanage opened) was a little boy named Gahungu, later called Sammy, who was four years old. His mother had dropped dead on a path near the house of a man who had ten children of his own and didn't want the little boy. We happily took him in, and he is very proud of his distinction as being our "first child." Among our original group was twelve-year-old Nizeyimana, called Commander, who is particularly loved and admired by the other children. His father was killed when his family fled to Gisenyi, and he was separated from his mother and sister when RPF soldiers began firing at crowds of refugees trying to flee to safety in Goma. Although several of his family members have been located, Commander steadfastly refuses to leave the loving environment of the Imbabazi and has told me that he wants to stay here "until he is all grown up." We have made a special exception in his case and allowed him to stay.

Soldiers found four-year-old Kadendeza in April of 1994, lying across the body of his dead mother. They brought him to their camp and kept him for several weeks. When their unit was relocated, they handed him over to a foster family in Ruhengeri. The head of the family was a drunkard who beat the little boy. He was so badly mistreated that neighbors reported it to Save the Children, who rescued him and brought him to us. For some time, Kadendeza had spells of crying and clung desperately to anyone who picked him up to comfort him. After several months, he was laughing and playing happily with the other children. His traumatism had faded, but he still needs more caresses and affection than many of the others.

Two of our most enchanting children were Didas and Olivia—brother and sister. At the age of three, Olivia was a joyful child—very pretty, with incredibly long eyelashes, lovely dimples, and a mischievous smile. She ran around gleefully hugging and kissing the other children, imitating me. Didas, at the age of five, was a bright and charming little boy. He was our best Intore dancer, and the other children wildly applauded his performances. Their father, who lost both his legs in the genocide, was located by Save the Children, and after fifteen memorable months with us, Olivia and Didas left the Imbabazi and were reunited with him. We still miss them terribly.

Ishimwe Pacifique saw both of her parents killed in Kigali during the genocide when she was only eleven years old. She picked up her baby sister Clemence and began walking toward Gisenyi, where she believed she had a grandmother named Agnes. With a one-year-old baby tied to her back, Ishimwe walked nearly seventy miles over a period of many weeks. She slept in fields and begged for food in order to survive. Just outside of Gisenyi, Clemence became ill and someone directed them to a dispensary. The baby's condition was considered extremely grave, and they were taken to a hospital in Ruhengeri run by Médecins Sans Frontiers. They remained at the hospital for more than a month, as Ishimwe had developed measles. When both girls had recovered, Save the Children brought them to us. Ishimwe is an exceptionally lovely girl and is doing well at school. Clemence is now a chubby four-year-old who has many "sisters and brothers" and is adored by everyone. We have never been able to locate their grandmother.

Save the Children and ICRC conduct extensive searches to locate the families of unaccompanied children, and very often, after months of tracing, relatives are found. Since the Imbabazi opened in December of 1994, we have cared for almost two hundred children, more than half of whom have been reunited with family members located through these agencies. But for every child who leaves, there are hundreds more to take his or her place. It is estimated that there are still approximately sixty thousand lost or orphaned children in Rwanda.

We employ a staff of ten women caretakers, two water carriers, two woodcutters, and a night watchman. Biriko is very proud of his role as orphanage cook, and dear old Micheli is his ever-loyal assistant. Together they prepare nourishing meals from dried beans, rice, and cooking oil provided by the World Food Program, supplemented by potatoes, cabbage, carrots, corn, and tomatoes which are grown on our own fields or nearby. Without a doubt, the most valued member of our staff is Sembagare. The young man I hired as houseboy in 1957 is now my business partner and codirector of the Imbabazi. Today, he does everything from coach soccer to bandage big and little wounds. It is under Sembagare's careful supervision that the children receive enormous amounts of love and comfort, spiritual guidance, emotional support, and discipline when necessary. He is father to all the children, and the Imbabazi couldn't possibly run without him.

All the children attend church on Sundays, and those age six and older attend the primary school located a short distance away. After many years of war and upheaval, they are all years behind in their schoolwork and are struggling to catch up. The school is woefully lacking in even the most basic materials and supplies, but most of the children enjoy school, and many are among the top students in their classes. It is my dream that all of our children will go on to complete secondary school.

The girls have learned to knit and crochet and have made beautiful afghans and shawls of many colors. The boys play soccer and basketball, which they learned from a Nigerian professional basketball player who was stationed in Rwanda. All the children help in the vegetable and potato gardens they have planted. They especially love to sing and dance and play the drums, and they never miss an opportunity to perform for visitors.

Many of the children we receive come to us with worms and scabies, and some are terribly malnourished. We are fortunate in that none of our children have serious physical disabilities, but they all bear deep emotional scars and demonstrate, at one time or another, symptoms of posttraumatic stress. There are cases of chronic bed-wetting, occasional outbursts of violence or uncontrollable crying, and some simply refuse to speak at all for long periods of time. It takes an enormous amount of patience, tenderness, and loving care before they begin to feel safe and secure and learn to laugh and play and be children again.

Our children have become very much a family, and it is always a bitter-sweet moment when one of them leaves us to return to relatives. Unfortunately, these family reunions are not always happy ones, as often the surviving parent or relative has already remarried and the new husband or wife does not accept the child. On the evening of November 1, 1995, in full moonlight, eight tired little boys who had left us in June to return to family members came back to the Imbabazi for a surprise visit. They had walked all the way from Ruhengeri—a distance of thirty miles. It was indeed a surprise, and it warmed our hearts to know they missed us as much as we missed them. It was a joyful reunion for everyone, and Sembagare told me the next morning that they stayed up laughing and talking well into the night. Our eight runaways remained with us for ten happy days (two ended up staying permanently). All of a sudden, we had two soccer teams again. Biriko baked bread, and I bought meat and other treats for Sunday dinner. On their last evening with us, they danced and sang a song in Kinyarwanda that was unfamiliar to me. Biriko translated it as follows: "We are the young ones of Rosa. We are growing up, but nothing bad will happen to us." I hope and pray that this is true.

Our children come from all three ethnic groups—Hutu, Tutsi, and Batwa. Many of the Tutsi children saw their parents, brothers, and sisters killed during the genocide, and many of the Hutu children lost their families to the cholera epidemic that swept through the refugee camps in Zaire. They are all very brave and have enormous faith in God. Their love for one another is extraordinary, and it is our fervent prayer that this love will last all their lives and that the Banyarwanda will one day live together in peace.

In a country torn apart by hatred and violence, every day brings new challenges and the future is always uncertain. The U.N. peacekeeping forces pulled out of Rwanda in the spring of 1996, and many of the relief agencies have been forced to reduce their presence or withdraw altogether, taking with them desperately needed food distributions, medical services, support systems, and a fragile perception of security and stability. In November 1996, Laurent Kabila, leader of the rebel forces in Zaire, abruptly dismantled the refugee camps, prompting eight hundred thousand Hutu refugees to return home to Rwanda in a period of several days. Among the returnees were the leaders of the genocide, the *interahamwe*, who continue to threaten the security and stability of the region.

* * *

There are times when I feel like the old woman who lived in a shoe. With so many children, each new day brings with it a new set of problems and surprises, but the joys have always far outweighed the difficulties. Our children are happy and healthy, and they are dearly loved. One of the few regrets in my life is that I never had children of my own. Today, at the age of eight-five, I am blessed with seventy-two.

Mugongo has been my home for forty-three years now, and it is here that I intend to spend the rest of my days. The little orphanage that began as a dream has become a haven of love and laughter and a symbol of hope to all who have been a part of it.

Every evening just before dusk, I say good night to the children and make my way slowly along the narrow path that leads to the house. The sounds of singing and laughter still ring in the cool evening air. Workers and friends call out, "*Kwa heri*, Madami." The dogs race ahead as I stop to survey the gardens and marvel at the dazzling sunset casting a golden glow on Lake Kivu in the distance. The crested cranes have come to roost on their leafy perches atop the dracaena trees. I turn toward the jagged peaks of Mikeno and the snowcapped dome of Karisimbi appearing as stark silhouettes against the falling darkness, and I know I am truly blessed.

I am weary as I mount the flagstone steps to my cozy, vine-covered cottage. Mikingo has lighted the oil lamps, and I settle into a chair beside a warm, crackling fire. My day is done, and I wonder with a flutter of anticipation what new adventures and surprises tomorrow will bring.

—August 1997

EPILOGUE

In a perfect world the story would have ended right there, with Roz and the children safely ensconced in the beauty and serenity of Mugongo. But few things in Rwanda are perfect nowadays.

In August 1997, I traveled to Rwanda to visit with Roz and the children and to work on this manuscript. I found that the house and orphanage had changed very little since my last visit in the spring of 1995, although the children had grown considerably and there were a great many more of them. Biriko had died in April of that year, and Micheli had taken over as orphanage cook. It was the height of the dry season, and despite the severe water shortage, the gardens looked lovely and the children were thriving.

In the fall of 1996, rebel leader Laurent Kabila launched a successful campaign to overthrow the Mobutu regime in Zaire and, in the process, dismantled the refugee camps in eastern Zaire, forcing eight hundred thousand Rwandan refugees to return to their homeland. Many of those returnees were members of the *interahamwe*—the perpetrators of the genocide. In the ensuing months, *interahamwe* murdered hundreds of Rwandan civilians, and any steps toward reconciliation that had been achieved in the years since the genocide quickly began to crumble. The *interahamwe* hid out in the volcanoes or blended into the general population during the daytime, emerging at night to continue their genocidal campaign against ethnic Tutsi—using clubs and machetes, sometimes guns and grenades. Their numbers were concentrated in the northwest region of Rwanda, between Gisenyi and Ruhengeri, and Roz and the children found themselves smack in the middle of the combat zone.

At Mudende, where the Seventh-Day Adventist university used to be, eight thousand Tutsi refugees from Zaire (now renamed Congo) were encamped in a sea of blue-and-white plastic tents. They had fled a civil war in the Masisi territory of the Congo and had sought refuge in Rwanda. As we drove up the Mutura road and passed by the camp, I couldn't help but think that these people were sitting ducks for the *interahamwe*, and I feared for their safety.

The week prior to my arrival, there had been a massacre at Kanama, approximately twelve kilometers from Mugongo. Hundreds of civilians had been killed and two hundred and fifty Hutu prisoners were released. Fear gripped the region, and an early curfew was imposed. Six military guards were assigned to protect Roz's house and the orphanage night and day.

During the night of Saturday, August 16, I was awakened by a barrage of gunfire outside my bedroom window. Stunned, I rolled out of bed and crawled across the floor to Roz's room, where she and I clung to one another as the onslaught continued for forty-five minutes—terrified for the lives of the children and the workers. We learned later that fifty *interahamwe* had surrounded the house, presumably in an attempt to rob us, and our six RPA guards had bravely fought them off, using twenty thousand rounds of ammunition. One member of the *interahamwe* was killed, and one of our guards was wounded. The children and workers, though terribly frightened, were unharmed. Sembagare and his family spent most of the night lying flat on the floor of his house as bullets whizzed all around them. Windows were shattered, and every tile on the roof of his house was broken.

From that moment on, Mutura became besieged in guerrilla warfare. Gunfire could be heard every day and every night—sometimes short bursts, other times for long durations. At 1:00 A.M. on August 21, *interahamwe* attacked the refugee camp at Mudende, killing one hundred and twenty Tutsi refugees and wounding hundreds more. They set fire to the tents, creating a conflagration that set the valley ablaze. In fear of retaliation, thousands of Hutu fled their homes in the middle of the night. Retaliation was swift. Within hours, Tutsi civilians began killing Hutu civilians at random, looting and setting fire to their homes. In the early dawn, Roz and I stood on the front porch and looked out over the valley at the massive destruction. Flames from hundreds of burning houses shot into the air, followed by long columns of thick, black smoke. Roz said it was like reliving the rebellion of '59 all over again, and we feared the outbreak of another full-scale ethnic war. Thousands of Hutu homes were looted or burned that day, and the sound of gunfire could be heard from all directions. Most of the workers and their families were missing and presumed to be in hiding. We feared that Micheli was dead. The women who had stayed at the Imbabazi that night were unable to leave and had no knowledge of where their families were. The children were ordered to remain indoors, and no one was allowed on the road.

That morning, Roz and I arrived at the Imbabazi to find a prayer service under way, led by Tamari, one of the women caretakers. The children were huddled together with their heads bowed, the older ones cradling the younger ones. Tamari led the singing, and the older boys read from their bibles. We all prayed for Micheli and for all the people of Mutura.

As the evening sun was setting, I looked out over the beautiful gardens and saw columns of smoldering fires rise up from every direction. The smoky air was punctuated by the sound of sporadic gunfire and periodic blasts of cannons and grenades. I heard a rumbling in the distance, and I thought, Please let it be thunder. Please let it rain! We had used the last of the water from the house cistern for the orphanage that day, and there was no more. As darkness fell, the sky over Mudende was crimson. I lay awake in bed listening to the stutter of machine guns in the distance and wept for this poor, sad country.

In the days that followed, some of the workers returned to Mugongo. All had heartbreaking tales of fleeing for their lives, being separated from their families, and finding their homes emptied of everything or burned to the ground. They all had lost everything for the second time. They were hungry and terrified. Some slept at the Imbabazi, and others slept on cots we set up in the back storeroom of the house.

For the remaining weeks of my stay, Mugongo remained the only "safe" haven in Mutura. We had seventy-four children at the Imbabazi, plus untold numbers of workers and their family members who had sought refuge there. One night, thirty people slept in Sembagare's small house. Apart from our six guards, there was no military presence in the area. We watched and waited for military help to arrive, but it never came. We listened for the sound of the water truck making its way up the Mutura road, but *it* never came. We were running perilously low on food.

Day after day there were reports of people killed. One morning, five bodies were found in the cornfield across the road from Mugongo. Another day, dozens of civilians were killed on the main road, including six members of Sembagare's wife's family, shot in the head execution style. Another night, two members of Sebashitzi's family were beaten to death with clubs and stuffed in a latrine. The woodcutter's wife and four children were killed. A week after the massacre, Batandarana, the head gardener, finally turned up at Mugongo, in shock and close to tears. His daughter and her three children had been killed the day after the massacre. Nzabanita, another of the gardeners, reported that more than one hundred houses had been torched where he lived, and he and his family had been sleeping in a corncrib.

Fear and grief were etched on the people's faces. Everyone seemed to be waiting to die. Sembagare said, "When God opens the door, we will walk through it." Only the children remained brave and cheerful. We did our best to keep them occupied with games and lessons, and every afternoon they converged on the lawn in the garden to jump rope and put on tumbling exhibitions and sing songs in beautiful harmonies, led by Tamari.

A few days before my scheduled departure, a frightened and weary Micheli returned to Mugongo, to everyone's immense joy and relief. The day before I left, a huge UNHCR water truck came rumbling up the road to fill the large rubber "bladder" which had been lying empty since long before my arrival. That night it rained for the first time in months.

Words cannot describe my sadness at leaving Roz and the children and all of those at Mugongo who have suffered so much and who seem to have been forgotten by the rest of the world, even by their own country. As we said good-bye, we reassured one another that the worst must surely be over. That the killing and dying would finally end and that Roz would spend her remaining years at her beloved Mugongo with her children and the people who are so dear to her. But that was not to be.

On October 8, 1997, more than a thousand *interahamwe* attacked Gisenyi and nearly captured the airport in a seven-hour battle. Many were killed. By the end of October, the number of Tutsi refugees at Mudende had swelled to eighteen thousand, where they remained frequent targets for the *interahamwe*. Countless massacres occurred throughout October and November. Taxi-buses were ambushed and burned, their occupants robbed and killed. *Interahamwe* attacked a prison at Giciye, killing three hundred (mostly civilians) and releasing more than a hundred prisoners.

New orphans arrived at the Imbabazi nearly every day, and Roz didn't have the heart to turn them away. The dry season that year continued through the end of October—the longest dry season in memory. Food was scarce. Finally, in early November, torrential rains came and continued unabated for many months. The Mutura road became impassable, and the main road to Gisenyi began to crumble from the deluge of water and mudslides.

For weeks there were no military guards at Mugongo. Roz's own night watchman, Joeli, remained in his tiny hut a few yards from Roz's bedroom, faithfully keeping watch over her house each night. Sixteen people slept in the chicken yard with just blankets to protect them from the cold. Sebashitzi and his family slept in a small stone cottage on the plantation, and Mikingo and several of the gardeners slept in the storeroom in Roz's house. Sembagare's house was overflowing with displaced people, and Micheli and others slept at the Imbabazi. Most of the women caretakers at the orphanage had fled, and those few who remained were living there with their families.

In December, the refugee camp at Mudende was evacuated and relocated to a more secure area some distance away. Mutura was now deserted, and Mugongo was completely isolated—cut off from all protection or assistance of any kind. The commune closed. The school closed. The military left. There were no markets, and there were no people. The harsh realization—that it was no longer possible to ensure the safety of the children at Mugongo, let alone obtain food, medical treatment, or other necessities—dawned with agonizing awareness. The children would have to be moved. Roz and Sembagare began the difficult search for another facility—one that was not too far away, and one that was large enough to keep them all together.

On the morning of January 8, 1998, workers from UNICEF arrived and packed up the orphanage—beds, mattresses, blankets, clothing, toys, cooking utensils—and most of the belongings in Roz's house, and loaded them onto four huge relief trucks. Roz and the children and all of the workers and their families—one hundred and forty people in all, plus dogs, cats, goats, and chickens—piled into two big buses, and the sad, frightened convoy left Mugongo and made its way slowly down the Mutura road. The building they had found for the children was a large school building in Gisenyi owned by the Catholic Church. Roz moved into a comfortable house on the shores of Lake Kivu, which had once been the home of Oswald du Chasteleer and later Sergio Bottazzi. The house has been loaned to her indefinitely through the kindness of friends at the Bralirwa brewery.

From the moment they arrived, Gisenyi became the target of repeated terrorist attacks. Massacres of Tutsi refugees, followed by retaliation killings of Hutu civilians, occurred daily. Buses and taxis were blown up, and a munitions depot in the center of town exploded. The hospital was overflowing with burn and amputee victims. Dozens of funerals were held each day. Roz worked tirelessly organizing the orphanage, enrolling more than a hundred children in school, and visiting the wounded at the hospital.

As the heavy winter rains continued, Gisenyi became a breeding ground for mosquitoes, and malaria struck with a vengeance. Almost a third of the children contracted malaria, as did many of the workers and their family members. Roz and Sembagare spent countless days and nights tending to the sick and searching for medicines and mosquito netting. A portion of the new building was turned into a sick ward as there was no room at the hospital. Mercifully, none of the orphans died. But many others did. Sebashitzi's two-year-old son, Shadrack, died of malaria. Three days later, Roz's longtime cook, Mikingo, died after a two-day illness. Roz was wracked with guilt and grief for bringing everyone to Gisenyi. Sembagare, as always, was a tower of strength, tending to the children and arranging the burials. In March, Roz herself came down with malaria and was very ill for many weeks. We all feared for her survival.

In the meantime, the gardeners and their families (eighty people in all) remained at Mugongo, living in the old orphanage building. On March 20, *interahamwe* attacked Mugongo. Thirteen people were killed, including three gardeners and Joeli, the night watchman. Dozens more were wounded. In a second attack two months later, Roz's house was robbed, vandalized, and set on fire.

In June, the Catholic Church announced that it wanted its building back and gave them thirty days to vacate. Once again, Roz and Sembagare began a frantic search for another facility. In a long-overdue stroke of good fortune, they managed to find an ideal building owned by the Pentacostal church which was formerly used as dormitories for secondary school students. It is a sturdy structure and very spacious, with four large rooms, an office and small bedroom for Sembagare, ample latrines, and a big shower room with ten white-tiled shower stalls and wash basins. The building is surrounded by eucalyptus trees and large open areas, with a huge football field and the primary school nearby. The only drawback is that it is very close to the Congo border, where war has broken out once again.

Although 1999 has seen a lessoning of terrorist activity in Gisenyi, northwestern Rwanda remains one of the most violent and politically unstable regions in Africa. It is estimated that more than ten thousand people—both Hutu and Tutsi—have been killed in ethnic fighting during the last two years. More than a million people have been forced to leave their homes and seek sanctuary in government-controlled resettlement camps. The wheels of justice turn slowly in a country shattered by so much hatred and bloodshed, but during the past two years the Rwandan judicial system has tried and convicted hundreds of prisoners accused of committing genocide and crimes against humanity. Some have been publicly executed. At the same time, the International Criminal Tribunal for Rwanda in Arusha, Tanzania, has indicted thirty-four suspects. Five have been convicted and sentenced to terms in prison.

During the past year, several of the children have been reunited with family members. At the same time, many new orphans continue to arrive—all dreadfully malnourished and traumatized. Sembagare works twenty hours a day as he is always on call for emergencies, such as illness or when there is audible gunfire. He is father to all the children, and they love him—as they do the dear women who are their substitute mothers. After years of upheaval and adversity, the children are remarkably happy and settled in their new home. Today, the Imbabazi is home to more than one hundred of Rwanda's lost or orphaned children, and it remains a haven of love and safety and a symbol of hope for them all.

Rosamond Carr, who happens to be my aunt, is one of the true heroes of this world, and my love and admiration for her are simply beyond measure. She would be the last to admit that her life has been characterized by greatness. But the young woman, so unsure of herself, who arrived in the Kivu fifty years ago, has certainly left her mark on this land and its people. Her courage and compassion have touched countless lives over the years and continue to inspire countless others. Although her life is in Gisenyi now with Sembagare and the children, her heart will always remain at Mugongo. She goes back to visit from time to time, just to wander through the empty rooms and sit in the garden and remember how good it all was. There is so very much to remember.

—Ann Howard Halsey

ACKNOWLEDGMENTS

Land of a Thousand Hills has been a true labor of love created from Rosamond Carr's extensive personal writings, letters, and diaries compiled over many years, in addition to firsthand accounts of her life and experiences and my own travels to Rwanda. This collaboration was achieved through a series of extraordinary efforts and unconventional methods. Completed chapters of the manuscript were sent by mail from my home in Downingtown, Pennsylvania, to the American Embassy in Kigali. From there they were delivered to Rwandex and placed on the coffee truck for its weekly run to Gisenyi. Along the way, the driver would drop them off at Sembagare's old house on the main road, where his grandchildren or foster children would carry the package twelve miles through the fields and hand deliver it to Roz. After reading, revising, and editing the chapters, the procedure was then reversed. This process took many weeks to complete and was repeated dozens of times during the past two years. For this, I owe a great debt of gratitude to Bonnie Harris, consular officer at the U.S. Embassy in Kigali; to Tony Wood, director of Rwandex in Kigali; to Saidi Seff, the ever-faithful driver of the coffee truck; and to the many children in Sembagare's extended family.

My thanks also go to Joe Wertheim for his assistance with research materials; and to Dorothy Halsey, the true historian of the family, whose insight, sense of humor, and remarkable memory were invaluable. Special thanks to our editor, Amanda Patten, who understood that this was a story that needed to be told; and to everyone at Viking who helped make it a reality. And to my family and friends, your encouragement and enthusiasm meant more than I can possibly express.

The authors acknowledge the contribution of Bruce E. Fleming.

—Ann Howard Halsey

EDITORIAL NOTE

Kinyarwanda, the local Bantu language of Rwanda, is one of the most complex languages in the world. Prefixes are used to indicate singular or plural with respect to ethnic groups. The prefix "Mu" denotes singular, the prefix "Wa" denotes plural, and the prefix "Ba" denotes the ethnic group as a whole. Accordingly, the grammatically correct term for Hutu or Tutsi in the singular is "Muhutu" or "Mututsi"; the term for Hutu or Tutsi in the plural is "Wahutu" or "Watutsi"; and the terms for the ethnic groups as a whole are "Bahutu" or "Batutsi." For the purposes of this manuscript and in the interest of simplification, the editorial decision was made to (in almost all cases) adopt the generally accepted abbreviated versions of the two primary ethnic groups of Rwanda—"Hutu" and "Tutsi"—to denote both singular and plural.

The term for whites in Rwanda is *"muzungu"* (singular) and *"wazungu"* (plural). The manuscript adheres to the correct usage of those terms, as well as any references to the Bahunde tribe (Muhunde in the singular).

GLOSSARY

Abiru: Royal council of the Tutsi monarchy
Baba: Father
Banyarwanda: People of Rwanda (Banyaruanda prior to 1962)
Bwana: Sir or mister
Capitas: Headmen on plantation
Casques bleus: U.N. peacekeepers (French for "blue helmets")
Cicatrix: Tribal scar
Circuit de Bugoyi: Scenic route through Ruanda and the Belgian Congo
Ikinimba: Traditional courtship dance
Imana: God
Iningiri: Single-corded musical instrument
Inkotanyi: Term for Rwandan Patriotic Front; literally "invincible ones"
Interahamwe: Extremist Hutu militia groups; literally "those who attack together"
Intore: Traditional dance of the Tutsi; literally "the chosen"
Inyambo: Sacred cows of the Tutsi king
Inyenzi: Cockroach (term used for exiled Tutsi infiltrators)
Jambo: Hello
Kalinga: Sacred drum of the Tutsi monarchy
Kanzu: Standard uniform of house servants in Africa
Karani: Plantation clerk
Kinyarwanda: Bantu language of Rwanda (Kinyaruanda prior to 1962)
Kurwana: Duel between two men using canes
Kwa heri: Good-bye, good night
Lapango: Thorn fence
Le grand monde: French for "the grand world"
L'ubu-hake: Feudal caste system in effect until 1957
Maradadi: To have a touch of elegance
Mille collines: A thousand hills (French)

Muzungu: White person (singular)
Mwami: Tutsi king of Ruanda
Mwamikazi: Tutsi queen
Pombi: Banana beer
Sale bête: Dirty beast (profanity)
Shamba: Field
Tipoy: Basket or litter for transporting people
Toto: Child
Uburozi: Poison
Ubutega: Special grass used for ornamentation
Uhuru: Freedom
Umulyango: Family
Umunzemze: Hardwood tree
Umwishywa: Plant believed to promote fertility
Unweko: Skin belt worn by married women
Wazungu: White people (plural)

INDEX